NAACP: Celebrating a Century
100 Years in Pictures

NAACP and *The Crisis* Magazine

GIBBS SMITH
TO ENRICH AND INSPIRE HUMANKIND
Salt Lake City | Charleston | Santa Fe | Santa Barbara

Acknowledgments

NAACP Photographers: Cecil Layne, Paul Greene, C.G. Taylor, and Richard McIntire.

Staffs of the NAACP and *The Crisis* Magazine, Angela Alexander, Krystle Cadogan, Angela Ciccolo, Paula Brown Edme, Victor Goode, Dennis C. Hayes, Pamela Horowitz, Ebony Jones, James Murray, and Tehra Williams.

Gibbs Smith and staff.

Library of Congress.

Books: Charles Flint Kellogg, *NAACP*, Baltimore, Maryland: The Johns Hopkins University Press, 1967.

First Edition
13 12 11 10 09   5 4 3 2 1

Published by
Gibbs Smith
P.O. Box 667
Layton, Utah 84041

Orders: 1.800.835.4993
www.gibbs-smith.com

Designed by Kurt Wahlner
Cover designed by Eric Oliver
Printed and bound in China
Gibbs Smith books are printed on either recycled, 100% post-consumer waste, or FSC-certified papers.

Library of Congress Control Number: 2008939456

ISBN 13: 978-1-4236-0527-0
ISBN 10: 1-4236-0527-6

the CRISIS

FEBRUARY 1977   SEVENTY-FIVE CENTS

Contents

The Crisis, February 1977 cover with images of some NAACP founders and early officials: (left to right): Arthur B. Spingarn, Mary White Ovington, John Haynes Holmes, Moorfield Storey, William Pickens, Oswald Garrison Villard, Mary Church Terrell, John Shillady, Henry Moskowitz, William English Walling, Joel E. Spingarn, W. E. B. Du Bois.

July 28, 1917: NAACP "Silent Protest Parade" down New York City's Fifth Avenue in protest to recent massacres, lynchings, and discrimination.

Foreword

By Julian Bond, Board Chairman, NAACP

On the commemoration of the NAACP's centennial, it is a special privilege for me to write a foreword for this special volume—a collection of historic photographs and documents, accompanied by text—highlighting the history of the National Association for the Advancement of Colored People (NAACP). I have been an active member of this organization since my college days.

NAACP: Celebrating a Century, 100 Years in Pictures reflects the rich history of the NAACP and its role in the pursuit of civil rights and social justice from its founding to the present day. There is no other such organized group today that has had greater influence on our societal structure. The NAACP has, indeed, served as America's conscience while consistently working to eradicate the deeply rooted idea of racial inferiority imposed by others.

The NAACP's story was and is a lengthy chronicle of a remarkable interracial army of ordinary men and women drawn from every walk of life and every race and class, dedicated to using every legal means to advance justice and fair play, engaging in extraordinary activity. They marched before marching for civil rights became popular. They successfully sued for fairness when most Americans did not dream of asking the courts for equality. They appeared before state and federal legislatures and registered fierce objections to racial affronts. They firmly insisted on equality in every aspect of American life. They defended African Americans in racially charged cases in the armed services, at home and abroad. They lobbied the United Nations and helped internationalize the struggle for civil rights. They helped a newly independent African nation write a constitution based on their hard experience of making the American charter a true contract of freedom. They made hard decisions that were not always popularly embraced.

The network of those whom they assisted in securing their rights ranges from sharecroppers to shareholders and from laborers to landlords; it encompasses all the vast complexity of the American population.

They did not only do these things, and more, years ago—the NAACP is doing them today and will do them tomorrow, if the need arises.

The NAACP stands out from its many strong partners in the fight for civil rights—it is the most democratic of them all, its leadership chosen by the votes of its members. It is the only national civil rights organization that reserves seats on its Board of Directors for young people, elected solely by the votes of the NAACP's young members.

Some fifty years ago, an extraordinary American of African descent, the late poet/playwright/author Langston Hughes, wrote *Fight for Freedom—The Story of the NAACP*. I own a copy today. In his postscript, Hughes proudly noted:

> I grew up in the NAACP, now in its second half century as I am in mine. I learned to read with *The Crisis* on my grandmother's knee. My poem, "The Negro Speaks of Rivers" was the first of my poems to be published in a national magazine. From that time on, over a period of forty years, my poetry and prose regularly appeared in *The Crisis*.

The then NAACP president and its oldest active member, Arthur B. Spingarn, wrote in his foreword to Hughes's *Fight for Freedom*:

From its beginning, the NAACP ignited a spark that has become a blazing flame, which cannot and will not be extinguished. But it should not be forgotten that the NAACP first lit this torch, which is now being carried by its spiritual sons and daughters and will continue to be carried by us and them until the final goal is reached.

My father, Dr. Horace Mann Bond, was also published in *The Crisis*, and I am proud to have been published there too. So too have a Who's Who of black American arts and letters whose words and illustrations graced the magazine's pages.

Now the NAACP, whose history Langston Hughes traced for a half century, is moving into its centennial year.

The Crisis that published young Langston Hughes fifty years ago was at one time the most widely circulated black-owned magazine in the country. Then and now it carried news of the NAACP's activities to every large city and small hamlet in America. And it is in those towns and cities in every state that the NAACP's real strength lives today—in its more than seventeen hundred branches and its state conferences, in its headquarters staff and its Board of Directors, but primarily in its individual members, people of every kind willing to put aside job and family for a few hours each week to address the serious challenges their community and country face in the exercise of civil rights.

We hope you will feel called to join this one-hundred-year-old crusade for justice by joining the NAACP. We believe that in the National Association for the Advancement of Colored People, "colored people" come in all colors; anyone who shares our values is more than welcome.

Come on in—we need you. American needs us together.

Introduction

By Roger Wood Wilkins
Chairman and Publisher
The Crisis *Publishing Company, Inc.*

The riot that broke out in Springfield, Illinois, in the summer of 1908 had roots in the American culture that were just shy of three centuries deep. During the first century on this continent, most of the descendants of the first black immigrants, who were brought to Virginia in 1619, had been assigned the lowest rung on the ladder of American life. At the end of the seventeenth century, almost all of the descendants and black newcomers as well had been reduced to lifelong, hereditary slavery.

In order to debase them, stifle the development of any real leadership among them, and to assure a docile labor force, the economic leaders of the colony introduced in about 1700 a method of indoctrination that they called "seasoning." It was a decision that would rumble through the decades of American life, destroying, mangling, and corrupting virtually everything that came in its path. The practice consisted of a survey of each group of newly arrived Africans to determine which members of the group seemed to have leadership potential or the spunk to oppose their role as slaves. Those identified would be "seasoned" by partial dismemberment: a toe, a finger, or an ear would be cut off. The purpose was to convince the slaves that they were not permitted to develop a will of their own: they were to be solely tools of the master's will. The lifelong scars of those "seasoned" would be lesson enough for most other slaves. A second prong of seasoning was the wholesale withholding of education from the blacks.

That regime also had psychic consequences for whites, particularly those who were major owners of slaves, but for lower-ranked whites as well. Their "superiority" to blacks became one of the measures of who they were—grand or petty masters of the universe, depending on their station. The owners of vast lands and squads of black workers had daily cultural "evidence" of their superiority and even the lowest white could find comfort in tough times by telling himself, "Well, at least I'm better than the blacks!"

The next century brought the Civil War, which erupted in 1860 over the issue of slavery. The war was a profoundly bitter experience for white Southerners. It shattered the economy of the region; killed or mutilated thousands and thousands of white men; devastated farms, cities, and factories; and, for the most part, scattered and freed the slaves. A majority of the bondsmen and women fled the farms, some entered politics, and others started learning so they could participate in this new America. The power of a few successful black politicians and the drastically improved financial status of entrepreneurial former slaves, piled on top of the other enormous losses the white Southerners sustained, were too much for some of them to bear, so they mounted a two-pronged counterattack.

On the political track, the Redeemers—as they called themselves—fought hard in Washington to bring about an end to Reconstruction and particularly sought the removal of Union troops from the South. On the home front—as the Yankee troops withdrew—many of the Redeemers chose terrorism. By 1875, bands of white men in groups such as the Ku Klux Klan and the Knights of the White Camellia bought down a reign of terror on successful blacks, on blacks seeking public office, and on those simply trying to vote. And, of course, on those whose attitude was deemed inappropriate (uppity). So they killed and they burned and they drove people out of their homes, their hometowns, and their states in order to remove blacks from public office and to return the conceit (and comfort) of white superiority to the center of their culture.

Consequently, in the decades after 1877 when the government in Washington turned its attention away from Reconstruction, the Redeemers continued to employ wide-scale murderous violence to nullify the majestic post–Civil War amendments to the Constitution: the 13th, which ended slavery; the 14th, which promised equal protection of the laws and due process of law to the former slaves; and the 15th, which gave the vote to black men. Their violence and the disinterest of the courts effectively nullified those amendments and other federal reconstruction efforts designed to aid former slaves.

Thirty years later—in the first decade of the twentieth century—the Redeemer strategy was still followed at the highest levels of intellectual and political thought and activity in the South. Senator Ben "Pitchfork" Tillman of South Carolina, enraged that President Theodore Roosevelt had entertained Booker T. Washington in the White House, proclaimed on the floor of the United States Senate that because of what Roosevelt had done "we'll have to kill a thousand niggers to get them back in their place."

In a similar vein, Paul B. Barringer, chairman of the faculty at the University of Virginia, the South's leading institution of higher learning, spoke to the convention of the Southern Education Association in 1900 about the nature of education blacks should receive. He observed that they should be given nothing more than "Sunday School training" because their lot in life was to serve as a fine source of "cheap labor for warm climate; everywhere else he is a foreordained failure, and as he knows this he despises his own color." The people who "seasoned" blacks by the use of physical harm and withholding of education in the seventeenth and eighteenth centuries could not have topped Senator Tillman and Professor Barringer.

Despite the horrific Southern backlash and the relative complacency with which the North observed it, some blacks achieved wholeness and effectiveness as human beings. William Edward Burghardt Du Bois, the brilliant scholar-activist who had earned (from Harvard) the first Ph.D. degree awarded to a black person in America, and his brave, crusading journalist colleague, Monroe Trotter, fiercely rejected Barringer's views of themselves and of black people generally. These men clearly had wills of their own. In 1905 they created an organization of black men who agreed to mount a movement to agitate for "full manhood rights" to black men and to struggle to make available to them the fullest and highest educational opportunities available to any other man in the country. Their approach was, in part, an answer to the accommodations approach of Booker T. Washington. They demanded all rights any other American possessed. In a sense, they were Senator Ben Tillman's worst nightmare. The group first met at Niagara Falls, New York, so their project was called "the Niagara Movement." Like most new movements, the Niagara group sputtered and started at the same time. But the men managed in their first three years to put together a manifesto, to stave off the enmity of Booker T. Washington, to forge some trust and respect among themselves, and to attract some white support.

As this work was proceeding, the country was still experiencing terrorism—largely in the form of lynching, but sometimes in the form of large-scale anti-lynching rioting by whites. In 1908 such a riot exploded in Springfield, Illinois, in which four whites were killed, one black was lynched, and more than two thousand black residents fled the city. A magazine article published in a liberal magazine and written by William English Walling, a wealthy white, described powerfully what had happened in Springfield. The article served as a catalyst that brought a number of activists to the task of seeking a way to deal with the racism and the violence in the country. The initial organizers of this group were Walling, Mary White Ovington (a social worker), and Oswald Garrison Villard (grandson of abolitionist William Lloyd Garrison). The group issued an appeal and a call to a meeting of people who wanted to end the deplorable treatment imposed upon blacks in most sections of the country. Three hundred people attended the first meeting of the group in May 1909. They quickly went to work dismantling the gross stereotype of the Negro as a congenitally inferior version of human being. That task was eased by the attendance of Du Bois, Trotter, and some of the other Niagara group's participants. Black participants brought their intellect, the fruits of their Niagara discussions, and their experiences as black Americans to the conference rooms. The meeting was not without its prickly moments, but in the end the biracial group held together and planned a second meeting for the following year.

The whites were dedicated to the idea that the leadership of the new organization would be biracial. Some thought that Du Bois ought to become the chairman of the group, but he opted to become director of publicity and research. He harbored the desire to create the voice of the new movement so that he could send the message of the group out to the country, and report on its activities and on black achievement in order to provide hope and inspiration for people around the country to initiate local action. These seeds of a new American organization were planted in the spring of 1909, almost exactly 290 years after the first Africans were bought to the Virginia colony.

The following year Du Bois got his wish to publish a magazine—the national voice of the new organization. He would name it *The Crisis, A Record of the Darker Races.* The magazine was not simply an arm

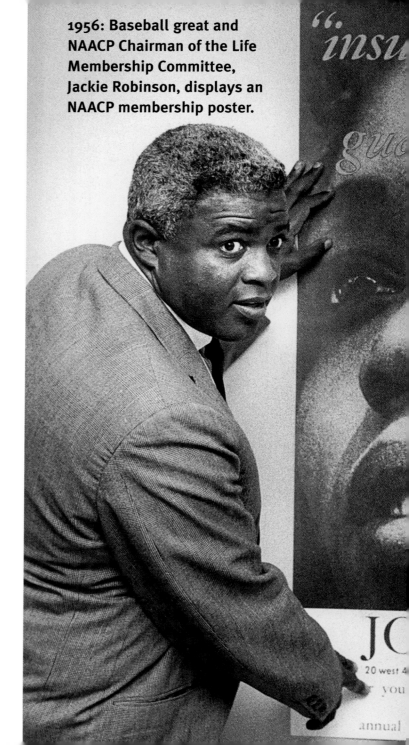

1956: Baseball great and NAACP Chairman of the Life Membership Committee, Jackie Robinson, displays an NAACP membership poster.

*my freedom...
and you
...ntee your own"*

N **NAACP**
York, N.Y.
branch — one in every area of the city
...onsult your telephone book
...rships: $2.00 / $3.50 / $5.00 / $10.00 and up

of the new organization; it was the trumpet through which Du Bois would attempt to knit opponents of racial subjugation together—to educate them and to empower them with ideas, information, and the knowledge that they were a part of a growing and inevitable movement toward justice. He was to be the commanding presence and major voice of the organization for the next twenty-four years.

In 1787, just after the Constitutional Convention had drafted a constitution for the United States, Benjamin Franklin encountered a woman who asked him, "What have you made for us, Dr. Franklin?" Franklin answered with the most elemental call for citizen activism that any of the founders offered: "A Republic, madam, if you can keep it."

The exhortation "If you can keep it" called for citizens of the country to honor, through the generations, the principles embodied in the Declaration of Independence and the Constitution of the United States. Ovington, Du Bois, Villard, Walling, Trotter, and others had taken up Franklin's challenge and had created a unique mechanism for driving the high ideals of the American creation into the daily realities of life as it was actually lived by black and white Americans. They had created the NAACP, the National Association for the Advancement of Colored People. Nothing could be so proudly American.

To commemorate the one hundred years of the oldest, largest, and most effective civil rights organization in the world, we are pleased to present you with this volume: *NAACP: Celebrating a Century, 100 Years in Pictures.* In a very short period, our small team viewed thousands of photos from the NAACP and *The Crisis* photo files, accessed our archived material at the Library of Congress, and perused hundreds of internal documents to produce this book. While it is most difficult to sum up one hundred years in a few hundred pages, we hope that the featured highlights and pictures impress upon you the impact this magnificent organization has had, and continues to have, in forging an equal America.

Image of the Spingarn medal. The Spingarn medal, created by Joel Spingarn in 1914, is the NAACP's highest honor awarded to an African American of distinguished merit and achievement.

How the NAACP Began

By Mary White Ovington, 1914

The National Association for the Advancement of Colored People is five years old—old enough, it is believed, to have a history; and I, who am perhaps, its first member, have been chosen as the person to recite it. As its work since 1910 has been set forth in its annual reports, I shall make it my task to show how it came into existence and to tell of its first months of work.

In the summer of 1908, the country was shocked by the account of the race riots at Springfield, Illinois. Here, in the home of Abraham Lincoln, a mob containing many of the town's "best citizens" raged for two days, killed and wounded scores of Negroes, and drove thousands from the city. Articles on the subject appeared in newspapers and magazines. Among them was one in the *Independent* of September 3rd, by William English Walling, entitled "Race War in the North." After describing the atrocities committed against the colored people, Mr. Walling declared:

"Either the spirit of the abolitionists, of Lincoln and of Lovejoy must be revived and we must come to treat the Negro on a plane of absolute political and social equality, or Vardaman and Tillman will soon have transferred the race war to the North." And he ended with these words, "Yet who realizes the seriousness of the situation, and what large and powerful body of citizens is ready to come to their aid?"

It so happened that one of Mr. Walling's readers accepted his question and answered it. For four years I had been studying the status of the Negro in New York. I had investigated his housing conditions, his health, his opportunities for work. I had spent many months in the South, and at the time of Mr. Walling's article, I was living in a New York Negro tenement on a Negro street. And my investigations and my surroundings led me to believe with the writer of the article that "the spirit of the abolitionists must be revived."

The NAACP Is Born

So I wrote to Mr. Walling, and after some time, for he was in the West, we met in New York in the first week of the year of 1909. With us was Dr. Henry Moskowitz, now prominent in the administration of John Purroy Mitchell, Mayor of New York. It was then that the National Association for the Advancement of Colored People was born. It was born in a little room of a New York apartment. It is to be regretted that there are no minutes of the first meeting, for they would make interesting if unparliamentary reading.

Mr. Walling had spent some years in Russia where his wife, working in the cause of the revolutionists, had suffered imprisonment; and he expressed his belief that the Negro was treated with greater inhumanity in the United States than the Jew was treated in Russia. As Mr. Walling is a Southerner, we listened with conviction. I knew something of the Negro's difficulty in securing decent employment in the North and of the insolent treatment awarded him at Northern hotels and restaurants, and I voiced my protest. Dr. Moskowitz, with his broad knowledge of conditions among New York's helpless immigrants, aided us in properly interpreting our facts. And so we talked and talked, voicing our indignation.

Lincoln's Birthday

Of course, we wanted to do something at once that should move the country. It was January. Why not choose Lincoln's birthday, February 12, to open our campaign? We decided, therefore, that a wise, immediate action would be the issuing on Lincoln's birthday of a call for a national conference on the Negro question. At this conference we might discover the beginnings, at least, of that "large and powerful body of citizens" of which Mr. Walling had written.

And so the meeting adjourned. Something definite was determined upon, and our next step was to call others into our councils. We at once turned to Mr. Oswald Garrison Villard, editor of the *Evening Post*. He received our suggestions with enthusiasm, and aided us in securing the co-operation of able and representative men and women. It was he who drafted the Lincoln's birthday call and helped to give it wide publicity. I give the Call in its entirety since it expresses, I think, better than anything else we have published, the spirit of those who are active in the Association's cause.

The celebration of the Centennial of the birth of Abraham Lincoln, widespread and grateful as it may be, will fail to justify itself if it takes no note of and makes no recognition of the colored men and women for whom the great Emancipator labored to assure freedom. Besides a day of rejoicing, Lincoln's birthday in 1909 should be one of taking stock of the nation's progress since 1865.

How far has it lived up to the obligations imposed upon it by the Emancipation Proclamation? How far has it gone in assuring to each and every citizen, irrespective of color, the equality of opportunity and equality before the law, which underlie our American institutions and are guaranteed by the Constitution?

Disfranchisement

If Mr. Lincoln could revisit this country in the flesh, he would be disheartened and discouraged. He would learn that on January I, 1909, Georgia had rounded out a new confederacy by disfranchising the Negro, after the manner of all the other Southern States. He would learn that the Supreme Court of the United States, supposedly a bulwark of American liberties, had refused every opportunity to pass squarely upon this disfranchisement of millions, by laws avowedly discriminatory and openly enforced in such manner that the white men may vote and that black men be without a vote in their government; he would discover, therefore, that taxation without representation is the lot of millions of wealth-producing American citizens, in whose hands rests the economic progress and welfare of an entire section of the country.

He would learn that the Supreme Court, according to the official statement of one of its own judges in the Berea College case, has laid down the principle that if an individual State chooses, it may "make it a crime for white and colored persons to frequent the same market place at the same time, or appear in an assemblage of citizens convened to consider questions of a public or political nature in which all citizens, without regard to race, are equally interested."

In many states Lincoln would find justice enforced, if at all, by judges elected by one element in a community to pass upon the liberties and lives of another. He would see the black men and women, for whose freedom a hundred thousand of soldiers gave their lives, set apart in trains, in which they pay first-class fares for third-class service, and segregated in railway stations and in places of entertainment; he would observe that State after State declines to do its elementary duty in preparing the Negro through education for the best exercise of citizenship.

"Silence . . . Means Approval"

Added to this, the spread of lawless attacks upon the Negro, North, South and West—even in the Springfield made famous by Lincoln—often accompanied by revolting brutalities, sparing neither sex nor age nor youth, could but shock the author of the sentiment that "government of the people, by the people, for the people; should not perish from the earth."

Silence under these conditions means tacit approval. The indifference of the North is already responsible for more than one assault upon democracy, and every such attack reacts as unfavorably upon whites as upon blacks. Discrimination once permitted cannot be bridled; recent history in the South shows that in forging chains for the Negroes the white voters are forging chains for themselves. "A house divided against itself cannot stand"; this government cannot exist half-slave and half-free any better today than it could in 1861.

Hence we call upon all the believers in democracy to join in a national conference for the discussion of present evils, the voicing of protests, and the renewal of the struggle for civil and political liberty.

This call was signed by: Jane Addams, Chicago; Samuel Bowles (Springfield Republican); Prof. W. L. Bulkley, New York; Harriet Stanton Blatch, New York; Ida Wells Barnett, Chicago; E. H. Clement, Boston; Kate H. Claghorn, New York; Prof. John Dewey, New York; Dr. W. E. B. Du Bois, Atlanta; Mary E. Dreier, Brooklyn; Dr. John L. Elliott, New York; Wm. Lloyd Garrison, Boston; Rev. Francis J. Grimke, Washington, D.C.; William Dean Howells, New York; Rabbi Emil G. Hirsch, Chicago; Rev. John Haynes Holmes, New York; Prof. Thomas C. Hall, New York; Hamilton Holt, New York; Florence Kelley, New York; Rev. Frederick Lynch, New York; Helen Marot, New York; John E. Milholland, New York; Mary E. McDowell, Chicago; Prof. J. G. Merrill, Connecticut; Dr. Henry Moskowitz, New York; Leonora O'Reilly, New York; Mary W. Ovington, New York; Rev. Dr. Charles H. Parkhurst, New York; Louis F. Post, Chicago; Rev. Dr. John P. Peters, New York; Dr. Jane Robbins, New York; Charles Edward Russell, New York; Joseph Smith, Boston; Anna Garlin Spencer, New York; William M. Salter, Chicago; J. G. Phelps Stokes, New York; Judge Wendell Stafford, Washington; Helen Stokes, Boston; Lincoln Steffens, Boston; President C. F. Thwing, Western Reserve University; Prof. W. I. Thomas, Chicago; Oswald Garrison Villard, New York *Evening Post;* Rabbi Stephen S. Wise, New York; Bishop Alexander Walters, New York; Dr. William H. Ward, New York; Horace White, New York; William English Walling, New York; Lillian D. Wald, New York; Dr. J. Milton Waldron, Washington, D.C.; Mrs. Rodman Wharton, Philadelphia; Susan P. Wharton, Philadelphia; President

Mary E. Wooley, Mt. Holyoke College; Prof. Charles Zueblin, Boston.

Conference Call

It was thus decided that we should hold a conference, and the next two months were busily spent arranging for it. Among the men and women who attended those first busy committee meetings were, Bishop Alexander Walters, Mr. Ray Stannard Baker, Mr. Alexander Irvine, Dr. Owen M. Waller, Mr. Gaylord S. White, Miss Madeline Z. Doty, Miss Isabel Eaton, besides many of the New York signers of the Call. It was agreed that the conference should be by invitation only, with the one open meeting at Cooper Union. Over a thousand people were invited, the Charity Organization Hall was secured, and, on the evening of May 30th, the conference opened with an informal reception at the Henry Street Settlement, given by Miss Lillian D. Wald, one of the Association's first and oldest friends. The next morning our deliberations began.

We have had five conferences since 1909, but I doubt whether any have been so full of a questioning surprise, amounting swiftly to enthusiasm, on the part of the white people in attendance. These men and women, engaged in religious, social and educational work, for the first time met the Negro who demands, not a pittance, but his full rights in the commonwealth. They received a stimulating shock and one which they enjoyed. They did not want to leave the meeting. We conferred all the time, formally and informally, and the Association gained in those days many of the earnest and uncompromising men and women who have since worked unfalteringly in its cause. Mr. William Hayes Ward, senior editor of the *Independent,* opened the conference, and Mr. Charles Edward Russell, always the friend of those who struggle for opportunity, presided at the stormy session at the close. The full proceedings have been published by the Association.

Membership in the Hundreds

Out of this conference we formed a committee of forty and secured the services of Miss Frances Blascoer, as secretary. We were greatly hampered by lack of funds. Important national work would present itself which we were unable to handle. But our secretary was an excellent organizer, and at the end of a year we had held four mass meetings, had distributed thousands of pamphlets, and numbered our membership in the hundreds. In May 1910, we held our second conference in New York, and again our meetings were attended by earnest, interested people. It was then that we organized a permanent body to be known as the National Association for the Advancement of Colored People. Its officers were:

National President, Moorfield Storey, Boston;
Chairman of the Executive Committee, William
    English Walling;
Treasurer, John E. Milholland;
Disbursing Treasurer, Oswald Garrison Villard;
Executive Secretary, Frances Blascoer;
Director of Publicity and Research, Dr. W. E. B.
    Du Bois .

The Role for Dr. Du Bois

The securing of a sufficient financial support to warrant our calling Dr. Du Bois from Atlanta University into an executive office in the Association was the most important work of the second conference.

When Dr. Du Bois came to us we were brought closely in touch with an organization of colored people, formed in 1905 at Niagara and known as the Niagara Movement. This organization had held important conferences at Niagara, Harpers Ferry, and Boston, and had attempted a work of legal redress along very much the lines upon which the National Association for the Advancement of Colored People was working. Its platform, as presented in a statement in 1905, ran as follows:

Freedom of speech and criticism.
An unfettered and unsubsidized press.
Manhood suffrage.
The abolition of all caste distinctions based simply
    on race and color.
The recognition of the principle of human brother-
    hood as a practical present creed.
The recognition of the highest and best training as
    the monopoly of no class or race.
A belief in the dignity of labor.
United effort to realize these ideals under wise and
    courageous leadership.

In 1910 it had conducted important civil rights cases and had in its membership some of the ablest colored lawyers in the country, with Mr. W. Ashbie Hawkins, who has since worked with our Association, on the Baltimore Segregation acts, as its treasurer.

The Niagara Movement, hampered as it was by lack of funds and by an absence of influential white friends, continued to push slowly on, but when the larger possibilities of this new Association were clear, the members of the Niagara Movement were advised to join, as the platforms were practically identical. Many of the most prominent members of the Niagara Movement thus brought their energy and ability into the service of the Association, and eight are now serving on its Board of Directors.

"The Present Crisis"

Our history, after 1910, may be read in our annual reports, and in the numbers of *The Crisis*. We opened two offices in the Evening Post building. With Dr. Du Bois came Mr. Frank M. Turner, a Wilberforce graduate, who has shown great efficiency in handling our books. In November 1910 appeared the first number of *The Crisis*, with Dr. Du Bois as editor, and Mary Dunlop MacLean, whose death has been the greatest loss the Association has known, as managing editor. Our propaganda work was put on a national footing, our legal work was well under way and we were in truth, a National Association, pledged to a nation-wide work for justice to the Negro race.

I remember the afternoon that *The Crisis* received its name. We were sitting around the conventional table that seems a necessary adjunct to every Board, and were having an informal talk regarding the new magazine. We touched the subject of poetry. "There is a poem of Lowell's," I said, "that means more to me today than any other poem in the world, 'The Present Crisis.'"

Mr. Walling looked up. "The Crisis," he said. "There is the name for your magazine, The Crisis."

And if we had creed to which our members, black and white, our branches, North and South and East and West, our college societies, our children's circle, should all subscribe, it should be the lines that are as true today as when they were written seventy years ago.

The Present Crisis

By James Russell Lowell

Once to every man and nation comes the moment to
    decide,
In the strife of Truth with Falsehood for the good or
    evil side;
Some great Cause, God's new Messiah, offering each
    the bloom or blight,
Parts the goats upon the left hand, and the sheep
    upon the right.
And the choice goes by forever 'twixt darkness and
    that light.

Then to side with Truth is noble when we share her
    wretched crust.
Ere her cause fame and profit, and 'tis prosperous to
    be just;
Then it is the brave man chooses, while the coward
    stands aside,
Doubting in his abject spirit, till his Lord is cruci-
    fied,
And the multitude make virtue of the faith they had
    denied.

Poem quoted in part

The Crisis "Opinion"

Excerpt from the first issue of The Crisis, *November 1910*
By W. E. B. Du Bois

The object of this publication is to set forth those facts and arguments which show the danger of race prejudice, particularly as manifested today toward colored people. It takes its name from the fact that the editors believe that this is a critical time in the history of the advancement of men. Catholicity and tolerance, reason and forbearance can today make the world-old dream of human brotherhood approach realization; while bigotry and prejudice, emphasized race consciousness and force can repeat the awful history of the contact of nations and groups in the past. We strive for this higher and broader vision of Peace and Good Will.

The policy of *The Crisis* will be simple and well defined:

It will first and foremost be a newspaper: it will record important happenings and movements in the world which bear on the great problem of inter-racial relations, and especially those which affect the Negro-American.

Secondly, it will be a review of opinion and literature, recording briefly books, articles, and important expressions of opinion in the white and colored press on the race problem.

Thirdly, it will publish a few short articles.

Finally, its editorial page will stand for the rights of men, irrespective of color or race, for the highest ideals of

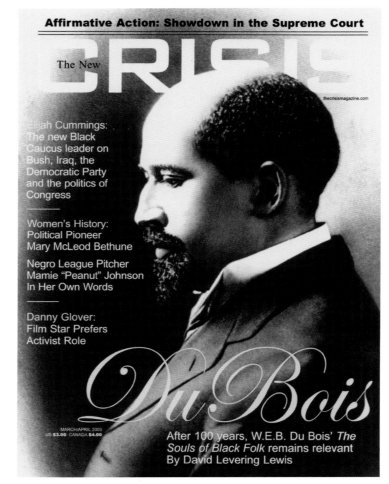

Affirmative Action: Showdown in the Supreme Court

The New CRISIS

thecrisismagazine.com

Elijah Cummings: The new Black Caucus leader on Bush, Iraq, the Democratic Party and the politics of Congress

Women's History: Political Pioneer Mary McLeod Bethune

Negro League Pitcher Mamie "Peanut" Johnson In Her Own Words

Danny Glover: Film Star Prefers Activist Role

Du Bois

MARCH/APRIL 2003
US $3.00 CANADA $4.00

After 100 years, W.E.B. Du Bois' *The Souls of Black Folk* remains relevant
By David Levering Lewis

The Crisis, **March/April 2003**

American democracy, and for reasonable but earnest and persistent attempts to gain these rights and realize these ideals. The magazine will be the organ of no clique or party and will avoid personal rancor of all sorts. In the absence of proof to the contrary it will assume honesty of purpose on the part of all men, North and South, white and black.

"*The battle we wage is not for ourselves alone, but for all true Americans.*"

Manifesto of the Niagara Movement, 1905

The mission of the National Association for the Advancement of Colored People is to ensure the political, educational, social, and economic equality of rights of all persons and to eliminate racial hatred and racial discrimination.

THOU
SHALT
NOT
KILL

July 28, 1917: The NAACP organized the 1917 "Silent March" to protest the East St. Louis, Illinois, massacre and lynchings in Texas and Tennessee. W. E. B. Du Bois is pictured third from right, with James Weldon Johnson to his left.

1909–1919

THE NEXT COLORED DELEGATION TO THE WHITE HOUSE

1909

• In January, Dr. Henry Moskowitz, Mary White Ovington, and William English Walling met in Walling's apartment to discuss the idea of creating a national, biracial organization to help right social injustices. Dr. Moskowitz was a socialist and social worker among New York immigrants. Mary White Ovington was a social worker and descendant of abolitionists. William English Walling was a wealthy Southerner, socialist, and writer, whose article on the 1908 Springfield, Illinois, riots in *The Independent*, aroused widespread sympathy over the treatment of Negroes. Also composing this nucleus were Charles Edward Russell, a close friend of Walling's, and Oswald Garrison Villard, publisher of the liberal *New York Evening Post*. It was agreed at the meeting that a public campaign should be opened on Lincoln's birthday to obtain the support of a much larger group of citizens.

Circa 1909: Dr. Henry Moskowitz, Jewish physician, civil rights activist, and NAACP Founder.

• This initial group was made biracial by the inclusion of Bishop Alexander Walters of the African Methodist Episcopal Zion Church and the Rev. William Henry Brooks, minister of St. Mark's Methodist Episcopal Church of New York. Augmenting this group were such other Negro leaders as W. E. B. Du Bois, Ida Wells Barnett, W. L. Bulkley, the Rev. Francis J. Grimke, and Mary Church Terrell, all of whom signed "The Lincoln Day Call."

• In a letter of encouragement to the conferees, William Lloyd Garrison, son of the Boston abolitionist, expressed the hope "that the conference will utter no uncertain sound

1915: "The Next Colored Delegation to the White House," a cartoon from the June issue of *The Crisis*.

Circa 1909: NAACP Founder and Chairman William English Walling.

Circa 1909: NAACP Founder and Secretary to the Board of Directors Mary White Ovington.

on any point affecting the vital subject. No part of it is too delicate for plain speech. The republican experiment is at stake, every tolerated wrong to the Negro reacting with double force upon white citizens guilty of faithlessness to their brothers. The rampant antipathy to the Oriental races is part and parcel of the domestic question. Safety lies in an absolute refusal to differentiate the rights of human beings."

• On February 12, 1909, over the signatures of sixty persons, the "Call" was issued for a meeting on the concept of creating an organization that would be an aggressive

Circa 1909: NAACP Founder Oswald Garrison Villard, who drafted the Lincoln Day Call.

Circa 1909: James Weldon Johnson, first black secretary to the NAACP Board of Directors.

watchdog of Negro liberties. This date marked the founding of the National Association for the Advancement of Colored People (NAACP).

• On May 31 and June 1, the National Negro Conference was held in the Charity Organization Hall in New York City. The theme was based on efforts to refute pre–Civil War beliefs that the Negro was physically and mentally inferior. A Committee of Forty on Permanent Organization was chosen to prepare for the incorporation of a National Committee for the Advancement of the Negro Race.

• Notably participating in this conference was Dr. William Edward Burghardt Du Bois, a signer of the "Call," who had organized the Niagara Movement in 1905 in an attempt to stem the curtailment of political and civil rights of Negroes.

69 black Americans are known to have been lynched in 1909.

1910

• On May 12, 1910, the Second Annual Conference of the National Negro Committee was held in New York City. The theme was "Disfranchisement." An Executive Committee selected the following as officers: Walling, chairman; John Milholland, founder of the Constitution League, treasurer; Villard, assistant treasurer. Frances Blascoer was the "incumbent secretary."

• On June 28, the Executive Committee hired W. E. B. Du Bois as director of publicity and research. He creates an official organ, which became known as *The Crisis*.

• In November, the first issue of *The Crisis* published with a circulation of 1,000. Taking its name from a poem by James Russell Lowell, "The Present Crisis," the magazine was created as the

Circa 1910s: William Edward Burghardt Du Bois, founder of the 1905 Niagara Movement, NAACP, and *The Crisis*.

official publication of the NAACP. Editor Du Bois declared, "the object of this publication is to set forth those facts and arguments which show the danger of race prejudice, particularly as manifested today toward colored people."

• The first legal action undertaken by the NAACP was the Pink Franklin peonage case, which involved the right of a farmhand to leave his employer after receiving advances in his pay. The Supreme Court was forced to rule on the rights of a black citizen and to state whether serfdom could legally be established in the U.S. The Court ruled that Franklin had not been denied his constitutional rights when a law officer attempted to serve a warrant and was killed by the farmhand. Because of this case, Villard persuaded the Executive Committee to establish a legal redress department in the NAACP.

• Du Bois and Booker T. Washington clashed in October when Washington declared in a speech to the Anti-Slavery and Aborigines Protection Society (which was meeting in Paris) that the condition of black people in the U.S. was being satisfactorily solved. Du Bois issued an

November 1910: First issue of *The Crisis*, official publication of the NAACP, edited by W. E. B. Du Bois.

THE CRISIS

A RECORD OF THE DARKER RACES

Volume One   NOVEMBER, 1910   Number One

Edited by W. E. BURGHARDT DU BOIS, with the co-operation of Oswald Garrison Villard, J. Max Barber, Charles Edward Russell, Kelly Miller, W. S. Braithwaite and M. D. Maclean.

CONTENTS

Along the Color Line   3

Opinion   7

Editorial   10

The N. A. A. C. P.   12

Athens and Brownsville   13
By MOORFIELD STOREY

The Burden . . .   14

What to Read . .   15

PUBLISHED MONTHLY BY THE

National Association for the Advancement of Colored People

AT TWENTY VESEY STREET   NEW YORK CITY

ONE DOLLAR A YEAR   TEN CENTS A COPY

"Appeal to Europe" that bitterly challenged that assertion.

• The National Negro Committee adopted the name National Association for the Advancement of Colored People (NAACP).

67 black Americans are known to have been lynched in 1910.

1911

• In January, a New York NAACP Branch was organized and Joel Spingarn became chairman. His brother, attorney Arthur B. Spingarn, became a member of the New York Branch vigilance committee, which sought to publicize and prosecute cases of injustices against Negroes in the metropolitan area.

• Publicity following investigation was the Association's weapon against lynching. In May, a lynching took place in a Kentucky opera house and those who paid admission were allowed to shoot the victim. The NAACP appealed to government officials with a resolution of protest demanding action against such atrocities.

• On June 20, the NAACP was incorporated; the bylaws provided for a Board of Directors of thirty members to be elected at the corporation's first meeting in

Circa 1909: Moorfield Storey, lawyer and civil rights activist who served as the NAACP's first president and co-chair of the National Legal Committee.

Circa 1909: Joel Elias Spingarn, university professor, civil rights leader and chairman of the NAACP Board of Directors. Spingarn established the Spingarn Medal in 1914.

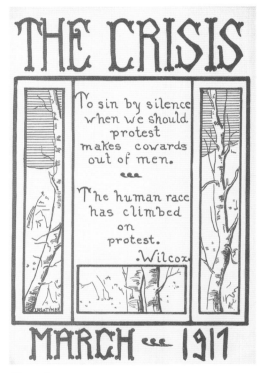

THE CRISIS

To sin by silence when we should protest makes cowards out of men.

The human race has climbed on protest. .Wilcox.

MARCH ⁓ 1911

March 1911

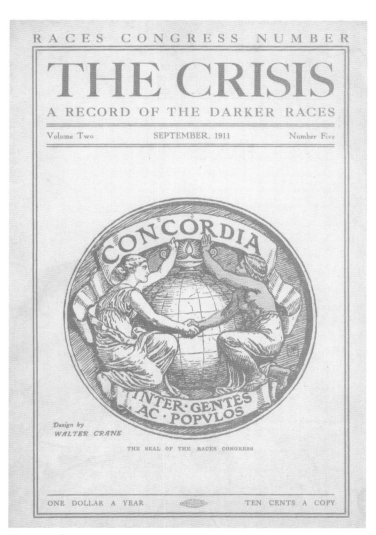

September 1911

November 1911

January 1912. The Board was to supplant the Executive Committee.

• After the meeting of incorporation, the following officers were elected: Moorfield Storey, president; John E. Milholland and Bishop Alexander Walters, vice presidents; Villard, chairman of the Board; Mary White Ovington, secretary; and Walter Sachs, treasurer. Du Bois was appointed director of publicity and research.

• That summer, the NAACP investigated the lynching and burning of Zach Walker, a Pennsylvania Negro who killed a policeman in self defense. The investigation by Mary Dunlop Maclean revealed an unfair trial and the Association employed the William J. Burns detective agency to secure evidence that was taken to Governor John Tener.

60 African Americans are known to have been lynched in 1911.

January 1912: NAACP New York Branch office.

Hon. Albert E. Pillsbury, attorney and NAACP supporter who interceded in the Pink Franklin case, recommending the Association appeal to South Carolina governor Martin Ansel.

1912

• On January 4, the Executive Committee met and presented a slate of thirty Board members for nomination and adjourned; the Board met and voted that the general committee (Committee of One Hundred) should be asked to serve on the new advisory committee; the annual meeting was held, and the thirty Board members were elected. The Association had 329 members.

• In February, at its first regular meeting, the Board elected its slate of officers, adding two vice presidents: Rev. John Haynes Holmes and Rev. Garnett R. Waller. May Childs Nerney replaced Ovington as secretary.

1912: Lynching by a mob of prominent citizens.

THE CRISIS

A RECORD OF THE DARKER RACES

Volume Four   SEPTEMBER, 1912   Number Five

Woman's Suffrage Number

ONE DOLLAR A YEAR   TEN CENTS A COPY

September 1912

November 1912: *The Crisis* **office at Vesey Street in New York City.**

November 1912: *The Crisis* **business force: Turner, Holsey, Allison, Jarvis and Sousa.**

Appointed as assistant secretaries were Martha Gruening, a volunteer social worker, and Paul Kennaday.

• The circulation of *The Crisis* reached sixteen thousand and went to every state except South Dakota. In October, it started publishing its annual children's number.

• Three branches were in existence: New York, New York; Chicago, Illinois; and Boston, Massachussets.

61 African Americans are known to have been lynched in 1912.

1913

• Early in the year, several northern state legislatures, including those in New York, Michigan, and Kansas, introduced anti-intermarriage Bills. As a result, the NAACP sought a Washington lobbyist.

• In April, at the annual conference in Philadelphia, Dr. Joel E. Spingarn instituted the Spingarn Medal, a gold medal which was to be awarded annually to an American Negro of "highest achievement" for the preceding year or years.

• In May, Villard personally presented to President Woodrow Wilson a plan for a National Race Commission. Members of this body would be appointed by the president, and their duty would be to conduct a nonpartisan, scientific study of the status of the Negro in the life of the nation, with particular reference to his economic situation.

• In July, the Wilson administration officially introduced segregation into federal government agencies, establishing separate work places, restrooms, and

September 1913

THE CRISIS

═══ FOR 1914 ═══

It is our determination to make THE CRISIS in the New Year absolutely indispensable to intelligent folk.

The news "ALONG THE COLOR LINE" will hereafter be so written as to furnish a complete summary of the history of colored folk and their struggles.

No important thought or comment on the Negro problem will be omitted from "OPINION."

Especial effort will be made to increase the number and weight of the ARTICLES published, and we expect contributions from some of the leading thinkers of the world, white and black.

We shall publish some interesting local STUDIES of great Negro cities and great Negroes of the past which you should read.

Our BOOK and MAGAZINE REVIEWS will be more complete, lively and critical than heretofore.

FICTION touching colored people will be given especial prominence, and now and then we shall publish a poem.

The EDITORIAL policy will be fearless and frank as usual. You may not agree with us (and that is your privilege), but you will have to admit that we know what we want and are not afraid to ask for it.

Finally, .we shall not forget the CHILDREN, their joys and sorrows and hopes.

All this for ONE DOLLAR.

Mention THE CRISIS.

December 1913: Advertisement for *The Crisis*.

April 1913

January 1913

lunchrooms for Negroes and whites. The NAACP, under Villard, therefore launched a full-scale battle against this spreading discrimination. In August, the NAACP Board authorized Villard to send an official letter of protest to President Wilson.

• The NAACP joined in filing *Guinn v. U.S. Supreme Court,* a voting rights case that held the Oklahoma "grandfather clause" invalid.

51 black Americans are known to have been lynched in 1913.

1914

• In January, Villard retired as Board chairman and was elected chairman of the finance committee. The NAACP had twenty-four branches and three thousand members.

• The NAACP moved into larger quarters at 70 Fifth Avenue, New York City. The first office was located at 20 Vesey Street in the *New York Evening Post* Building.

• August 15 was the official opening of the NAACP campaign against segregation within the Federal government with an "Open Letter to Woodrow Wilson." After a series of meetings, Mary Childs Nerney was sent to investigate conditions of segregation in Washington, D.C., and her report was widely publicized.

• The NAACP also protested against the drawing of the color line in the American Bar Association (ABA). Moorfield Storey, during a meeting of the ABA, was successful in having the organization rescind a two-year-old resolution that barred the admission of black lawyers.

• The NAACP won the admission of Negroes to the women's suffrage parade in Washington.

March 1914: The NAACP and *The Crisis* offices at 70 Fifth Avenue, suites 518 and 521, New York City.

1914: Maud Cuney Hare, pianist, author, and editor of *The Crisis* music notes.

March 1914

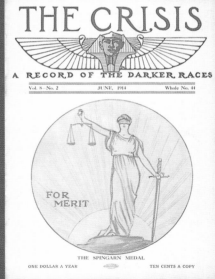

June 1914

1914: The leading colored residential street, Druid Hill Avenue in Baltimore, Maryland, site of the NAACP 6th Annual Conference in May 1914.

1914: Washington, D.C., Branch Legislative Advocacy Meeting. In foreground: Neval H. Thomas, Dr. C. W. Childs, G. W. Cook, Branch President and NAACP Founder Archibald Grimke, Oswald Villard, and U.S. Senator Moses E. Clapp.

• Villard personally intervened with the Judge Advocate General of the Army and eventually won freedom for a black soldier, Private Anderson of Honolulu, Hawaii, who had been sentenced by a court-martial to five years in prison for burglary.

• The NAACP hired two newsmen as lobbyists for each branch of Congress to report on the introduction of hostile Bills.

• The sixth annual NAACP conference was held in the Lyric Theatre in Baltimore, Maryland.

51 African Americans are known to have been lynched in 1914.

1915

• In February, *The Birth of a Nation*, probably the most controversial and racially biased film in the history of the motion picture industry, was released. A vigorous campaign had been launched in California to halt its production inasmuch as it was known to be based upon Thomas Dixon's notorious anti-Negro novel, "The Clansman." The novel, as did the film, glorified the Ku Klux Klan and vilified the role of Negroes in the Reconstruction period following the Civil War.

• With the release of the film, the NAACP, only six years old, launched a nationwide campaign to expose the

1915: The NAACP protested against racial stereotyping by launching a nationwide boycott against the movie *The Birth of a Nation*.

May 1915

falsity and infamy of the story and to halt showing of the film on the grounds that it distorted history and libeled the entire Negro race.

• In June, the Supreme Court ruled in *Guinn v. U.S.* that the grandfather clause violated the Fifteenth Amendment. This provision, which was adopted in a 1910 amendment to the Oklahoma Constitution, effectively barred illiterate men from voting except those whose ancestors were eligible to vote prior to January 1, 1866.

July 1915: Officers of the Howard University NAACP College Chapter, 1915.

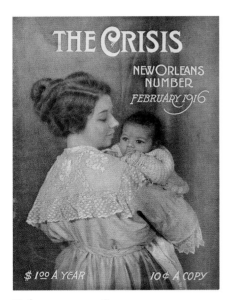

February 1916

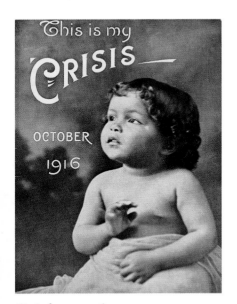

October 1916

The effect of this trick was to bar black men while permitting white men to vote. This case, argued before the Supreme Court by Moorfield Storey, in which the NAACP filed an *amicus curiae brief,* marked the Association's first significant involvement in the legal battlefront.

56 African Americans are known to have been lynched in 1915.

1916

• Following the death of Booker T. Washington in 1915, W. E. B. Du Bois proposed that the regular annual meeting be postponed as a memorial meeting for the Tuskegee leader that was scheduled for that day. At his suggestion, a meeting of reconciliation, known as the Amenia Conference (held on Joel Spingarn's Troutbeck Estate at Amenia, New York) was held instead and included the heads of all large Negro organizations.

• On January 10, at the NAACP Board meeting, Mary White Ovington became acting secretary, replacing Mary Childs Nerney. Royal Freeman Nash was appointed secretary in February.

1916: The automobile phalanx in St. Louis, Missouri, where the February 29 election was three to one in favor of segregation.

• In May, the lynching of an illiterate seventeen-year-old farmhand, Jesse Washington, who was mutilated and burned by a white mob in Waco, Texas, for the rape and murder of a white farmer's wife, was dubbed the "Waco Horror." The day after the lynching, NAACP secretary Nash, wired Elisabeth Freeman in Fort Worth, Texas, that her suffrage work throughout Texas would give her a cover to investigate the lynching and an excuse for being in Waco.

Freeman spent ten days investigating. Her report was carried in *The Crisis* July 1916 edition with an eight-page story and pictures of the horrific torture that outraged America and she toured lecturing on her investigation. The piece was distributed to 42,000 *Crisis* subscribers, 700 white newspapers, Congressmen, and 500 affluent New Yorkers in an effort to gain support for the Association's Anti-lynching fund.

• In an attempt to raise funds to end the widespread brutality against blacks, an anti-lynching committee was formed. The five-member committee determined that the NAACP should gather and compile facts on lynching, investigate such cases, and, organize Southern business and political leaders willing to speak out against the crime. A fund-raising drive was launched, and more than $10,000 was collected. The development of the public's consciousness of lynching as a national problem was regarded as the year's most important achievement.

51 African Americans are known to have been lynched in 1916.

1917

• Joel Spingarn led the NAACP fight to have the War Department provide a training camp to train Negro officers. In April, the NAACP was notified that this facility would open on June 17 at Des Moines, Iowa.
• On July 2, the East St. Louis, Illinois, riots broke out. As a result of the widespread brutality against black residents, the NAACP sent Martha Gruening and W. E. B. Du Bois to investigate. The Association also raised special funds to finance the legal defense and provided assistance for Negroes left destitute.

1917: Officers and Executive Committee of the NAACP Atlanta Georgia Branch.

• On July 28, the NAACP led a "Silent Protest Parade" of nearly ten thousand individuals to only the sound of muffled drums down New York City's Fifth Avenue to protest the mass murders, discrimination, and segregation in East St. Louis, Illinois, and other parts of the nation.

• In October, the NAACP Board of Directors appointed Du Bois as chairman of the Tercentenary Committee to Commemorate the Landing of the Negro at Jamestown.

• Following widespread rioting in Houston, Texas, in which members of the 24th Infantry were involved, the NAACP sent Martha

June 1917

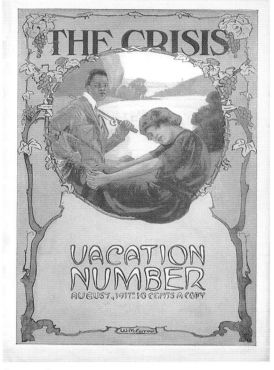

August 1917

Gruening to conduct an investigation. In her report, published in the November *Crisis*, she found that the soldiers had been provoked into violence by widespread racial prejudice. Thirteen of the soldiers were summarily hanged on December 11.

• Baltimore, Maryland, became the first of a number of cities to enact ordinances that segregated Negroes into residential districts. Several state courts, including the Maryland Supreme Court, threw out these ordinances on the grounds that they were unconstitutional. Other state courts, however, upheld them. So, on November 15, in

Buchanan v. Warley, an NAACP case originating in Kentucky (often referred to as the Louisville case), the U.S. Supreme Court ruled unequivocally that these ordinances were "in direct violation" of the Fourteenth Amendment.

• The NAACP won the battle to allow African Americans to be commissioned as officers in World War I. Six hundred officers were commissioned.

36 African Americans are known to have been lynched in 1917.

Christmas 1917

1918: Youngsters holding NAACP banner.

July 1918

June 1918

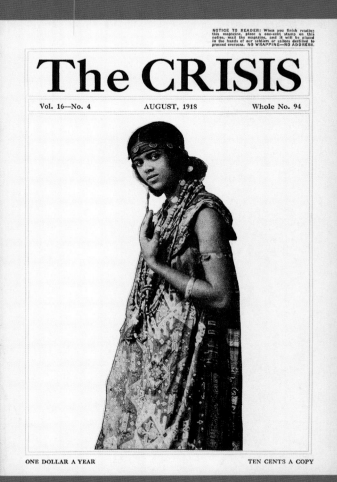

August 1918

May 1918

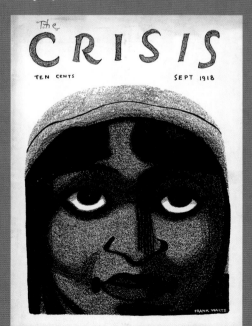

September 1918

Easter 1918

1918

• In January, John R. Shillady was appointed Executive Secretary and Walter White was appointed assistant secretary.

• Throughout the year, the Association continued its anti-lynching campaign with pressure on state officials and publicity on their activities. By this time, the NAACP was sending out press releases to nearly four hundred newspapers.

• Progress was made when an amendment to the New York State Civil Rights Law, drafted by the legal committee of the NAACP, was enacted into law on April 13. Thus, the Association had a model law on the books to secure legislation in other states.

• On July 26, due to NAACP pressure, President Wilson finally made a public statement against lynching. The Association distributed fifty thousand copies of the message.

• Following the summary execution of thirteen members of the 24th Infantry who had been accused of participating in the Houston riot, sixteen more were condemned to die. Consequently, the NAACP collected twelve thousand signatures on a petition presented to President Wilson on February 19. On September 3, the president commuted ten of the death sentences and affirmed six. A total of nineteen soldiers were executed.

• On December 1, Du Bois left for France on a three-fold mission: (1) as representative for the NAACP and *The Crisis* to the Peace Conference following the end of the World War; (2) to collect material for an NAACP history

Circa 1900s: John R. Shillady and Richetta Randolph in NAACP office.

Circa 1900s: John R. Shillady, Executive Secretary from 1918–1920 is severely beaten in Austin, Texas, for his civil rights work.

of the American Negro in the War; and (3) to summon a Pan-African Congress as a representative of the NAACP.

• Upon the recommendation of NAACP President Moorfield Storey, the NAACP argued that the anti-lynching bill known as the Dyer Bill was unconstitutional, but Storey revised his position, and from 1919 onward, the NAACP supported the legislation.

• Mob vengeance resulted in the deaths of innocent Negroes. During a five-day span in Georgia, eight Blacks were lynched including an innocent man, Haynes Turner. As his pregnant wife, Mary, proclaimed his innocence, she, too, was lynched and as she burned, her baby fell to the ground. Walter White and James Weldon Johnson investigated and Shillady forwarded the information to Governor Hugh Dorsey for prosecution.

60 African Americans are known to have been lynched in 1918.

1919

• In January, at the annual meeting, Mary White Ovington was elected chairman of the Board. Arthur B. Spingarn was elected a vice president.

• Also in January, the Pink Franklin case finally ended nearly nine years after the

Happy New Year

The Crisis

One Dollar a Year   Ten Cents a Copy

New Year edition, 1919

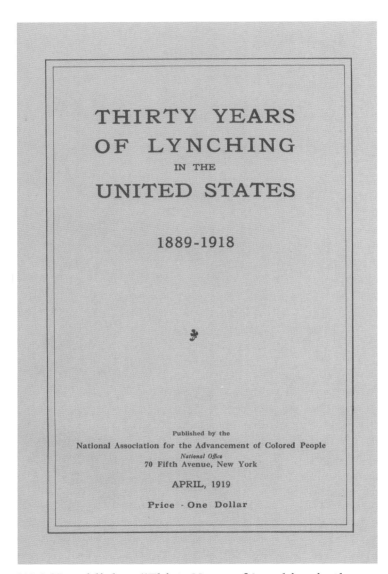

NAACP publishes "Thirty Years of Lynching in the United States," which lists the names, by state, of Negroes lynched from 1889–1918.

NAACP started the fight to free the farmhand who had killed a white law officer who broke into his cabin at 3 a.m. to arrest him for breaking his contract. In this month, South Carolina Governor Richard I. Manning paroled Franklin for good behavior. This was the first legal redress case undertaken by the Association.

• In April, the NAACP published its "Thirty Years of Lynching in the United States," which covered the years 1889 to 1918. An anti-lynching conference was held the first week of May at Carnegie Hall in New York City with 2,500 attending.

• James Weldon Johnson stated that the race problem was not only one of saving black men's bodies but of saving white men's souls. Following the conference, John Shillady and the committee drew up "An Address to the Nation on Lynching," signed by 130 prominent citizens including former President William Taft.

• Johnson deemed the summer of 1919, "The Red Summer" as twenty-six vicious and intense race riots erupted with the most violent occurring in: Chicago, Illinois, Washington, D.C., Elaine, Arkansas. When a race riot erupted in Elaine, Walter White, who with blond hair and blue eyes could pass for white, was sent to investigate. White was granted credentials from the *Chicago Daily News* and was able to speak with members of both communities. Black sharecroppers and tenant farmers, some members of the Progressive Farmers and Household Union of America, met at a church to discuss demanding better prices from whites for their crops. White officers went to the meeting location, shots were exchanged and the rioting began. Walter White's identity was discovered and he was soon on his way back to New York. When the train conductor told him he was leaving just when the fun was going to start because it was discovered a black man was "passin," White asked what they would do to him and the conductor responded, "when they get through with him he won't pass for white no more!"

• Tired of being easy targets for lynching and mass murders, Negroes began to strengthen their defense against the opposition. Because of this new fighting spirit that was displayed in several cities, beginning with Longview, Texas, as well as the NAACP investigations and campaigns, efforts were begun to curtail the Association's work. The first move was made by the Texas attorney general, who subpoenaed the Austin NAACP Branch president to turn over all of the Association's records to the court. Such a move threatened the existence of all thirty-one NAACP branches in Texas. The NAACP National Office stepped in to protect its operation. To lead the fight against the subpoena, NAACP Executive Secretary John Shillady went to Austin. But he was beaten unconscious by a group of men one morning on the courthouse steps as he left the attorney general's office where he, himself, was questioned in a "court inquiry." The mob was led by County Judge Dave J. Pickle.

• When Ovington wrote to police officials, the deputy sheriff responded that Shillady had been "received by red-blooded white men," who did not want "Negro-loving white men" in Texas. Shillady, who never recovered physically or psychologically from the beating, resigned.

• NAACP membership grew to around ninety thousand and the circulation of *The Crisis* grew to 100,000 after Du Bois published "Returning Soldier," an official document that reported the indignities black servicemen endured in France by the U.S. military.

76 African Americans are known to have been lynched in 1919.

In the last century, this nation has been transformed, and the leadership and vision of the NAACP has been a defining force in the founding of this New America. The NAACP has been a beacon of light in the midst of the storms of separation and discord that could have torn this nation apart. Born out of the crisis of racial violence during the riots of 1908, the NAACP has labored, sacrificed, and some of its members have even died struggling to lead this nation toward a more just, more peaceful society. The courage of this one organization to stand in the gap and call for justice has made this a better, more fair, more deeply democratic America. Congratulations to all my colleagues and fellow members in the struggle. Congratulations on a century of work well done.

Representative John Lewis
87th Spingarn Medalist

1923: Dr. Vada Somerville, W. E. B. Du Bois, Anita Thompson, Beatrice Thompson, and Mrs. F. M. Roberts are entertained by Ernest Morrison ("Sunshine Sammy") at Hal Roach Studios in Hollywood.

1920–1929

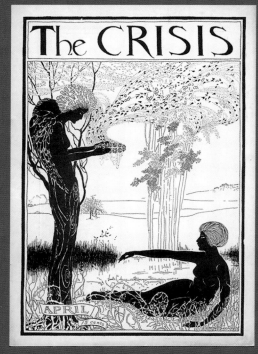

April 1920

May 1920

1920

• Following the United States takeover of Haitian finances in 1915 and the occupation of the Caribbean nation the following year by Uncle Sam's Armed Forces, the NAACP began receiving reports of widespread atrocities. In Du Bois's words, the NAACP was concerned because Haiti was "a continuing symbol of Negro revolt against slavery and oppression, and capacity for self-rule." The Board sent James Weldon Johnson to investigate the actions of the U.S. Armed Forces. He spent six months in Haiti and his findings were published in *The Nation, The Crisis, The Christian Herald,* and other magazines. Through his and other efforts to publicize these U.S. atrocities of slavery and oppression, the Wilson Administration's policies toward Haiti became a heated campaign issue. The NAACP fought for the restoration of independence to Haiti.

• Upon the adoption of the 19th Constitutional Amendment granting the vote to women, the NAACP launched an expanded voter education campaign to bring black people into the political process. The NAACP dramatized black people's political impotence in its pamphlet "Disfranchisement of Colored Americans in the Election of 1920."

• James Weldon Johnson became the first African American Executive Secretary of the NAACP.

• Led by Johnson and Walter White, NAACP representatives testified in Washington, D.C., before the House Committee on the Census on the vicious tactics that Southern states used to bar Negroes from the ballot boxes. They demanded that Congress investigate the 1920 elections of those states. Where it was found that the vote was denied black people, they demanded that no representative from those areas should be seated in the House.

• The Ku Klux Klan was revived under the leadership of Imperial Wizard William Joseph Simmons. Through its publication, *The Searchlight*, the Klan announced that the NAACP was its arch enemy.

• The 11th Annual Conference of the NAACP, regarded as the greatest up to its time, was held in Atlanta, the hotbed of the Klan.

• *The Crisis* launched "The Brownies' Book," which was designed for "all children and especially ours" and aimed "to be a thing of Joy and Beauty, dealing in Happiness, Laughter and Emulation, and designed for Kiddies from Six to Sixteen. It will seek to teach Universal

Love and Brotherhood for all little folk—black and brown and yellow and white." Unfortunately, it lasted for only two years.

• In August, John Shillady, who never fully recovered from the beating in Austin, Texas, resigned as Executive Secretary.

53 African Americans are known to have been lynched in 1920.

1921

• Newly appointed NAACP Secretary James Weldon Johnson visited President-elect Warren G. Harding at his home in Marion, Ohio, informing him that black people were primarily interested in the enactment of measures to relieve the oppressive conditions under which they lived. He also arranged a meeting with the President for a group of black Southerners. Johnson pressed for action on lynching, disfranchisement, peonage, and the end of American atrocities in Haiti; he called for the abolition of segregation in federal agencies and offices; and he also asked for the appointment of Negro assistant secretaries in the Departments of Labor and Agriculture.

• As a measure of the NAACP's unrelenting fight against lynching, forty-five thousand pieces of literature were sent out by the national office on lynching in 1921 alone.

• The NAACP presented a petition signed by fifty thousand persons to President Harding, requesting the pardon of soldiers from the 24th Infantry who had been imprisoned at Fort Leavenworth on charges arising from a riot in Houston, Texas, in 1917.

59 African Americans are known to have been lynched in 1921.

1922: Winners of special award for outstanding service to NAACP are shown at 13th North Carolina convention in Winston-Salem. Left to right: An unidentified branch representative, Rev. L. W. Wertz, Mrs. L. B. Michael, W. R. Saxon, Emma Johnson, Dr. P. H. Brandon and state treasurer N. L. Gregg.

1922

• During the previous year, on April 11, Congressman L. C. Dyer of St. Louis reintroduced his anti-lynching Bill at the opening of the 67th Congress. On January 26, 1922, the House passed this Bill by a vote of 230 to 119. The following day, the Bill was sent to the Senate Judiciary Committee. The NAACP was the lone force pushing for the passage of anti-lynching legislation and is to be credited for bringing the issue to the forefront of the nation's consciousness during fourteen years of unrelenting work. The NAACP's greatest single stroke in this fight was the placing of full and half-page advertisements entitled "The Shame of America" in nine major dailies and two weeklies across the nation to present the facts of this crime to the world.

• On June 30, the Judiciary Committee reported the Bill to the Senate floor, where it died in November because of a filibuster by Southern democrats. The NAACP, however, won four ancillary but decisive victories as a result of this fight. In Delaware, New Jersey, Michigan, and Wisconsin, congressmen who had voted against the Dyer Bill were defeated at the polls as a result of their stand in Washington.

• The fight against peonage reached a significant stage after the NAACP assumed the defense of twelve Arkansas farmers near Elaine who had been sentenced to death for rioting in 1919. The NAACP had twice won reversals of death sentences imposed by Phillips County Circuit Court for six of the men in the Arkansas Supreme Court. (The men first had been sentenced to die in October 1919.)

51 African Americans are known to have been lynched in 1922.

May 1922

The CRISIS

JULY 1922

FIFTEEN CENTS A COPY

July 1922

The CRISIS

Vol. 23—No. 5   MARCH, 1922   Whole No. 137

ONE DOLLAR AND A HALF A YEAR

FIFTEEN CENTS A COPY

March 1922

1923

• The NAACP won a significant victory in its fight for due process when the Supreme Court reversed a lower court order dismissing a petition for a writ of habeas corpus in the Arkansas riot case. Moorfield Storey argued the case of the six men before the Supreme Court on January 9, 1923. On February 19, the Supreme Court handed down its decision in the case, *Moore v. Dempsey*, reversing the convictions. The majority opinion was delivered by Justice Oliver Wendell Holmes.

• By this decision, the Supreme Court also reversed itself on the principle that federal courts had no right to interfere in certain cases even though it was shown that the trial was dominated by a mob atmosphere. The six men subsequently pleaded guilty to lesser charges. Their sentences were commuted on November 11.

• In the case of the other six whose convictions by Phillips County Circuit Court in 1919 had been twice reversed, the NAACP appealed to the Arkansas State Supreme Court for dismissal of the charges after the statute of limitations had run out and no further action had been taken against them in the local courts. The State Supreme Court handed down its decision, freeing the men on June 25.

• These decisions favorably influenced the fate of sixty-seven other men who had received long prison terms as a result of the 1919 riot. Consequently, all but eight of them were freed.

• In September, 558 delegates attending the NAACP 14th Annual Conference in Kansas City, Missouri, led by James Weldon Johnson, journeyed to Leavenworth Federal Prison in Kansas to visit fifty-four members of the 24th Infantry who had been convicted for rioting in Houston in

THE CRISIS ADVERTISER   231

COME TO KANSAS CITY
TO THE

FOURTEENTH ANNUAL CONFERENCE
OF THE

N. A. A. C. P.

AUGUST 29 to SEPTEMBER 5

Speakers of National repute will discuss all phases of America's Race Problem.

Representative L. C. Dyer who will reintroduce his Federal anti-lynch bill in the next Congress, will address the conference and help make new plans to carry the

JUST OUT

13th ANNUAL REPORT OF THE N. A. A. C. P. FOR 1922

PRICE 25 CENTS

TELLS THE STORY OF OUR YEAR'S WORK WITH FULL RECORD OF THE DYER BILL IN THE SENATE

WRITE FOR YOUR COPY TODAY

DYER ANTI-LYNCHING BILL TO VICTORY
"WE'VE JUST BEGUN TO FIGHT"

WE OUGHT TO BE A MILLION STRONG
HELP US GET THERE

FOR INFORMATION ABOUT THE KANSAS CITY CONFERENCE
WRITE TO
THE N. A. A. C. P.   69 FIFTH AVENUE
NEW YORK CITY
Mention THE CRISIS

1923: Cartoon from *The Crisis*: "Mr. Bryan Lends a Hand."

1923: The NAACP 14th Annual Conference, Kansas City, Kansas, where delegates journeyed to Leavenworth Federal Prison to visit fifty-four members of the 24th Infantry convicted of rioting in Houston, Texas, in 1917.

1917. November 11 was designated "Houston Martyrs' Day." Thirteen members of the 24th Infantry had been summarily hanged in 1917 and another six at a subsequent date.

29 Negroes are known to have been lynched in 1923.

1924

• On June 2, the Court of Appeals of the District ruled in *Corrigan et al. v. Buckley*, known as the Curtis case, that residential covenants were not unconstitutional. The NAACP appealed to the Supreme Court.

• Another important case was *Emmett J. Scott et al.* It differed from the Curtis action in that the deed for the property was already in effect and Mr. Scott had moved onto his property. An injunction to have the deed cancelled was being obtained. The NAACP filed a motion attacking the covenant on behalf of the defendants.

• At the White House on February 7, President Calvin Coolidge received a delegation of fourteen Negroes headed by James Weldon Johnson. They presented the president with a petition of 124,454 signatures requesting the release of the 24th Infantry soldiers from the Leavenworth prison. As a result of this long campaign, which began in 1917, the sentences of the men remaining in prison were reduced. Twenty of these men were released during the year; all the others received reduced sentences. Thus, the NAACP won reductions for a total of fifty-five soldiers.

• The extended legal struggles of the NAACP resulted in saving the lives of Elias Ridge, a thirteen-year-old accused of killing the wife of a white farmer, and Luther Collins, accused by a white woman of criminal assault.

• NAACP Director of Branches Robert Bagnall was sent

1924: NAACP Annual Convention in Philadelphia.

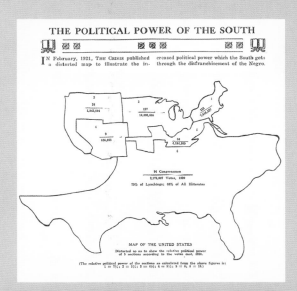

From *The Crisis*, November 1924: Map of the U.S.—distorted to show political power according to the votes cast.

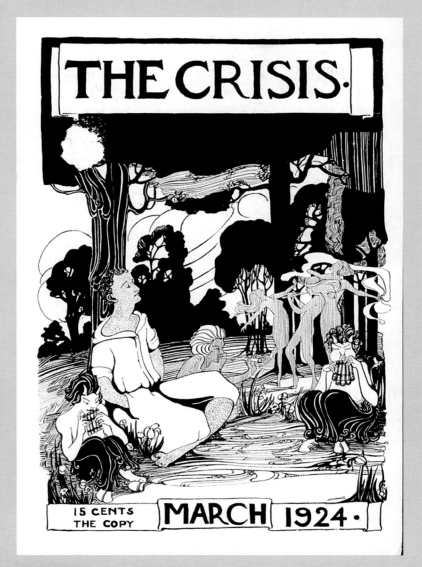

March 1924

1924: The NAACP Junior Branch of Detroit, Michigan.

1924: Caledonia Robinson of New York City, the "NAACP Prize Baby" for 1924.

July 1924

Christmas 1924

to Dayton, Ohio, where the Board of Education, in violation of Ohio law, was attempting to establish a Jim Crow school system. The NAACP continued to monitor the Sterling-Reed Education Bill which, if enacted, would have lent the sanction of federal funds to the system of discrimination against colored children.

• On May 10, a group of New York women organized "The Committee of One Hundred" to promote benefits for the NAACP.

Walter Nelson, Julian W. Perry, Cecil O. Rowlette, and Charles Mahoney, was retained by the NAACP to take charge of the defense. The first trial ended November 27 with the jury deadlocked.

• The system of permitting only whites to vote in the Texas Democratic primaries was challenged by Dr. L. A. Nixon, a Negro living in El Paso, after he was barred from voting. The El Paso Branch of the NAACP filed suit against

17 African Americans are known to have been lynched in 1924.

1925

• On September 9, one member of a mob attacking the Detroit, Michigan, home of Dr. Ossian H. Sweet was killed. Dr. Sweet and his family had just moved into their newly bought home in a white neighborhood. Sweet, his wife, two brothers, and seven other persons were arrested and jailed on charges of murder in the first degree. Clarence Darrow, assisted by Arthur Garfield Hays of New York and Detroit attorneys

January 1925: South Carolina per-capita expenditure according to average attendance 1920–21. Top figures=white children; Bottom figures=colored children. (Map copied from the official "Statistical Atlas of South Carolina" 1922.)

1925: The NAACP 16th Annual Convention, Denver, Colorado, which focused on voting rights and the elimination of "Whites Only" primaries in which blacks were not permitted to vote. Front row: James Weldon Johnson, Robert Bagnall, and Walter White.

local election officials. The case was dismissed and the national NAACP was asked to enter.

• The NAACP led successful fights against anti-intermarriage Bills in Ohio, Michigan, and Iowa.

• Thirteen more members of the 24th Infantry were released. Three of these soldiers had been sentenced to die and the others to life imprisonment. Twenty-two soldiers now remained in prison.

• The NAACP saw the end of the Arkansas case in which twelve black men were sentenced to death and sixty-seven others were given long prison terms for alleged rioting. However, investigation showed it was a plot to impress upon the country that these Negroes had organized to massacre white people and seize their land. Through the NAACP's investigation, the men organized to secure legal redress against exploitation under the share cropping system. Some 250 men, women, and children were killed in the rioting. Moorfield Storey, along with Scipio Jones of Little Rock, took the case to the Supreme Court and won.

• James Weldon Johnson was presented the Spingarn Medal as "author, diplomat, and public servant."

17 Negroes are known to have been lynched in 1925.

May 1925

1926

• The outstanding legal victory of the year was the acquittal of Dr. Ossian Sweet by a Detroit jury.

• Congressman L. C. Dyer introduced a new anti-lynching Bill in the House in December of the previous year, and this was followed by the introduction of another in the Senate by William B. McKinley. On February 16, James Weldon Johnson testified on the McKinley Bill before the subcommittee of the Senate Judiciary Committee and submitted facts on lynching.

• Assistant Secretary Walter White delivered a most telling blow against this crime by conducting a bold investigation on October 8 in Aiken, South Carolina, into the murder of three persons—Bertha, Demon, and Clarence Lowman. White obtained a detailed story of the lynchings and sworn affidavits with the names of persons, including law enforcement officers, who had been members of the mob or had assisted it. He then sent these names to South Carolina Governor Thomas McLeod and turned over details of the mob action to the *New York World*. The newspaper consequently sent its correspondent Oliver H. P. Garrett to Aiken. His stories aroused not only the

South Carolina press but also won the support of the nation's editors, who joined the demand for a federal anti-lynching Bill.

23 Negroes are known to have been lynched in 1926.

1927

- On March 7, in *Nixon v. Herndon*, the U.S. Supreme Court in a unanimous decision ruled the Texas white primary unconstitutional.
  - The NAACP carried the *Harmon v. Tyler* case to the Supreme Court and won on March 14. This case involved residential segregation in New Orleans, Louisiana, where a black was prohibited from occupying a house in an all-white block unless the prospective occupant obtained written permission from a majority of the residents.
  - In July, a Michigan judge dismissed all remaining cases in the Sweet trial.
  - The NAACP Board of Directors established the $500 Life Membership Program to provide another source of funds.

16 Negroes are known to have been lynched in 1927.

1928

- Although the courts had earlier ruled that black people could not be barred from voting in Texas Democratic primaries because of their color, the party devised alternate means to continue their illegal actions in Texas and other

February 1927

states. Political committees and party members now personally prevented qualified Negro Democrats from voting. Four cases in which the Association participated during this year challenged the constitutionality of enabling acts in Virginia (*West v. Bliley*); Texas (*Nixon v. Herndon*); Florida (*H. O. Goode v. Thomas Johnson et al.*); and Arkansas (*Robinson et al. v. Holfman et al.*).

10 Negroes are known to have been lynched in 1928.

1929

$10,000 a Year
For Its 20 Years' Work

Is the N.A.A.C.P. Worth This to America?

Will You Help Raise $200,000 in Its 20th Anniversary Year for the Oldest Organization Since the Civil War Championing the Cause of the American Negro?

5 Fundamental Victories Before the U. S. Supreme Court Profound Changes in Public Sentiment Stand to Its Credit ALL SAFEGUARDING BASIC CITIZENSHIP RIGHTS

Strengthen Your Organization the N.A.A.C.P. Increase the Power of its Organ *The Crisis* By Raising Its Subscription List to 50,000 Names

GIVE FOR YOURSELF AND FOR THOSE WHO CANNOT

J. E. SPINGARN, *Treas.*, 69 FIFTH AVENUE, NEW YORK, N. Y.
I enclose $............... as my contribution toward the $200,000 Fund being raised in the 20th Anniversary Year of the N.A.A.C.P. to carry forward and extend its work.

NAME_____
ADDRESS_____

1929: NAACP appeal for donations to continue its work.

• Now twenty years in existence, the NAACP had demonstrated the wisdom and prescience of its founders and the need for its continuing existence. When it was founded, many people thought the race relations problems could be solved by concentrating on the economic question alone. But now, having confronted racism on a determined and organized basis for twenty years, there was the realization that a broad attack upon phases of the problem was required.

• As lynchings declined, emphasis was shifted away from a concern about racial brutality. The NAACP resources were now being concentrated on gaining free access to the ballot for black voters and fighting residential segregation and employment discrimination.

• In West Virginia, Negroes were being denied access to the public libraries. Local attorney and Charleston West Virginia Branch President T. Gillis Nutter enlisted the help of colored attorney C. E. Kimbrough; together they filed a petition for a writ of error and supersedeas to the Supreme Court of Appeals of the state. The court ruled that the public library was not a part of the school system as the Board of Education tried to make it, and that the Board of Education could not establish a "Jim Crow" system there.

• Louis Marshall, who had worked with Moorfield Storey to win the five great victories for the NAACP in the U.S. Supreme Court and had participated in a number of other significant cases, died in September in Zurich, Switzerland. Replacing Marshall on the NAACP Board was New York Lt. Gov. Herbert H. Lehman. Harvard Law School Professor Felix Frankfurter joined the National Legal Committee.

7 Negroes are known to have been lynched in 1929.

> *For a century the NAACP has been a stalwart guide in helping black Americans achieve the full measure of their American citizenship. In doing so, it has also helped the American nation to pursue the equality of opportunity that is its greatest promise. All who value American democracy owe the NAACP gratitude for a job well done.*
>
> ## Vernon E. Jordan, Jr.
> *86th Spingarn Medalist*

Circa 1920s: W. E. B. Du Bois in the offices of *The Crisis*.

1937: Group of Detroit delegates to the NAACP Youth Council.

1930–1939

1930

• The political strength of the NAACP was dramatically displayed when Walter White engineered the strategy and led the successful fight against the nomination of Judge John J. Parker of North Carolina to the U.S. Supreme Court. The series of fast-moving events lasted just five weeks from the time the NAACP launched an inquiry into the record of President Herbert Hoover's nominee. But the consequences were of such great importance that the fight could have been nothing less than one of the most bitter in the nation's political history.

The NAACP's opposition to Judge Parker was sparked by a speech he had made ten years earlier in which he approved an amendment to his state's constitution that provided for a poll tax, literacy tests for voters, and a grandfather clause. The Supreme Court had already declared the grandfather clause unconstitutional. This clause, like the other two aspects of Judge Parker's proposals, violated basic equal rights of Negro Americans.

The NAACP urged President Hoover to withdraw the nomination, citing a precedent that was set on February 8, 1912, when President William Taft withdrew the nomination of Judge William Hook after the NAACP protested. In the face of President Hoover's adamant support of his man, however, the NAACP launched a public campaign. The result was that the Senate rejected Parker's confirmation on May 7 by a vote of 41 to 39.

• At its December meeting, the NAACP Board of Directors elected Joel E. Spingarn to succeed Moorfield Storey as president. Spingarn had served as chairman of the Board from 1914 to 1919 and as treasurer from 1919 to this time.

• On December 19, James Weldon Johnson resigned as secretary to devote himself to his creative work. He had been on a year's leave of absence from November 1929 under a fellowship for creative writing from the Julius Rosenwald Fund.

• The foundation for a full-time legal staff was laid when the NAACP received a two-year grant to study the legal status of the Negro. The study recommended that the Association retain the full-time services of legal counsel and Charles Hamilton Houston, dean of Howard University Law School, was chosen. He set the pattern for fundamental attacks on barriers to equal justice. Previously, the practice was to meet emergencies and opportunities as they arose.

20 Negroes are known to have been lynched in 1930.

1931

- On March 30, 1931, nine black youth, known as the "Scottsboro Nine," were returned to the Scottsboro Courthouse in Alabama to be charged with raping two white girls.

  The "Scottsboro" case arose on March 25 when the youth, aged 14 to 20, were removed from a freight train at Pain Rock, Alabama, after a fight with a group of white boys who were also traveling on the train in search of work.

  Eight of the youth were tried and sentenced to death in April. For the fourteen-year-old, the state asked for life imprisonment. The boys were at first represented by the NAACP, but, because of conflicts with Communists who were operating through the International Labor Defense (ILD), the NAACP lawyers, Clarence Darrow and Arthur Garfield Hays of New York, withdrew from the case.

- Roy Wilkins, former managing editor of the *Kansas City Call*, joined the NAACP staff as assistant secretary.

- The NAACP released the *Margold Report*, which challenged segregation in public schools.

12 Negroes are known to have been lynched in 1931.

OCTOBER, 1931　　　FIFTEEN CENTS THE COPY

THE CRISIS

Reg. U. S. Pat. Off.

Professor Herbert Miller
ON
INTERMARRIAGE
—
TWO TEACHERS
ON
CHILDREN'S
PREJUDICES
—
THE MINNEAPOLIS
RIOT
—
DELTA SIGMA
RHO

20th ANNUAL CHILDREN'S NUMBER

Is The N. A. A. C. P. Lying Down On Its Job?

October 1931

During the late twenties into the early thirties, W. E. B. Du Bois' writings become more militant and controversial, thus leading to conflicts with the NAACP. In 1934, he resigned and Roy Wilkins assumed the position. Wilkins continued Du Bois' mission of addressing the race issue while incorporating more news on the NAACP's activities.

May 1930

August 1931

March 1930

1932: The 23rd NAACP Conference in Washington, D.C., included a trip to Harpers Ferry, West Virginia, to lay the "Great Tablet" in honor of abolitionist John Brown; however, the NAACP was turned away by Storer College President Henry T. McDonald.

December 1934: Members of the Richmond Virginia Branch.

PILGRIMAGE OF THE 23RD
CONFERENCE OF THE N.A.A.C.P.
HARPER'S FERRY W.VA., MAY 22
SCURLOCK PH

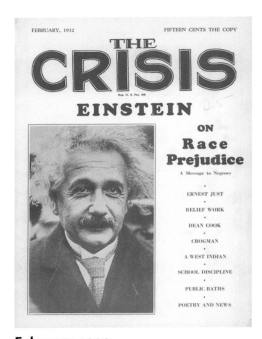

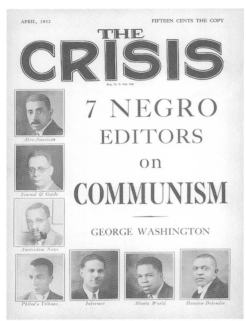

February 1932   **April 1932**   **September 1932**

1932

• In 1932, the NAACP vigorously protested to President Hoover the inhuman conditions under which Negroes had to work on the Mississippi Flood Control Project. Hoover responded to repeated complaints by appointing a commission to investigate the charges. New York Senator Robert F. Wagner promised to introduce in the Senate a resolution demanding an investigation of conditions. The NAACP also joined the National Bar Association (NBA) in protesting the refusal of the Hoover Dam Contractors to hire black workers.

• The second Texas white primary case was concluded when the Supreme Court, in a 5 to 4 decision, declared the Democratic Party's actions unconstitutional. This decision made it possible for state party committees to bar black voters from the primaries. Nevertheless, a third Texas white primary case developed when the election judges refused to allow Dr. L. A. Nixon of El Paso, Texas, to vote in the general run-off primaries.

• In July, the NAACP Board of Directors authorized a contribution of $1,000 to the Legal Defense Fund for use in the defense of the Scottsboro boys. The cases were argued before the Supreme Court on October 10, and on November 7, a decision was handed down reversing the death sentences. The court granted a new trial.

• W.E.B Du Bois led a delegation from the NAACP 23rd Annual Convention in Washington, D.C., to Harpers Ferry, West Virginia, to lay a tablet at the fort in honor of

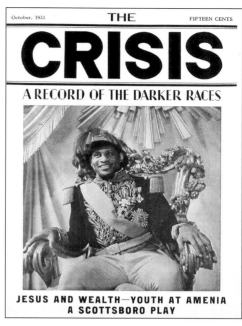

JANUARY, 1933 THE FIFTEEN CENTS

CRISIS
A RECORD OF THE DARKER RACES

Will the NEGRO Rely on FORCE
NEW RACIAL PHILOSOPHY

January 1933

June 1933 THE FIFTEEN CENTS

CRISIS
A RECORD OF THE DARKER RACES

ROLAND HAYES · THE NEGRO VOTER
McGHEES of ST. PAUL · SLATER FUND

June 1933

October, 1933 THE FIFTEEN CENTS

CRISIS
A RECORD OF THE DARKER RACES

JESUS AND WEALTH—YOUTH AT AMENIA
A SCOTTSBORO PLAY

October 1933

the abolitionist John Brown; however, the Storer College president and board of trustees refused to allow the tablet to be laid because of its inscription.

6 Negroes are known to have been lynched in 1932.

1933

• At the height of the Great Depression, Franklin D. Roosevelt began his first term as president. His revolutionary programs for social and economic development—the New Deal—held an initial promise for the betterment of black as well as white Americans.

• The NAACP stepped up its fight, with the passage of the National Recovery Act on June 16, to have blacks appointed to committees and boards related to the program.

• NAACP Assistant Secretary Roy Wilkins and journalist George S. Schuyler investigated working conditions on the Mississippi Flood Control Project. They spent three weeks there disguised as laborers. Earlier investigations had been conducted by Helen Boardman in 1932. As a result of this work, the secretary of war announced that unskilled workers would have their pay raised and hours shortened.

• The NAACP continued contributing funds to the ILD for the defense in the Scottsboro case.

• NAACP member Thurgood Marshall graduated at the top of his class from Howard University and began a career with the NAACP.

• Until February 1933, *The Crisis* was published by the National Association for the Advancement of Colored People. The February 1933 issue was published under the imprimatur of Crisis Publishing Company Inc., a wholly owned subsidiary of the NAACP.

• On August 7, an accord was signed between the U.S. and Haiti providing for the withdrawal of American troops by October 1, 1934, and for modification of U.S. control of Haitian finances. The NAACP had been fighting the battle for Haitian sovereignty since 1920.

• A second "Amenia Conference" was held on the "Troutbeck" estate of Joel E. Spingarn from August 18–21. The conference was called to consider the role of the Negro in a changing America and the world; it concluded that a union of white and black workers was needed in the labor movement to direct economic and political life. The conference condemned the traditional labor movement in America as ineffective.

24 Negroes are known to have been lynched in 1933.

1934

• With the effects of the Great Depression now being felt in every corner of society, the NAACP found itself increasingly involved in fighting to end employment discrimination. The Association continued its militant opposition to the numerous codes of fair competition created under the National Industrial Recovery Act that blatantly discriminated against black people. The NAACP's position was that the NRA was condemning the Negro to industrial slavery.

Most of the NAACP's effort to end these injustices was waged through the Joint Committee on National Recovery, which was composed of twenty-two national, racial, and interracial member organizations.

The Joint Committee on National Recovery also fought for jobs and benefits in the Civil Works Administration, Public Works Administration, Agricultural Adjustment Administration, Division of Subsistence Homesteads, and the Federal Emergency Relief Administration.

Through the Joint Committee on National Recovery, the Association sought to have industrially stranded black families integrated into various subsistence homestead colonies that were being established with federal funds.

• The NAACP continued protesting discrimination on the Boulder Dam Construction Site near Las Vegas, Nevada, and reported to President Roosevelt similar employment discrimination on the Tennessee Valley Authority Construction Project.

• On February 7, a federal district court judge defeated, for the third time in seven years, efforts to bar black voters in Texas Democratic primaries. Furthermore, the court awarded damages to Dr. L. A. Nixon for his having been denied his right to register and vote in the spring 1933 primary. Negroes were still barred, however, from voting in Texas primaries during the year.

• Hearings were held February 19–20 on the newly introduced Costigan-Wagner Anti-lynching Bill. The Senate Judiciary Committee reported out the bill, but it was not called up on the floor because of lack of support. Among the supporters of the bill were the Young Women's Christian Association (YWCA) and the Women's International League for Peace and Freedom (WILPF).

Consequently, by year's end, organizations representing more than forty-two million persons were openly committed

1935: NAACP Assistant Secretary Roy Wilkins at the NAACP National Office, 69 Fifth Avenue, New York City.

1935: NAACP Assistant Special Counsel Thurgood Marshall shown discussing the Donald Gaines Murray case filed to gain admission for Murray to the University of Maryland Law School.

to its passage and planned to support it the following January when it was again scheduled to be reintroduced in Congress.

• In March, the NAACP fought the closed shop provisions of the Wagner Labor Disputes Act, which was aimed at providing bargaining machinery. The NAACP felt that thousands of black workers who were shut out from membership in AFL unions would also be excluded from jobs by the closed shop provisions.

• On June 26, W.E.B. Du Bois tendered his resignation as editor of *The Crisis* because he strongly differed with the Board of Directors on many issues, particularly over what stance the Association should take on segregation. The resignation followed extended discussion on the issue by the Board and in columns of *The Crisis*. On July 9, the Board accepted the resignation "with the deepest regret" and with "our sincere thanks" for the services he had rendered.

• In August, the NAACP hailed the withdrawal of the last contingent of U.S. troops from Haiti.

• The San Francisco California NAACP Branch began

picketing the American Federation of Labor (AFL) on October 5, because of its racial discrimination. NAACP Secretary Walter White telegraphed William Green, president of the AFL, at the convention in San Francisco, urging that his unions end segregation and discrimination against blacks and warning the labor leaders that the AFL could never win job security for whites as long as black workers were excluded from bargaining units.

15 Negroes are known to have been lynched in 1934.

1935

• The Association accelerated its fight to end racial discrimination on federal construction and relief projects. NAACP Vice President James Weldon Johnson, who was now a Fisk University professor, was offered a high post with the National Works Progress Administration (WPA) in October. But the offer was suddenly withdrawn, and no satisfactory explanation was ever given by the Roosevelt Administration.

• The NAACP's fledgling legal staff, under the direction of attorney Charles H. Houston, won its first major victory when the Baltimore City Court ordered the University of Maryland Law School to admit Donald Gaines Murray if he was qualified. Baltimore attorney Thurgood Marshall worked with Houston on the case.

• NAACP Assistant Secretary Roy Wilkins was named acting editor of *The Crisis* on January 7, at a time when circulation dropped to between 8,500 and 10,500 as a result of the Depression, the exit of Du Bois, and the expanded coverage offered by other black publications. Wilkins continued his duties as assistant secretary. In dealing with the

"issues of the day" such as fascism, the rise of Hitler, and discrimination in the armed services, Wilkins gave more editorial attention to the work of the branches. During the fifteen years of his editorship, Wilkins sought to maintain the standards set by Du Bois and began to showcase the works of younger writers and leaders such as Thurgood Marshall, Pauli Murry, and Chester Himes.

• On March 1, the Association launched a nationwide drive to enlist public support for passage of the Costigan-Wagner Anti-lynching Bill. But after protracted and bitter debates, a Senate filibuster killed the bill for this session on May 1.

• In June, the Board of Directors adopted, at the 26th annual conference in St. Louis, Missouri, a broadened and more intensive program encompassing a universal concern for economic, legal, and educational problems. A new legal offensive arose from this approach that was directed against the fundamental basis of racial discrimination in education, thus marking a turning point in NAACP strategy—from a chiefly defensive stance against the onslaught of racism to an aggressive offensive upon segregation and other forms of discrimination.

• On July 19, the American Civil Liberties Union (ACLU), the ILD, the League for Industrial Democracy (LID), and the NAACP formed the Scottsboro Defense Committee and provided funds for an attorney in the case.

• On December 13, the NAACP warned the League of Nations about the dangers of the proposed Franco-British Peace Agreement, which would have settled the Italo-Ethiopian War by giving half of the African nation to Italy.

18 Negroes are known to have been lynched in 1935.

June 1935: The New Orleans Louisiana Branch.

THE CRISIS

JUNE, 1935

FIFTEEN CENTS

BROWN BOMBER JOE LOUIS
(Stone-faced, lethal robot bids for title—See page 165)

UNIONISM OUR ONLY HOPE
By Frank R. Crosswaith

RELIGION AND THE RACE PROBLEM
By John M. Cooper

SHARECROPPERS DROP COLOR LINE
By Ward H. Rodgers

June 1935

APRIL, 1935

THE CRISIS

FIFTEEN CENTS

SHIELDS, ELLINGTON AND BROWN
(Escaped Mississippi noose, but Death trails them—See page 119)

THUMBS DOWN ON UNIONS!
BY J. WELLINGTON EVANS

THE GEORGE CRAWFORD CASE
A STATEMENT BY THE N.A.A.C.P.

UPON THIS ROCK
BY EDWARD ARBOR

April 1935

SEPTEMBER, 1935

THE CRISIS

FIFTEEN CENTS

JUANITA E. JACKSON
(Leader of Young People Joins N.A.A.C.P. Staff—See page 272)

ETHIOPIA AWAKENS
By Reuben S. Young

September 1935

1936

• The NAACP waged a sustained fight against educational barriers to blacks. In a case similar to Donald Gaines Murray's, the NAACP sought the court's assistance to have the University of Missouri Law School admit twenty-three-year-old Lloyd L. Gaines; but the judge ruled that the state had a right to separate black from white students in schools.

• The Association opened an attack on unequal salary scales for black teachers in Maryland. NAACP Assistant Special Counsel Thurgood Marshall appeared before the state board of education to argue the case.

• The Scottsboro Defense Committee now also included the Church League for Industrial Democracy and the Brotherhood of Sleeping Car Porters. A request for a change of venue from Decatur, Alabama, was denied. At the conclusion of his fourth trial for rape charges, Haywood Patterson was found guilty and sentenced to seventy-five years in prison.

March 1935: The Charleston West Virginia Branch.

1936: The NAACP picketing of Eagle department store succeeded in the hiring of Negro salesmen.

1936: The NAACP 27th Annual Conference in Baltimore, Maryland, where the Association opened an attack on unequal salary scales for black teachers in the state.

1936: The NAACP flag "A Man Was Lynched Yesterday" was suspended from the window of the NAACP National Office at 69 Fifth Avenue with each lynching.

April 28, 1936: The lynching of Lint Shaw hours before his trial for an attempted assault.

1937: The Jamaica New York NAACP Branch Negro History Week Committee.

1937

- In January, Roy Wilkins was named editor of *The Crisis*.

- On April 15, a major victory was won when the House approved the Gavagan Anti-Lynching Bill by a vote of 277 to 119. Opponents in the Senate succeeded in blocking any decisive action on the measure by waging a filibuster. The Association took heart in the fact that support for such a law had increased considerably.

- Also in 1937, the NAACP continued its fight to open up state universities to black students by challenging the University of Tennessee's policy of providing professional training for whites but denying it to Negroes. In response to an

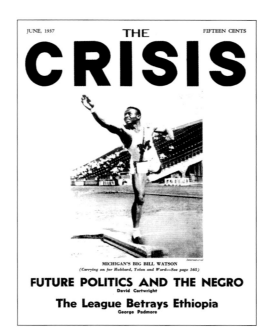

JUNE, 1937   THE   FIFTEEN CENTS

CRISIS

MICHIGAN'S BIG BILL WATSON
(Carrying on for Hubbard, Tolan and Ward—See page 165)

FUTURE POLITICS AND THE NEGRO
David Cartwright

The League Betrays Ethiopia
George Padmore

June 1937

NAACP suit against the university, the legislature subsequently passed a bill that provided scholarships for black students attending universities outside Tennessee.

- In another case, NAACP Counsel Charles H. Houston pushed forward the court battle to have the University of Missouri admit Lloyd Gaines to its law school. But the state supreme court upheld a lower court decision that dismissed Gaines's petition. The NAACP then began work to take the case to the U.S. Supreme Court.

- Among the new members who were elected to the National Board of Directors was William H. Hastie, Esq.

- Walter White was awarded the 23rd Spingarn Medal.

1937: Juanita Mitchell, NAACP national youth director, shown visiting the Scottsboro Boys.

1938

• In 1938, the Association continued its fight to end segregation at the Tennessee Valley Authority. Charles Houston and Thurgood Marshall conducted a third NAACP investigation of working conditions there and submitted a report to a joint committee of Congress that was appointed to study repeated complaints of racial discrimination.

• Thurgood Marshall was appointed NAACP special counsel after Charles H. Houston returned to private practice.

• On April 19, the last two Houston martyrs were freed from Leavenworth Federal Penitentiary after twenty-one years of imprisonment.

• Donald Murray graduated from the University of Maryland Law School in June.

• The U.S. Supreme Court ruled on December 12 that the University of Missouri Law School could not exclude a student (Lloyd Gaines) because of his color. It also ruled

December 1936: The Richmond Virginia NAACP Branch membership campaign members.

January 1947: The P.O. 400 Club of Chicago had 100 percent NAACP membership.

P.O 400 CLUB 1936.

R D JONES
PHOTO

May 1937: First Annual NAACP Youth Council - Oklahoma Conference of Branches (105 youth delegates from 18 Youth Councils and College Chapters).

February 1937: The Boston Massachusetts NAACP Youth Council.

April 1937: The Chicago Illinois NAACP Youth Council.

SEPTEMBER, 1937   FIFTEEN CENTS

THE CRISIS

SCOTTSBORO BOYS IN NEW YORK
(Montgomery, Roberson, Leibowitz, Williams, Roy Wright—See page 263)

HITLER, MUSSOLINI AND AFRICA
George Padmore

TOO MUCH OF RACE
Langston Hughes

URBAN HOUSING PROBLEMS
Samuel Lafferty

September 1937

June 1937: A young Clarence Mitchell Jr., who later became NAACP Washington Bureau director.

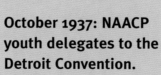
October 1937: NAACP youth delegates to the Detroit Convention.

December 1937: Officers of Newark Ohio NAACP Youth Council.

September 1937: James Weldon Johnson at the NAACP Detroit Convention.

that states must provide equal educational facilities for black students and that the provision of scholarships outside the states did not constitute equality.

1939

• In 1939, the most concerted drive ever by the NAACP was made to gain enactment of an anti-lynching law. Despite the continued backing of groups like the CIO and the AFL, Congress adjourned without acting on a measure.

• The Missouri legislature appropriated $200,000 to provide graduate study for black students at Lincoln University. The NAACP at once opposed the establishment of such a school, because it was felt that it would be inadequate.

• The NAACP provided resources and support to more than one thousand Negro residents in Miami, Florida, who were facing intimidation and threats of violence from KKK members on election day.

• After being appointed to the U.S. Supreme Court, Justice Felix Frankfurter resigned from the National Board of Directors.

• On April 9, after the Daughters of the American Revolution barred Marian Anderson from performing at their Constitution Hall in Washington, D.C., the NAACP successfully moved to have her appear at the Lincoln Memorial that Easter Sunday where more than seventy-five thousand people attended the open air concert broadcast nationally by radio.

• On October 11, the NAACP Legal Defense and Educational Fund, Inc., was formed. Its incorporators were

The CRISIS September 1938 • Fifteen Cents

BATTALION CHIEF WESLEY WILLIAMS
(Highest ranking Negro fireman in the nation—See page 286)

LABOR TROUBLE IN JAMAICA
GEORGE PADMORE

JAMES WELDON JOHNSON
MEMORIAL TRIBUTES FROM THE NATION

September 1938

Dr. William Allan Nielson, president of Smith College; Arthur B. Spingarn; Federal Judge William H. Hastie; New York Gov. Herbert H. Lehman; Mary White Ovington;

May 1939: The Columbus Ohio NAACP Youth Council.

Municipal Judge Charles E. Toney; and New York City Tax Commissioner Hubert T. Delany. On April 30 the following year, the U.S. Treasury Department certified the fund, enabling it to receive tax-deductible donations.

• Arthur B. Spingarn was elected NAACP president in December to succeed his late brother, Joel.

> *My wife Billye and I are pleased to celebrate the many accomplishments of the NAACP. Over the past one hundred years, it has stood as a strong beacon of hope for justice and equality for African Americans. We applaud this stalwart organization, as it continues to fight and advocate for those whose civil rights are being denied.*
>
> ## Hank Aaron
> *60th Spingarn Medalist*

The CRISIS   July, 1939   •   Fifteen Cents

CONDUCTOR ON CITY-OWNED SUBWAY
He hauls millions of New Yorkers—(See page 198)

July 1939

1939: At the 30th Annual NAACP Convention in Richmond, Virginia, Eleanor Roosevelt, wife of President Franklin D. Roosevelt and NAACP National Board member, presents the 24th NAACP Spingarn Award to distinguished vocalist Marian Anderson.

The CRISIS

September, 1939 ● Fifteen Cents

Morgan Smith Photo

JUSTICE JANE M. BOLIN
(First Negro woman judge in the U.S.A. — see page 262)

September 1939: New York mayor Fiorello La Guardia appoints Jane M. Bolin judge of the Domestic Relations Court, making her the first black woman to don the robes in the United States. Judge Bolin would serve for forty years.

September 1939: Walter White addresses the NAACP 48th Annual Convention.

December 1945: NAACP Baltimore Maryland Youth Council Christmas party.

1940–1949

May 1945

1940

• As the nation became more involved in World War II, the NAACP found it necessary to step up its efforts to end discrimination in the armed services and win justice for the black serviceman. Walter White, along with A. Philip Randolph, president of the Brotherhood of Sleeping Car Porters, and T. Arnold Hill, an executive officer with the National Youth Administration, led a series of nationwide demonstrations to publicize their opposition to segregation in the military.

• In response to such protests, the Roosevelt Administration promoted Col. Benjamin O. Davis Sr. of the 369th New York Infantry to brigadier general, the first such office ever held by a black man in the army. William H. Hastie, who was dean of the Howard University Law School, was named a civilian aide to the secretary of war. Another black man, Maj. Campbell C. Johnson, was named administrative assistant to the selective service director.

The CRISIS March, 1940 ● Fifteen Cents

DANCER KATHERINE DUNHAM
"She is not only lovely to look at, but has style and authority."—New York Times

March 1940

• On September 9, the NAACP Board of Directors passed a resolution offering the NAACP's legal services to any American who found it difficult to enlist in the army or navy because of his race or color.

• The NAACP wrote seventy-five senators, urging them to amend the Selective Service Act before its passage, to provide for the drafting of Negroes into the army and navy without consideration of race. The Association, later in the year, urged its branches to seek the appointment of Negroes to local draft boards. Consequently, a greater number of people were appointed to draft boards than during World War I.

• When the first defense contracts were awarded in mid-July, the NAACP immediately urged Negro workers to apply for jobs in plants that were benefiting from these contracts and offered its assistance to persons who were barred from employment because of their race. Walter White presented a clear picture of the problems black workers faced in the defense industry in the December 11 issue of the *Saturday Evening Post*.

• In June, Brownsville, Tennessee was the scene of an "off the record" lynching of NAACP leader Elbert Williams after he raised the ire of local whites by getting blacks out to vote.

• In September, Assistant NAACP Field Secretary Amos Brown was arrested at Savannah Beach, Georgia following a "wade-in" to protest discrimination at a public beach.

• The NAACP joined in the filing of *Hansberry v. Lee*. The U.S. Supreme Court decided Chicago, Illinois' restrictive covenants to sell or rent to blacks was unlawful.

• The NAACP reported eighty thousand blacks voted in eight Southern states but acknowledged only five percent of voting-age blacks were registered.

Pre-1945: The NAACP National Headquarters in New York City.

The CRISIS April, 1940 • Fifteen Cents

HATTIE McDANIELS
Her "Mammy" in GWTW won coveted film "Oscar"

April 1940

The CRISIS May, 1940 • Fifteen Cents

ERSKINE HAWKINS
The nation dances to his "Tuxedo Junction"

May 1940

February 1941

July 1941

1941

• On June 18, Walter White and A. Philip Randolph met at the White House with President Roosevelt, Secretary of War Henry L. Stimson, Secretary of Navy Frank Knox, and other officials to discuss the threatened march on Washington as a protest against employment discrimination. Finally, to avoid the march, the president issued Executive Order No. 8802 on June 25, which set up the Committee on Fair Employment Practices and banned discrimination in industries receiving government contracts.

• The NAACP's role in *Mitchell v. United States* led to a Supreme Court decision that ended segregated facilities in railroad travel.

• At Fort Benning, Georgia, the body of a black soldier was found hanging from a tree in a wooded area. Four months later, in August, black soldiers riding a bus to Fort Bragg were stoned and one was shot. Shortly after the Fort Bragg clash, forty black members of the 94th Engineers Division went AWOL from Camp

1941: NAACP National Youth Director Madison Jones Jr. addresses the 32nd Annual Conference of Branches in Houston, Texas.

May 1941: An NAACP Youth Council sound truck at the Ford strike.

Robinson, Arkansas, in protest over insults and threats by state troopers.

• The NAACP protested to the War Department about these acts of violence and the many other forms of discrimination that the black soldiers experienced. The navy, however, refused to enlist Negroes in any category other than messman.

• The NAACP continued its fight against segregation in graduate schools and the discriminatory practice prevalent in the South of paying black teachers considerably less than their white counterparts. Nevertheless, progress was slow. In Missouri, the state supreme court upheld a lower court decision of the previous year against Lucile Bluford, who had been barred from registering in the state university's graduate school of journalism. The courts refused to issue an order to have the university register her and dismissed her damage suit. The NAACP consequently filed a new suit in federal court to have her admitted. Other institutions that the NAACP was actively battling included the universities of Tennessee and Kentucky.

1942

• The NAACP maintained its strong opposition to the creation of a Jim Crow blood bank by the American Red Cross. The Association also fought the creation of segregated service clubs by the Red Cross.

• In February, the NAACP protested the many forms of discrimination in the war industries. The Association

1942: The NAACP St. Louis Missouri Branch representatives protesting lynching in Sikeston, Missouri.

demanded that the AFL permit thirty Negro workers who had been restricted to jobs as painters' helpers to sign up for better-paying jobs.

• In June, the NAACP Washington Bureau was established.

• As a result of NAACP demands, Dorie Miller, a black mess attendant, was commended by the secretary of the navy for his bravery during the attacks on Pearl Harbor.

• The navy modified its practice of restricting black enlisted men to the mess halls, but the NAACP still protested the new policy as racially restrictive, since blacks were still generally barred from serving on ships as sailors, gunners, and technicians. With the establishment of the Women's Army Auxiliary Corps (WACS), the NAACP demanded that enlistments and assignments should not be based on color.

• The NAACP continued to fight against voter discrimination in three areas: white primaries, poll tax, and general registration barriers. The Association sought passage of the Geyer anti-poll tax bill, which passed the House but was defeated by a filibuster in the Senate.

• The NAACP joined in the filing of *Hill v. Texas.* The U.S. Supreme Court reversed the case because of key systemic exclusions of blacks from jury cases.

• The Association worked with studio executives and politicians to establish an ad hoc committee with the major film studios to monitor the image and portrayal of African Americans on the silver screen.

1942: NAACP junior drummers and majorettes, Santa Clara County, California.

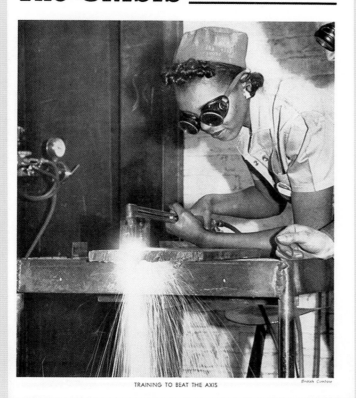

April 1942

September 1942

1943

• Job opportunities and racial discrimination in the armed services were the principal concerns this year. The NAACP repeated its demands several times that the War Department establish a mixed voluntary unit. Other actions included protesting the exclusion of Negroes from army and navy specialized programs that were being offered in colleges and defending several soldiers who had been convicted on various charges.

• The Association filed several informal complaints with the Interstate Commerce Commission on the refusal of railroads to serve black passengers in dining cars. The NAACP also began preliminary steps to challenge interstate commerce segregation in the courts. Cases challenging dual pay scales were now pending in Southern states.

• NAACP branches in Detroit, Michigan, and Harlem, New York, worked to quell violent race riots that erupted. The riots were a response to inadequate housing, education, and job discrimination. In Detroit, Walter White and Thurgood Marshall worked with local NAACP officials to protect the rights of black residents. In Harlem, where the police were not as violent, White and Roy Wilkins helped Mayor LaGuardia end the disturbance. Riots also broke out in Beaumont, Texas; Mobile, Alabama; Los Angeles, California; and Philadelphia, Pennsylvania.

• Ruby Hurley of Washington, D.C., was appointed NAACP youth director.

March 1943

June 1943

July 1943

1943: The NAACP Baltimore Maryland Branch membership drive committee.

1940s: NAACP Executive Secretary Roy Wilkins with Negro GIs in Louisiana during World War II.

1943: An apartment destroyed during the Detroit, Michigan, riot.

1944

• Walter White spent three months touring the European and Mediterranean Theatres to observe the U.S. war machine in operation. Upon his return to the U.S., he submitted to the war department a 14-point memorandum in which he made recommendations that the services create nonsegregated bomber crews and a special court-martial review board. He left in December for a similar tour of the Pacific Theatre.

• The NAACP led a legal battle to gain release of African American servicemen facing disciplinary action for protesting discriminatory practices in the armed services.

• On April 3, the U.S. Supreme Court ruled in the NAACP case *Smith v. Allwright* that the right to vote was protected by the Constitution. Consequently, black citizens were able to vote in Texas, where the case originated; they had been barred from participating in democratic primaries.

• Despite the ruling in *Smith v. Allwright,* the South Carolina legislature continued its attempts to disfranchise black residents by abolishing its laws on primaries and thus providing election officials with unlimited discretion as to who should vote. And in Alabama, Georgia, Florida, and Mississippi, Negroes were still openly and officially barred from voting in democratic primaries.

• The Washington Bureau vigorously protested discrimination by the Federal Housing Administration (FHA) by submitting to President Roosevelt a comprehensive statement on the agency's racial policies and actions.

• In September, W. E. B. Du Bois returned to the staff of the NAACP as director of special research after an absence of ten years, during which he taught at Atlanta University.

1944: The NAACP Detroit Michigan Branch parade for victory over "Jim Crow."

1944: World War II veteran Isaac Woodard, whose eyes were gouged out by a Negro-hating police chief in Batesburg, South Carolina (accompanied by his wife and NAACP attorney Franklin Williams to his left).

1944: Washington, D.C. leaders launch
1944 NAACP membership campaign.

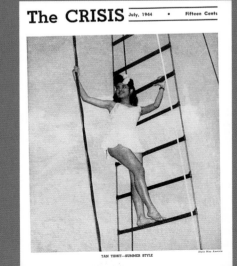

July 1944

February 1944: NAACP membership campaign captains of the Elizabeth New Jersey Branch.

The CRISIS — August, 1944 • Fifteen Cents

33rd Annual Education Number

August 1944

1945

- Continuing its attack on discrimination against black soldiers, the NAACP demanded that the Veterans Administration end hospital segregation and other forms of racial bias. The Association fought to free fifty seamen who had been convicted of mutiny at Port Chicago, California, and had the convictions reversed of fifty-two soldiers who had also been convicted of mutiny in Hawaii.

- When the Daughters of the American Revolution again barred a black artist, this time pianist Hazel Scott, from performing at Constitution Hall, the NAACP prepared and had introduced in Congress a bill that sought to deny tax-exempt status to any organization that discriminated because of race, religion, or color.

- Walter White and W. E. B. Du Bois proposed at the San Francisco, California, meeting of the United Nations Conference on International Organization that the colonial system should be abolished and the equality of races recognized. In October, Du Bois attended the Pan-African Congress in London, which met to consider the problems of African people around the world.

- The NAACP led the outcry when Congress refused to fund the federal Fair Employment Practices Commission (FEPC).

1946

- The U.S. Supreme Court handed the Association an important legal victory when it held in *Morgan v. Virginia* that a state law requiring separation of races on motor carriers could not be applied to interstate passengers. The bus companies attempted to circumvent this ruling by creating their own regulations.

PRESS RELEASE   JANUARY 25, 1945

NAACP PROTESTS "BIRTH OF NATION" SHOWING AT MUSEUM OF MODERN ART

New York -- The NAACP has demanded immediate withdrawal of the race-baiting film Birth of a Nation being shown now, by the New York Museum of Modern Art. In a wire protesting use of the film banned 30 years ago, Roy Wilkins, Acting Secretary said: "National Association for Advancement of Colored People vigorously protests showing of Birth of a Nation under any pretext whatsoever. This film was ordered withdrawn by City of New York in 1915 and has been barred by city councils, mayors, and even state legislatures in many sections of the country because it stirs racial prejudice and hatred and has been judged to be an inciter of violence. At this time when America and the world are fighting racial bigotry and attempting to build mutual respect and unity between peoples, Museum of Modern Art should not interfere by showing this film. We have received protests from indignant Negro soldiers and sailors and from some whites who have seen film at Museum recently. We demand immediate withdrawal of film."

January 25, 1945: Press release announcing NAACP's protest of the racebaiting movie *The Birth of a Nation*.

- The NAACP launched a new attack on segregation in universities in these cases: *Sweatt v. University of Texas, Sipuel v.*

June 1945: Purple Heart recipient Staff Sgt. Dave Hira speaks to the NAACP convention.

The CRISIS

April, 1945 • Fifteen Cents

SOME OF THE NAVY'S NEW WAVES

Official U. S. Navy Photo

NEW YORK BARS ECONOMIC JIM CROW
JULIA E. BAXTER

THE NEGRO SOLDIER BETRAYED
AN EDITORIAL

April 1945

NATIONAL ASSOCIATION FOR THE
ADVANCEMENT OF COLORED PEOPLE

Report of the Youth Secretary
(For the May Meeting of the Board)

NAACP YOUTH WEEK: The annual observance of NAACP Youth Week
was held April 8-14. Reports from many of the councils and college
chapters show that the program as outlined in the March report to the
Board was carried out successfully. Because of the death of President
Roosevelt, some of the groups postponed activities scheduled for the
latter part of the week until the following week. Twenty-seven
thousand tags were distributed to groups that sent in requests.

PLANNING AND ADVISORY COMMITTEE TO YOUTH COUNCILS AND COLLEGE
CHAPTERS: The National Planning and Advisory Committee to Youth
Councils and College Chapters met on Saturday, April 28 and Sunday,
April 29 at the Church of the Master, New York City. Ten of the
thirteen representatives were in attendance together with Mr. Dudley,
Miss Black, Miss Jensen, Mr. Madison S. Jones and Rev. James H.
Robinson who acted as consultants.

The meeting opened at 10:00 A.M. Saturday with a statement of
purpose by the Youth Secretary. The representatives were charged
with the duty of fulfilling the obligation as set forth by the Youth
Conference; to set up for accomplishment specific objectives and to
keep youth in local communities informed of legal decisions, legislative enactments, political trends and issues and furnish information
and guidance as to the most effective way to utilize all poortuni-
ties and resources available to the end that they may contribute
substantially to the advancement of minority rights.

Following the prepared agendum which incorporated suggestions
from the delegates the discussions began with Educational Projects.
It was felt that there should be a nation-wide project in the form
of an Essay Contest to stimulate the thinking of young people and to
point up the work of the Youth groups.

It was recommended that such a contest with the topic "Problems
of Minority Youth in Our Community and the Solutions" be held September 20 - October 15, 1945. Information and publicity on the contest
would be released as soon as approval is given by the National Office.
The dates set were for the time when the three best manuscripts from
local groups must be into the regional judges. The regional judges
will then select the three best to be submitted to the National
Office for final judging by October 31.

Regions set up were the West Coast, Southeast, Northeast,
North Central and South Central. Representatives present were named
chairmen of their regions and it was recommended that a person be
secured to represent the West Coast.

The National Office was asked to be responsible for nationwide publicity, in the form of posters and initial announcements. The
regions will seek ways and means of securing regional and local
publicity. National prizes were recommended to be (1) $100.00 war
bond (2) $50.00 war bond (3) $25.00 war bond. For regions (1) $50.00
war bond (2) $25.00 war bond (3) $15.00 in stamps. For local prizes
(1) $25.00 war bond (2) $10.00 in stamps (3) $5.00 in stamps. Regional
judges would be National Board Members located in the areas and the
Youth Work Committee would be the final judges. Other details of age
limits, etc. were left to the discretion of the Youth Work Committee
and the National Office.

1945: NAACP Youth Secretary Ruby
Hurley leads a group discussion.

1945: NAACP Youth Secretary
Ruby Hurley's report for the
May 1945 Board meeting.

1945: The NAACP Pancas—Chicago Branch members.

The CRISIS — June, 1946 • Fifteen Cents

JACKIE ROBINSON

June 1946

AUGUST, 1946 — 35th ANNUAL EDUCATIONAL NUMBER — 15¢

HONOR GRADUATE

August 1946

SEPTEMBER, 1946 — DID NEGROES ELECT TALMADGE? — See page 266 — 15¢

ICE CREAM HOUR — THEN SCHOOL

September 1946

University of Oklahoma, *Hatfield v. Louisiana State University*, and *Johnson v. Louisiana State University*. In each of these cases, no separate law or medical school had been established for Negroes. In another case, *Mendez v. Westminister School District*, in which the NAACP participated, a federal court declared for the first time that segregation was a denial of the equal protection clause of the Constitution.

• The NAACP negotiated pardons for eleven of twenty-six servicemen by petitioning the secretary of war for clemency in their behalf and gaining a review of their court-martial convictions.

• The Association made some progress in its fight against discrimination in the Veterans Administration. These positive steps included the hiring of a black assistant to the administrator, the certification of a veteran for educational benefits to attend Harvard University, and the admitting of Negro patients by eleven of twenty-two veterans hospitals that had previously refused to do so.

• Clarence Mitchell Jr. was appointed NAACP national labor secretary, assisting Walter White.

• Gloster B. Current, who had been executive secretary of the Detroit Michigan NAACP Branch since 1941, was appointed director of branches.

1946: NAACP secretary's report for the September 1946 Board meeting.

NATIONAL ASSOCIATION FOR THE
ADVANCEMENT OF COLORED PEOPLE

Report of the secretary
For the September 1946 Meeting of the Board
————————

GEORGIA LYNCHINGS: On July 25th two Negro men and their wives were lynched in Walton County, Georgia. On July 14th one of the Negroes, Roger Malcolm, had stabbed Barney Hester, his white employer, because of Hester's continued attentions to Malcolm's wife. Immediately following this an attempt was made to lynch Malcolm but the sheriff came and placed him in jail. On July 25th, Lloyd Harrison (wealthy white farmer) brought George Dorsey, his wife and Malcolm's wife to post bond of $600 for Roger Malcolm. (Dorsey's wife was Malcolm's sister.) The bond was arranged shortly after 2 P.M. but Malcolm was not released from the jail until 5:30. Then Harrison and the four Negroes started back to his farm. En route they were stopped by two cars and approximately 25 to 30 men dragged the two men from the car and shot them. When one of the women cried out the name of one of the mob, the women were taken from the car and drilled with bullets also. Harrison reported this to the sheriff and an inquest was held on the scene where it was found the four came to their death at the hands of parties unknown. Harrison said he did not recognize any members of the mob.

The NAACP proceeded at once to send investigators to the scene to obtain as much first hand information as possible. Unofficial information has been secured as to the identities of some of the mob and this has been turned over to the FBI. It is generally thought that Lloyd Harrison was a party to the crime as well as the jailer and sheriff of the county.

Oliver Harrington, Director of Public Relations of the Association, spent ten days in Georgia gathering additional data on the lynching and the general situation there. It is generally believed that the lynching was a direct result of the winning of the election by Talmadge.

A man who claims he was an eye witness to the lynching was located by the Afro-American newspaper and after several days was brought to the NAACP to tell his story. The Administrative Assistant in the National Office took him to the FBI where his story was taken and checked.

The Association's Secretary called on the President to reconvene Congress to enact anti-lynching legislation immediately. Passage of such legislation was urged by Major W. E. Spence, Chief of the Georgia Bureau of Investigation and Governor Ellis Arnall.

On July 31st the NAACP announced on behalf of the National Office and branches rewards totalling $10,000 were being offered for information leading to the arrest and conviction of the lynchers. Request was sent to the branches for contributions toward this reward and they responded immediately by sending checks and accounts of their activities in connection with the lynchings. A telegram was received from Governor Arnall congratulating the NAACP on its offer of the $10,000 reward.

November 1946: Baritone Todd Duncan (5th from left) at the NAACP Honolulu Hawaii Branch.

January 1946: Recently organized NAACP Lexington Kentucky Youth Council.

1946: Members of the executive committee of the NAACP Washington, D.C. Branch.

1946: The NAACP Nashville Tennessee Branch membership drive committee.

1947

• W. E. B. Du Bois organized the preparation of a 155-page petition, "An Appeal to the World," documenting the history of racism in America. This petition was presented to the United Nations. The issue was raised before the world body just after it held a debate on the treatment of blacks and minorities in South Africa, Southwest Africa, Palestine, and Asia. The NAACP petition was debated for two days at a meeting in Geneva of the drafting committee of the U.N. Human Rights Commission.

• On March 1, the NAACP Church Department was established to coordinate its civil rights activities with

January 1947: The NAACP 38th Annual Board of Directors Meeting led by Executive Secretary Walter White.

similar work by religious institutions.

• In June, there was a significant development in the nation with a shift in the federal government's attitude toward segregation and discrimination. This shift was brought about by President Harry S. Truman when he addressed the NAACP 38th Annual Conference in Washington, D.C. He was the first U.S. president to address an NAACP convention. The President declared: "We can no longer afford the luxury of a leisurely attack upon prejudice and discrimination. There is much that state and local governments can do in providing positive safeguards for civil rights. But we cannot, any longer, await the growth of a will to action in the slowest state or the most backward community. Our national government must show the way."

• Three bodies appointed by the president further clarified the government's policies on race: the Commission on Higher Education, the Civil Rights Committee, and the Advisory Commission on Military Training. The Civil Rights Committee was particularly significant to the NAACP, because it was the direct result of a meeting between Mr. Truman and civil rights groups of which the NAACP was the leader.

• The U.S. Supreme Court had established nine years earlier in *Lloyd Gaines v. the University of Missouri* the right of black students to equal public educational facilities. Nevertheless, graduate schools around the nation still barred them. The NAACP there-fore began creating a legal strategy to tear down the entire structure of segregation in all levels of education.

• Because of the persistence of restrictive housing covenants, the NAACP won the support of several other ethnic groups and started moves to make its case to the U.S. Supreme Court. A national conference of lawyers

1947: NAACP staff working at the 56th Annual Convention in Washington, D.C.

and sociologists sponsored by the NAACP Legal Department met in New York on September 6. Four cases were subsequently prepared for the high court. These were *Hurd v. Hodge* and *Urciolo v. Hodge*, which were handled by private lawyers, and *Shelley v. Kraemers* and *McGhee v. Sipes*, which were handled by the Association.

April 1947: The NAACP Durham North Carolina Branch membership campaign brought in 829 new members.

1948

• Twenty-two national black organizations responded to an NAACP call and met in New York to formulate a "Declaration of Negro Voters," which was a guide on candidates for the November elections. This strategy paid off well and demonstrated that black voters were not wedded to a single party or special candidate. Consequently, President Truman was reelected with the help of three key states—Ohio, California, and Illinois—where the sizeable margin of black votes for him were crucial to his victory.

• The U.S. Supreme Court sounded the death knell of racially restrictive housing covenants when it decided unanimously on May 3 that these agreements that barred blacks from purchasing homes in white neighborhoods could not

March 1948: Delegation from New York City boards a bus to attend the NAACP Youth Legislative Conference at Howard University in Washington, D.C.

be enforced by state or federal courts. The decision was the result of the *Shelley v. Kraemer, Urciolo v. Hodge,* and *McGhee v. Sipes* cases.

• The NAACP further positioned itself for an all-out attack on school segregation when the Board of Directors approved a legal strategy in which the Association would file only those cases that challenged the constitutionality of racial separation. The professional and graduate school cases were all tried on this issue, so various precedents had been established. Attention was therefore turned to extending these principles to secondary schools.

• The Association won fights for equalization of teachers' salaries in several cases.

• In an attempt to evade the Supreme Court's decision that ended discrimination in primary elections, South Carolina repealed its law in this area. But the Democratic party was now restructured as a private, voluntary association with powers to choose its members. In *Elmore v. Rice* and *Brown v. Baskin,* the NAACP won a district court injunction against this move on July 12. The South Carolina plan was declared unconstitutional.

• South Carolina then attempted to devise other means of disfranchisement. But, once more at the NAACP's insistence, the district court declared them unconstitutional.

• The NAACP succeeded in having President Truman issue Executive Order No. 9980, prohibiting racial discrimination in federal service. Although the practice of discrimination did not end, at least eighteen agencies

1948: The NAACP National Staff.

established procedures for handling complaints by the end of the year.

• On July 26, President Truman issued Executive Order No. 9981, which established the Committee on Equality of Treatment and Opportunity in the Armed Forces. This order did not meet the NAACP's demand for an end to racial segregation in the military, but it was viewed as a step in that direction.

• The NAACP supported the creation of the Fair Practices Board of the Civil Service to handle workplace discrimination complaints.

• Henry Lee Moon was appointed NAACP director of public relations.

• W. E. B. Du Bois left the NAACP for a second time. Sparking this second departure was the refusal of the Board of Directors to renew his contract because he supported certain ideologies that were alien to the Association.

1949

• The NAACP submitted a twenty-one-page memorandum to President Truman on February 1 in which it was charged that the Federal Housing Administration (FHA) was supporting and perpetuating residential segregation. As a result of such pressures, the U.S. solicitor general announced

April 1948: Amy Spingarn pins an orchid on Mrs. Arthur Spingarn at the 70th birthday celebration for NAACP president Arthur Spingarn, as NAACP Board Chairman Dr. Louis T. Wright looks on.

1948: During a court recess visit to lend support, Ike Williams (left), world lightweight boxing champion, shakes hands with Collis English, one of the defendants in the Trenton Six Trial. The other defendants are seated.

1948: The Rosa Ingram case where Ingram, a black sharecropper, was accused along with three of her sons of killing a white farmer.

AMERICUS, GEORGIA
MARCH 26, 1948

I hereby authorize National Association for the Advancement of Colored People, through Attorney A. T. Walden of Atlanta, Georgia, and his associates, to take complete and exclusive charge of the defense of myself and my minor sons, namely, Wallace Lee Ingram and Sammie Lee Ingram, in the cases in which we have been convicted of Murder in the Superior Court of Schley County, Georgia.

Said Association is hereby given exclusive authority to raise funds for our defense, and no other person or organization is so authorized, unless permission is granted by National Association for the Advancement of Colored People.

All contributions for our defense coming from outside the State of Georgia may be sent to that Association at Number 20 West 40th Street, New York, New York. All other contributions shall be sent to Attorney A. T. Walden, Suite 200 Walden Building, Atlanta, Georgia, for deposit to Ingram Defense Fund of Georgia Conference of N. A. A. C. P., Branches.

Official receipts shall be given for all contributions. Disbursements shall be made by vouchers and checks signed and countersigned by the proper officials of the Association. The accounts shall be audited by certified public accountants and certified reports of the same made public.

My sons join in this authorization.

Signed: *Rosa Lee Ingram*
MRS. ROSA LEE INGRAM
WALL ISGRAM
SAMMIE LEE INGRAM (14)   WALLACE LEE INGRAM (15)

1948: Rosa Ingram's statement granting the NAACP exclusive charge of the defense of her family, who were convicted of murder.

1948: Rev. William H. Borders, NAACP vice president, Daniel E. Byrd, NAACP assistant field secretary, and C. L. Harper, NAACP Atlanta Branch president discuss raising funds for the Ingram defense.

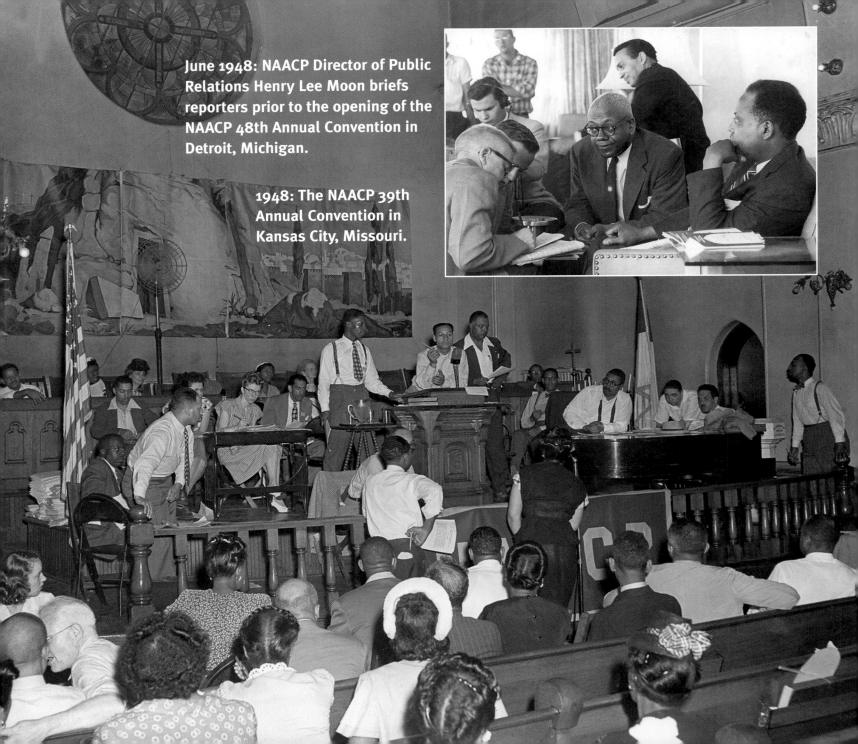

June 1948: NAACP Director of Public Relations Henry Lee Moon briefs reporters prior to the opening of the NAACP 48th Annual Convention in Detroit, Michigan.

1948: The NAACP 39th Annual Convention in Kansas City, Missouri.

June 1948: NAACP members lead a membership drive in the Cordornices Village, California, housing project.

on December 2 that the federal government would end policies that directly contributed to the creation of racial ghettos.

• The Joint Committee on Civil Rights, which was organized by the NAACP on February 5, served as the coordinating arm of twenty-two organizations seeking enactment of civil rights legislation. The Joint Committee gave priority to the enactment of a fair employment practices law by the federal government. The Committee also supported efforts to enact bills against lynching, poll tax, and Jim Crow travel. Also supported were omnibus civil rights and equal rights bills.

• A major bar to the speedy enactment of legislation in these areas, however, was the filibuster. So the committee first set its sights on getting the Senate rules revised so that it would be easier to invoke cloture. After the February 5 conference, Walter White, Roy Wilkins, Thurgood Marshall, Gloster Current, Clarence Mitchell, Leslie S. Perry, and representatives of the other organizations began lobbying on Capitol Hill in support of anti-filibuster resolutions.

• They suffered a setback, though, and the Hayden-Wherry resolution was approved over their bitter objections. This resolution was a "compromise" sponsored by senators Carl Hayden (D-Ariz.) and Kenneth Wherry (R-Neb.) and did the opposite of what the NAACP sought. It tightened the cloture rule. The NAACP National Board of Directors, therefore, changed its strategy and voted that the enactment of FEPC laws was now its priority. Following this lead, local branches succeeded in having several states enact such laws.

February 1949: The Crisis Publishing Company, Inc. finance report.

• President Truman established a Federal Fair Employment Board that immediately responded to some of the issues the NAACP had raised.

• On April 8, an NAACP-sponsored conference on colonialism was held in New York. Nineteen organizations attended and adopted a statement prepared by Dr. Rayford Logan, a consultant to the NAACP, in support of establishing an international trusteeship for Southwest Africa

July 1949: Ralph Bunche arrives in Los Angeles, California, to receive the NAACP Spingarn Medal, accompanied by Roy Wilkins and Henry L. Moon to his left.

and the former Italian colony of Somaliland. They also called for the independence of Indonesia.

- Because of ill health, Walter White submitted his resignation as Executive Secretary, effective June 1. But the National Board of Directors rejected it, and, instead, gave him a year's leave of absence beginning June 1. Roy Wilkins was then appointed acting secretary.

- The Association won its twenty-fifth victory before the Supreme Court on July 22, when the murder conviction of Austin Watts was reversed. The high court held that the Marion County, Indiana, police had denied Mr. Watts due process in preparing their case.

- The NAACP's Emergency Civil Rights Committee invited some sixty national organizations involved in civil rights to join in a national emergency civil rights mobilization that would organize a lobbying blitz and conference for Washington in mid-January the following year. The Civil Rights Committee met in New York City on October 15 and announced its objectives for calling "upon the American people to join in a crusade to remove the stigma of discrimination and segregation from our national life."

- The goals of the Emergency Civil Rights Committee were announced to the branches of the NAACP by Roy Wilkins, a key strategist. Following the October 15 meeting, a conference was held on November 10 with twenty-two national church, labor, civic, and trade organizations to map plans for developing widespread support for their civil rights programs.

- The NAACP urged the repeal of the Taft-Hartley Act, because it felt that its union shop requirement was a bar to the employment of black workers in the construction industry.

- The NAACP filed suits in federal courts attacking public segregation in Lumberton, North Carolina, and Irwin County, Georgia. A petition against segregation was also filed with the school board in Clarendon County, South Carolina.

- On October 2, Oswald Garrison Villard died. He was author of the NAACP's "Call" in 1909.

I am not only honored but challenged to have been cited by the NAACP with the Spingarn Medal. It connects me to so many people who have contributed to social justice in our country. I always try to justify the confidence it represents.

Dorothy I. Height

78th Spingarn Medalist

1949: Delegates leaving New York City for the NAACP Youth Legislative Conference.

July 1957: NAACP members attend the NAACP 48th Annual Convention in Detroit, Michigan. Pictured: Mrs. Charles Foggie; Rev. Foggie, president of the Pittsburgh Pennsylvania NAACP Branch; Marion Bond Jordon, Branch executive secretary; Matthew Moore, Branch executive committee; and Mildred Bond, NAACP field secretary and sister to Marion Jordon.

1950–1959

50

NAACP
1909-1959

YEARS
FREEDOM
CIVIL RIGHTS
PROGRESS
NAACP

1950

- In 1950, more than four thousand delegates, led by NAACP Executive Secretary Roy Wilkins, representing one hundred organizations that composed the National Emergency Civil Rights Mobilization, met in Washington from January 15 through January 17 to demonstrate for civil rights laws. Wilkins, general chairman of the demonstration, led a delegation that met with President Truman at the White House to secure his support in passage of the Fair Employment Practices Commission (FEPC) Bill being considered in the Senate. Mr. Truman assured the delegation that he would support the civil rights program.

- The U.S. Supreme Court took decisive steps toward ending the "separate but equal" doctrine that was established in 1896. In one case, the Court ruled that the University of Texas could not bar Herman Marion Sweatt from its law school because of his race. It further ruled that the separate law school that the state had established to accommodate Sweatt was not and could not be equal to that at the University of Texas.

- In another case, the High Court ruled that the University of Oklahoma could not segregate G. W. McLaurin within its graduate school once he had been admitted. In a third case, which was brought by Elmer Henderson against the Southern Railway Company, the Supreme Court declared that segregation of dining car facilities was unconstitutional.

- The Sweatt and McLaurin cases were NAACP actions, while the Association supported the Henderson action by filing a brief.

- On August 1, Clarence Mitchell Jr. was appointed director of the Washington Bureau.

- The NAACP requested a review by the U.S. Supreme Court of the affirmation by the Alabama Supreme Court of the conviction of James Arrington, an illiterate Negro sentenced to death for assaulting a white woman, on the grounds he was denied due process of law when his court-appointed counsel failed to defend him adequately.

- A polylingual scholar, James W. Ivy, was named editor of *The Crisis*. Ivy, who brought a sense of international solidarity, had a profound interest in the cultural development of colored peoples around the world. He translated pertinent writings by persons of African descent from the French, Spanish, and Portuguese for republication in *The Crisis*.

NAACP 50th Annual Convention program, New York City.

January 1950

January 1950: NAACP holding a National Emergency Civil Rights Mobilization meeting. After the event, Congressman Franklin D. Roosevelt, Jr., of New York commented, ". . . Your project was handled in such a dignified and capable manner that the net result was, in this instance, a beneficial one for the civil rights program."

June 1950: Six-year-old Charles Houston Jr. accepts the 35th Spingarn Medal from Dean Erwin Griswold of Harvard University Law School, awarded posthumously to his father, the late Charles Hamilton Houston, at the NAACP 41st Annual Convention in Boston, Massachusetts. NAACP Special Counsel Thurgood Marshall and Mrs. Houston look on.

February 8, 1950: Joe Louis, retired heavyweight champion, presents a $500 check to Franklin H. Williams, assistant special counsel of the NAACP, to aid in the legal defense of three Florida youth whose conviction on a trumped-up rape charge is being appealed by the NAACP. James Collier, chair of the Orlando Florida Branch Legal Redress Committee and J. P. Ellis, Orlando Florida Branch president, look on.

May 1950

1950: Gregory Hayes Swanson, who was denied entrance to the University of Virginia School of Law until the NAACP stepped in, stands by a statue of Thomas Jefferson at the university.

1950: World War II veteran Frank Cole is congratu-
lated by NAACP assistant special counsel Jack
Greenberg upon exoneration of a court-martial
conviction on charges of participating in a mutiny
in Germany in 1946. The NAACP's work won Cole
an honorable discharge.

1950: NAACP Acting Secretary Roy Wilkins receives
a Life Membership Certificate from NAACP
President Arthur Spingarn.

December 1950: At the cocktail party launching the NAACP benefit concert given by Duke Ellington are Mollie Moon, wife of NAACP's Henry L. Moon; Christiane Halle; Kitty Hemming; Mrs. Edward Dudley, wife of the American ambassador to Liberia; and Ruth Bryan Rohde, former American minister to Denmark, also serving as chair of the sponsoring committee for the concert.

1950: Entertainers Sarah Vaughan and Duke Ellington purchase the NAACP's first Christmas seals in the 1950 drive.

1951

• In 1951, encouraged by U.S. Supreme Court decisions invalidating segregation in state-supported professional and graduate schools, the NAACP launched a well-planned "Equality Under Law" campaign to overturn racial separation at its roots—in elementary and secondary schools. The drive was launched with the filing of lawsuits against school districts in Atlanta, Georgia; Clarence County, South Carolina; Topeka, Kansas; and Wilmington, Delaware.

• On February 28, the NAACP filed their case as *Oliver L. Brown et al. vs. The Board of Education of Topeka, (KS)* based on a black third grader, Linda Brown, who had to walk a mile to her black school when the white school was only three blocks away. Making its way to the U.S. Supreme Court, the combined cases from other states became known as *Oliver L. Brown et al. vs. The Board of Education et al.*

• Special Counsel Thurgood Marshall responded to complaints from black GIs by personally investigating the conditions of segregated units in Korea. He conferred with soldiers and top-level army personnel in Japan and Korea, including General Douglas MacArthur, and uncovered a shocking pattern of racial discrimination.

• NAACP lawyer Jack Greenberg was successful in securing the exoneration of four Negro GIs, Corporal Verlon S.

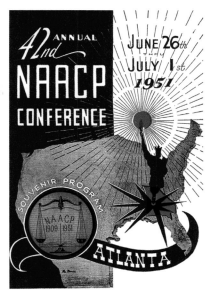

June 1951: 42nd Annual NAACP Convention program.

White and Privates Willie Martin Jr., Hardy E. Sanders, and Bernell Gordon, sentenced to ten years imprisonment for violation of Article of War 75 and "misconduct before the enemy."

• In October, entertainer Josephine Baker secured the help of the NAACP when she was given the "run-around" after requesting service at New York City's segregated Stork Club. Walter White asked Walter Winchell, who had a reputation for championing minorities and was seated a few tables from Baker at the time, to denounce the Stork's Jim Crow policy. Winchell hinted he would but later reneged and launched an attack on Baker, suggesting she was a "fascist," a Communist fellow-traveler, and a lewd dancer. The NAACP picketed the club.

• November 6 marked the brutal slaying of Samuel Shepherd and the critical wounding of Walter Lee Irvin, defendants in the Groveland, Florida, case defended by the NAACP. The Association called upon Florida Governor Fuller Warren to remove McCall and Deputy James Yates and try them for murder.

• On Christmas day, Harry T. Moore, who founded the first NAACP chapter in Florida, was killed by a firebomb in his home in Mims, Florida. His wife, Harriet, died days later from the bombing.

1951: Plaintiff in the Prince Edward County, Virginia, school segregation cases, Irene Jefferson, with Virginia State NAACP Executive Secretary W. Lester Banks and Prince Edward County NAACP coordinator Rev. L. Francis Griffin.

March 1952: Delegates attending the NAACP North Carolina Conference of Branches Emergency Registration and Get Out the Vote conference in Raleigh, North Carolina.

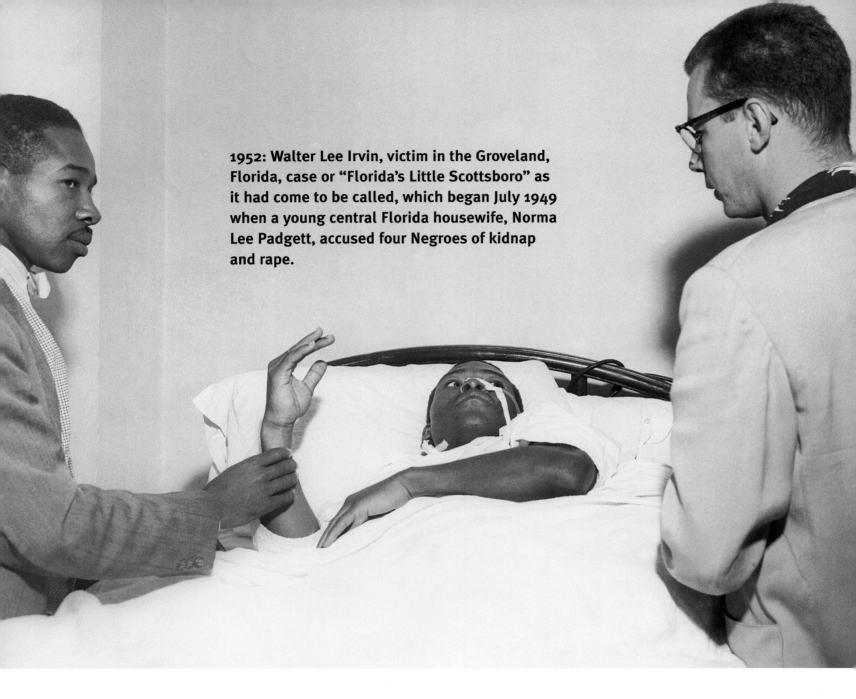

1952: Walter Lee Irvin, victim in the Groveland, Florida, case or "Florida's Little Scottsboro" as it had come to be called, which began July 1949 when a young central Florida housewife, Norma Lee Padgett, accused four Negroes of kidnap and rape.

1952

- An NAACP delegation consisting of Arthur B. Spingarn, president, Channing H. Tobias, assistant treasurer, Theodore Spaulding, board member, and Walter White, executive secretary called upon President-elect Dwight D. Eisenhower, who gave assurance that he would use his executive powers to eliminate racism in federal establishments.

- The five precedent-shattering school desegregation cases reached the Supreme Court and were argued on December 9-11. The cases now involved Clarendon County, South Carolina; Topeka, Kansas; Prince Edward County, Virginia; Wilmington, Delaware; and Washington, D.C.

- In his annual report, Executive Secretary White announced the NAACP had doubled the number of Negro voters in the South between the 1948 and 1952 presidential elections. White stated that progress during the year included work towards ending segregation in the armed services; decrease in mob violence; and indictments in Florida for perjury in connection with bombings of homes and places of worship.

- The NAACP Pennsylvania State Conference convened on the problems of migrant labor in Pittsburgh with fifty-seven churches and labor and welfare groups to form the Pennsylvania State Citizens Committee on Migrant Labor. They issued a five-point legislative program to ensure just treatment. NAACP Labor Relations Assistant Herbert Hill gave accounts of child labor, filthy living conditions, and the exploitation of workers.

AN AMERICAN TRAGEDY

THE STORY OF JESSE DUKES

Jesse Dukes was sentenced to 15 to 25 years on the chain gang when he was twelve years old, at a trial that lasted a few minutes, without a lawyer, without defense. He escaped and is now in a New Jersey prison awaiting extradition to the State of Georgia.

THE "COMMITTEE OF 100"
20 West 40th Street
New York 18, N. Y.

1952: NAACP "Committee of 100" pamphlet seeking support for Jesse Dukes, who, at twelve years of age, was arrested for stealing five cars and was beaten, tortured, and sentenced to a chain gang in Georgia.

CRISIS

NOVEMBER, 1952   15¢

NAACP Mourns Dr. Louis T. Wright

His Town
KEN MACRORIE

Great Negro Author Rediscovered
WILLIAM L. GROSSMAN

Wanted A Compulsory Federal FEPC
CONSTANCE MOTLEY

Brotherhood On The Campus
FREDERICK OLSON

The Arabs In Israel
IRENE DIGGS

NAACP

43rd

Annual Convention

Calvary Baptist Church

Oklahoma City, Oklahoma

June 24-29, 1952

NATIONAL ASSOCIATION FOR THE ADVANCEMENT OF COLORED PEOPLE
National Headquarters: 20 West 40th Street, New York 18, N. Y.

November 1952

June 1952: Program for the NAACP 43rd Annual Convention in Oklahoma City, Oklahoma.

1952: Strategizing at the NAACP Annual Meeting in New York City: President Arthur Spingarn; Executive Secretary Roy Wilkins; Washington Bureau Director Clarence Mitchell; Board Member Dr. Montague Cobb; and Board Member Dr. Robert Weaver (seated).

1953: NAACP Washington Bureau Director Clarence Mitchell Jr. and wife, Juanita Jackson Mitchell, attending the NAACP "Great Night" benefit, co-chaired by Oscar Hammerstein II and Lena Horne, at Madison Square Garden in New York City.

1953

• On February 25, Mack Ingram, the sharecropper defended by the NAACP and convicted of "assault by leering" at a white girl, was freed by the North Carolina Supreme Court on the grounds that he could not be convicted "for what may have been in his mind."

• Financially pressed by the heavy load of legal cases and other aspects of the civil rights battle, Dr. Channing H. Tobias, newly elected chairman of the NAACP Board of Directors, launched the "Fight For Freedom Fund" campaign at the annual convention in St. Louis, Missouri. The slogan was "Free by '63," and the goal was to eliminate all state-imposed racial discrimination and segregation by the centennial of Lincoln's Emancipation Proclamation. The convention unanimously adopted a resolution to raise $1 million annually.

• Membership in the NAACP continued to climb for the fourth consecutive year, reflecting the increased tempo of activity and expectation throughout black communities.

• That summer, the NAACP investigated the lynching and burning of Zach Walker, a Pennsylvania Negro who killed a policeman in self defense. The investigation by Mary Dunlop Maclean revealed an unfair trial, and the Association employed the William J. Burns detective agency to secure evidence taken to Governor John Tener.

• The ninety-nine-year prison term imposed on nineteen-year-old John Taft Rosenburough of Brownwood, Texas, convicted for the alleged rape of a white woman, was reversed by the Court of Criminal Appeals in Austin as a result of NAACP attorneys appealing the conviction on two counts: the refusal of the trial court to allow Rosenburough to testify as to the conversation and the promise of a

July 1953: NAACP's Roy Wilkins greets singer and film star Dorothy Dandridge at the Association's 44th Annual Convention in St. Louis, Missouri.

bondsman; and the error in admitting the alleged confession, citing he was beaten, threatened, and forced to sign a confession while in custody without the advice of a lawyer.

1954

- On May 17, the U.S. Supreme Court handed down its decision, *Brown v. Board of Education*, overturning the "separate but equal" doctrine of the land. This historic victory for the NAACP marked the dramatic opening of a new, intensified front in the battle for equality. Six days later, the NAACP issued its "Atlanta Declaration," offering to negotiate so that segregated schools could be eradicated in a spirit of "calm reasonableness."

- Following the delivery of a petition calling for desegregating the public schools, the Sulphur Springs, Texas, home of NAACP official H. W. Ridge was blasted by gunfire.

- The White Citizens Council was formed, first in Mississippi, then in other states, with the aim of maintaining the separate school system and continuing the restriction on civil rights for blacks. Economic reprisals were invoked in several communities in Mississippi, South Carolina, and Alabama, against the signers of desegregation petitions.

- To counter this pressure, the NAACP induced churches and fraternal, civic, and labor organizations to make deposits in the Tri-State Bank of Memphis, Tennessee, a black-owned bank, to enable it to expand its loans to persons in need.

- The NAACP's Ruby Hurley called in the FBI to investigate the interruption of a Branch meeting and confiscation of Branch records by Sheriff Robert Jenkins.

- Washington Bureau Director Clarence Mitchell asked the Defense Department to investigate and halt acts of brutality against black soldiers by white soldiers and civilians stationed in the South.

- The NAACP denounced the Department of Health, Education and Welfare (HEW) for continuing to provide funds to hospitals that would not staff black physicians and nurses.

- In August, the NAACP honored the first Negro to vote in the United States after the Fifteenth Amendment went into effect in 1870, David A. Strother of El Paso, Illinois, at his graveside funeral.

1954: Pictured at the steps of the U.S. Supreme Court Building is the battery of attorneys for the NAACP who argued the school desegregation case *Brown v. Board of Education,* which resulted in the May 17, 1954, U.S. Supreme Court decision banning segregation in public education. Left to right: Howard Jenkins, James M. Nebrit, Spottswood W. Robinson, III, Frank Reeves, Jack Greenberg, Thurgood Marshall, Louis Redding, U. Simpson Tate, and George E. C. Hayes. Not pictured is Robert L. Carter, who argued the Topeka, Kansas, case.

1954: NAACP President Arthur Spingarn and NAACP Board Chairman Dr. Channing H. Tobias confer at the Association's 45th Annual Meeting in New York City.

July 1954: NAACP Executive Secretary Walter White greets the Rev. Ernest Estell Jr., pastor of St. John Baptist Church, Dallas, Texas, at the Association's 54th Annual Convention.

1954: Members of a panel on working with school boards at an NAACP Emergency Conference on School Integration in Philadelphia, Pennsylvania. Left to right: Dr. Harry J. Greene, president, Philadelphia NAACP; Spottswood W. Robinson, attorney for the Virginia State NAACP; Dr. Margaret Just Butcher, member, District of Columbia Board of Education and consultant to the NAACP Legal Department; Robert L. Carter, NAACP assistant special counsel; and Wagner Jackson, president, Wilmington Delaware NAACP.

1954: Preceding the 46th Annual Convention in Atlantic City, New Jersey, fifty-two NAACP lawyers from twenty-one states meet to map an action plan to bring about school integration in line with the U.S. Supreme Court's decision in states that seek to maintain segregated schools in violation of the May 1954 decision.

1954: Baltimore artist Anne Beadenkopf presents an oil painting, "Innocent Prisoner," to NAACP chairman Dr. Channing Tobias.

1955

• In 1955, the NAACP continued to grow despite an unprecedented level of attacks from die-hard segregationists. For the first time since 1947, memberships passed 300,000 to a record high of 309,000.

• On May 7, NAACP Mississippi leader Rev. George Lee, who organized an NAACP Branch and used his pulpit and printing press to urge people to register and vote, was murdered. NAACP Mississippi Field Director Medgar Evers and Regional Director Ruby Hurley visited Belzoni, Mississippi, to investigate.

• On May 31, the U.S. Supreme Court handed down its ruling outlining the procedures to be followed in implementing its May 17, 1954, decision. The May 31 order stated that "all provisions of federal, state or local law requiring or permitting" segregation in public education "must yield to" the principle announced in the 1954 decision.

• The August murder of fourteen-year-old Emmett Till in Money, Mississippi, sent shockwaves through the nation, galvanized the African American community, and became a major catalyst for the Civil Rights Movement. Evers and Amzie Moore, president of the Bolivar County NAACP Branch, disguised themselves as cotton pickers to investigate.

• On December 1, NAACP Branch Secretary Rosa Parks was arrested after she refused to give up her seat on a city bus to a white person, thus leading to the Montgomery Bus Boycott.

March 24, 1955: NAACP staff at NAACP Executive Secretary Walter White's funeral. Henry Lee Moon (front), Lucille Black, Bobbie Branch, Gloster Current, Ruby Hurley (rear). Roy Wilkins is named by the Board of Directors to succeed him.

• On November 25, the Interstate Commerce Commission banned segregation in interstate travel, including railway, bus stations, and airports. This action was taken in response to a petition from the NAACP filed in December 1953 giving carriers until January 10, 1956, to cease all such segregation. Branches were actively involved in the Montgomery, Alabama, bus boycott, launched in December.

• The NAACP, led by Evers, filed a complaint with the Federal Communications Commission (FCC) stating that the local television station, WLBT, presented the news in a racially biased manner that did not serve the public interest. After years of litigation, WLBT's broadcast license was revoked, marking the only time in the FCC's history a television station's license was revoked for racially biased programming.

• Historian, journalist, and scholar Henry Lee Moon was named editor of *The Crisis* and returned to a format that included lengthy analytical essays on blacks.

• Black teachers in Georgia were forced to give up their NAACP memberships or forfeit their teaching licenses.

• NAACP attorneys filed two housing discrimination suits in Philadelphia, Pennsylvania: Levitt and Sons Development Corporation for not allowing blacks to purchase homes in Levittown developments in New York and Pennsylvania was filed by NAACP legal counsel Constance Baker Motley and attorney Walter Gay Jr., NAACP Philadelphia, Pennsylvania

June 1955: Vice President Richard Nixon greets the sons, Clarence III and Michael, of NAACP Washington Bureau Director Clarence Mitchell Jr. at the NAACP 46th Annual Convention in Atlantic City, New Jersey.

Branch housing committee member; and a lawsuit was filed in federal court to prevent federal housing officials from discriminating against blacks seeking federally funded rental housing. The first suit was dismissed in federal court, citing that neither the Federal Housing Authority nor the Veterans Administration "has been charged by Congress with the duty of preventing discrimination in the sale of housing project properties."

• The NAACP filed a suit in the federal district court in Charleston, South Carolina, citing the ban in public recreational facilities was a violation of the Fourteenth Amendment; however, Governor George Timmerman, Jr. responded that he would rather close the parks and beaches to blacks than integrate them.

• The NAACP Youth and College Division sponsored the second annual National Youth Legislative Conference for three days in Washington, D.C. to discuss their role in breaking down discrimination and segregation.

• The NAACP came to the defense of and won full exoneration for Theodore Griffin, president of the Asbury Park, New York NAACP Branch. Griffin was suspended from his post as a civilian employee of the U.S. Air Force for alleged association with Communists. NAACP leader Roy Wilkins rejected the theory of "guilt by association" and stated that his acquaintance and association with alleged Communists, who were members of his Branch, involved his duties as Branch president.

June 1955: NAACP Executive Secretary Roy Wilkins congratulates Texas "Queen of Freedom," Barbara Caviel, at the NAACP 46th Annual Convention in Atlantic City, New Jersey.

June 1955: Mrs. Walter White greets NAACP members at the NAACP 46th Annual Convention in Atlantic City, New Jersey.

June 27, 1955: The NAACP Cleveland Ohio Branch sponsors an "amateur day" baseball classic. Pictured: Indians center fielder Larry Doby, Cleveland Youth Council Vice President Alberta Belton, Indians pitcher Mike "Big Bear" Garcia, Cleveland Branch promotion committee co-chair Ester Threat, Indians manager Al Lopez, and Cleveland Branch President Dr. James E. Levy.

1955: The NAACP conducts a public relations techniques workshop during the Eastern Regional Conference in New York City.

June 1955: NAACP national staff meet in New York City to chart future civil rights work immediately following the Association's 46th Annual Convention in Atlantic City, New Jersey.

1955: At an NAACP Baltimore Maryland Branch meeting, Mr. and Mrs. Adolphus Pugh with their children, David, Diane, and Deborah, one of the first set of triplets to hold NAACP memberships.

1956

• The first attempts to outlaw the NAACP came in late March when the Louisiana attorney general dusted off a 1924 anti-Ku Klux Klan law requiring the filing of membership lists by organizations and attempted to use it against the NAACP. But the Louisiana NAACP Branches refused to file their lists. The following month, the state obtained an injunction barring the NAACP from operating in Louisiana. Similar injunctions were obtained in Georgia and Virginia.

• Following a yearlong boycott, prompted by the arrest of NAACP Secretary and Youth Council Advisor Rosa Parks, the desegregation of the Montgomery bus system was decided, and the U.S. Supreme Court held that segregation in intra-state travel was also unconstitutional.

• Roy Wilkins's effort to bring various civil rights and labor organizations under one umbrella came to fruition when in early March, fifty national organizations cooperated to bring two thousand delegates from thirty-eight states to Washington, D.C. to attend a three-day National Delegate Assembly for Civil Rights.

• This event, an outgrowth of the 1948 coalition organized in part by Walter White, marked the founding of the Leadership Conference on Civil Rights (LCCR).

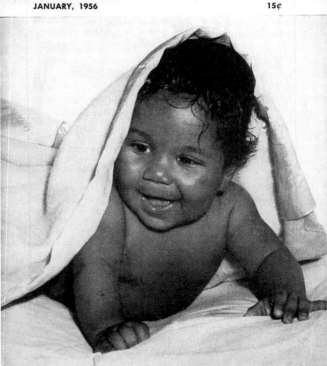

JANUARY, 1956   15¢

January 1956

1956: Autherine Lucy, denied admission to the University of Alabama's graduate school, at a New York City press conference with NAACP Special Counsel Thurgood Marshall. In October, Lucy was admitted by court order. The NAACP Youth and College Division took an active role by encouraging letters of protest. Riots ensued and she was expelled on a technicality.

July 1956: Lulu White, director of branches for the NAACP Texas State Conference, gets a big hug from NAACP Special Counsel Thurgood Marshall at the Freedom Fund Dinner during the Association's 47th Annual Convention in San Francisco, California.

July 1956: The NAACP West Coast Regional Office welcomes the NAACP national staff to San Francisco, California, for the Association's 47th Annual Convention.

July 1956: NAACP Anchorage Alaska Branch member Blanche McSmith presents a gavel made by Eskimos from the tooth of a walrus to Executive Secretary Roy Wilkins at the NAACP 47th Annual Convention in San Francisco, California.

July 1956: President of the Brotherhood of Sleeping Car Porters and Vice President of AFL-CIO, A. Philip Randolph, addresses the 47th Annual NAACP Convention urging unity between Negro and white wage earners.

July 1956: Congressman Sidney Yates and Hugh Scott discuss the civil rights legislative program with NAACP Washington Bureau Director Clarence Mitchell Jr. at the Association's 47th Annual Convention in San Francisco, California.

December 1956: TV Host Ed Sullivan presents the Spingarn Medal to Jackie Robinson in New York City as NAACP Executive Secretary Roy Wilkins looks on.

1956: Youth enjoy themselves at a teenage talent show sponsored by the Bronx New York NAACP Youth Council.

1957

May 17, 1957: **NAACP members at the NAACP Prayer Pilgrimage for Freedom in Washington, D.C. on the third anniversary of the *Brown* decision, organized to demonstrate unity, protest violence against "Freedom Fighters," and urge passage of pending civil rights legislation.**

May 17, 1957: **NAACP Public Relations Director Henry Lee Moon at the NAACP Prayer Pilgrimage for Freedom in Washington, D.C.**

• Foremost among the year's achievements was enactment of the Civil Rights Act of 1957, the first civil rights legislation passed by Congress since the Reconstruction era. Aided by local and state units, Roy Wilkins and Clarence Mitchell Jr. worked tirelessly to secure passage of this legislation that provided for expanded registration and voting in the South.

• The Rev. Richard S. Emrich, Protestant Episcopal Bishop of Michigan, presented the 42nd Spingarn Medal to the Rev. Dr. Martin Luther King Jr. at the annual convention in Detroit, Michigan. Dr. King was awarded the medal for "his inspired leadership of the Montgomery, Alabama, bus protest movement of 1955-56."

• A federal court order to desegregate Little Rock, Arkansas, schools sparked widespread violence as the first nine Negro students attempted to enter Central High School. President Dwight Eisenhower federalized the Arkansas National Guard and ordered one thousand members of the 101st Airborne Division into Little Rock to restore and maintain order. Courageously directing the desegregation strategy that eventually led to victory over arch-segregationist Gov. Orval Faubus were local NAACP leaders Mr. and Mrs. L. C. Bates. All nine students remained in Central High until graduation.

• Students at Alcorn A&T University staged a campus boycott after they discovered that a college history professor, Clennon King, wrote a *Jackson State Times* article criticizing the activities of the NAACP. The boycott caused the school's closure.

1957: A meeting of NAACP Youth Council and College Chapter officers planning the 1957 Spring Membership Drive.

September 1957: Milwaukee Braves players Henry Aaron, Billy Bruton, and Felix Mantilla sign up as NAACP life members as Membership Chair R. C. Townsend and Milwaukee Wisconsin Branch President Fred Hickman look on.

July 1957: NAACP Executive Secretary Roy Wilkins at a press conference prior to the opening of the NAACP 48th Annual Convention in Detroit, Michigan.

February 1957

November 1957: Mrs. Jackie Robinson, Mrs. Channing H. Tobias, and NAACP Board Chairman Dr. Tobias at the Association's November 1957 Freedom Fund Dinner in New York City honoring Duke Ellington.

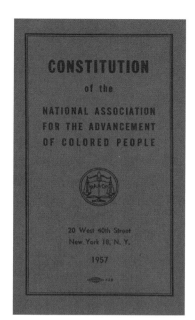

NAACP Constitution and By-laws.

November 1957: Senator John F. Kennedy and Dr. Benjamin Mays at the NAACP Freedom Fund Dinner in November 1957.

1958

• The year 1958 was probably the most significant for the NAACP since the historic 1954 Supreme Court desegregation decision. The Supreme Court, in *Cooper v. Aaron*, stated in even stronger language than in 1954 that state-imposed segregation violated the Constitution.

• Another significant victory was the Supreme Court's reversal of the $100,000 contempt fine that Alabama had levied against the NAACP for refusing to turn over its membership lists to the state.

• A major threat arose from efforts to bar the NAACP from providing Negroes with legal aid. Virginia led the way by accusing the NAACP of barratry—unlawful solicitation of clients—and passed statutes that would have subjected the Association to heavy fines and its attorneys to disbarment. But a U.S. district court ruled in *NAACP v. Patty* that these laws were unconstitutional.

• The Oklahoma City, Oklahoma NAACP Youth Council launched the forerunner of the sit-in demonstrations that were to gain nationwide attention two years later by protesting segregation in lunchrooms, soda fountains, and department stores. A similar sit-in was conducted by the Wichita Kansas Youth Council.

• Daisy Bates and the nine students who desegregated Little Rock's Central High School were awarded the 43rd Spingarn Medal.

• On November 4, two black boys ages eight and ten, Fuzzy Simpson and Hanover Thompson, were terrorized in jail for six days and sentenced to the Morrison Training School for Negroes after participating in a kissing game with a white girl. Under pressure from the Monroe North Carolina NAACP Branch led by the controversial Robert Williams, the boys were released. Known as the "Kissing Case," Williams embarked on a major publicity campaign to bring attention to the race problem and managed to get the case on the front pages of newspapers around the world.

• The day before he was to move into his new home in an all-white suburb, Chester, Pennsylvania NAACP Branch President George Raymond's home was burned down.

1958: Daisy Bates and the Little Rock Nine are awarded the Spingarn Medal at the 49th Annual NAACP Convention in Cleveland, Ohio. This was the first time the medal was awarded to a group.

November 1958: The NAACP transports citizens to the polls to vote in 1958.

July 1958: The NAACP Housing Committee prepares to assign delegates attending the NAACP 49th Annual Convention in Cleveland, Ohio.

September 1958: Duke Ellington and Marguerite Belafonte, co-chairmen of the NAACP 1958 Freedom Fund Drive, at a press conference at NAACP New York City headquarters.

THE NEW
LINCOLN SCHOOL

·31·

1958: Minnie Jean Brown, one of the Little Rock Nine, with her mother.

July 1958: Bishops Frank Madison Reid and Joseph Gomez confer with NAACP Executive Secretary Roy Wilkins at the Association's 49th Annual Convention in Cleveland, Ohio.

1959

• The NAACP celebrated its golden anniversary. The year opened with the launching of a full-scale assault upon what was thought to be the remaining vestiges of discrimination in organized labor and closed with an intensified campaign to increase the number of black registered voters in the South by more than one million.

• Other highlights of the year:

• Winning of a lower court decision invalidating the Florida Pupil Placement Act, which sustained segregation.
• Publication of the U.S. Civil Rights Commission Report, which the NAACP supported.
• Gaining of an exhaustive FBI probe of a Mississippi lynching.
• Conviction of four white men for the rape of a black student at Florida A & M College at Tallahassee.
• Winning of a Supreme Court decision reaffirming that juries from which black people were excluded on the basis of color were invalid.

• The NAACP chapter at Washington University in St. Louis, Missouri, leveled the color bar at a popular off-campus restaurant by conducting sit-in demonstrations.
• The NAACP and Ministerial Alliance of Boston called for an investigation after the Boston Red Sox's only black player, Jerry "Pumpsie" Green, was switched to their minor league.
• Daisy Bates' home was, again, firebombed.

> *It is a pleasure to add my voice to that of others congratulating the NAACP as it celebrates its Centennial Anniversary. It was a high honor for me to receive the distinguished Spingarn Medal in 1965. It is always very gratifying when my artistry merits such prestigious recognition. I wish the NAACP and its oracle* **The Crisis** *continued success in the future.*
>
> ## Leontyne Price
> *50th Spingarn Medalist*

July 1959: Mrs. Roy Wilkins, Eleanor Roosevelt, and Marguerite Belafonte, honored guests at the Wilkins NAACP 50th Anniversary Convention reception in New York City.

1959: NAACP Executive Secretary Roy Wilkins shares a warm moment with nephew Roger Wilkins and wife, Eve, and great-niece, Amy.

1959: NAACP St. Louis Missouri Branch President Margaret Bush Wilson presents the Association's Life Membership Scroll to Nellie Wilkins, stepmother of NAACP Executive Secretary Roy Wilkins.

NAACP GOLDEN JUBILEE, 1909-1959 — NEW YORK CITY JULY 13-19

the CRISIS

MARCH, 1959   15¢

March 1959

1959: NAACP ladies launching a nationwide membership campaign for half a million members in 1959 at the NAACP headquarters at the Freedom House in New York City.

WE MUST ESTABLISH BEYOND ANY DOUBT THE EQUALITY OF MAN

The Goal: ½ Million IN '59

August 1959: NAACP Youth Council and College Chapter officers and advisors from New York and New Jersey at a meeting at National Headquarters in New York City to plan a fall membership campaign.

1959: Martin Luther King Jr., NAACP Executive Secretary Roy Wilkins, and Dr. George Cannon, vice chairman of the National Life Membership Committee at the NAACP Youth Night event at the 1959 convention in New York.

November 1959: *Look* magazine Publisher Gardner Cowles introduces his wife to Marian Anderson at the 3rd annual NAACP Freedom Fund Dinner in New York City.

December 1959: Eager faces await the arrival of Santa and NAACP Executive Secretary Roy Wilkins at a Christmas party for 1,700 Negro students barred from attending public schools in Prince Edward County, Virginia.

June 12, 1966: The Medgar
Evers Memorial Observance
in Jackson, Mississippi.

1960–1969

1960

May 1960

- The NAACP proudly saluted the involvement of its youth in the sit-in demonstrations that began on February I in Greensboro, North Carolina, in an effort to desegregate lunch counters. These protests desegregated lunch counters at more than sixty stores.
- Langston Hughes, first published in *The Crisis*, was awarded the 45th Spingarn Medal.
- Dr. Robert C. Weaver was elected chairman of the NAACP National Board of Directors. Subsequently, he resigned to become administrator of the Federal Housing and Home Finance Agency, the highest position ever held by a black man in the federal government up to that time.
- A week before the Democratic convention, NAACP Executive Secretary Roy Wilkins met before the Democratic platform committee to make a case for civil rights and hold the party to a more honest platform. Wilkins, along with Martin Luther King Jr., led a peaceful march of 2,500 from the Shrine Auditorium to the Los Angeles Arena, where Democrats were to meet for their convention.
- NAACP leaders opened two training centers to teach black children in Prince Edward County, Virginia, after the public schools were closed to prevent integration.
- After an NAACP protest threat, casino and club owners in Las Vegas, Nevada, dropped their unwritten ban against African Americans.
- White merchants in Jackson, Mississippi, claimed their businesses had dropped by 75 percent as a result of NAACP boycotts.
- Wilkins announced that only 6 percent of the South's black students had been integrated into white schools since the 1954 *Brown* decision.

1960: Senator John F. Kennedy addresses an audience of seven thousand at the NAACP Civil Rights Rally at the Shrine Auditorium in Los Angeles, California, just four days before he secured the Democratic nomination.

May 1960: B. Elton Cox and members of the NAACP Kansas City Youth Council picket chain stores in support of the southern sit-ins.

1960: Edgar Young, student sit-in leader from LeMoyne College in Memphis, Tennessee, and head of the NAACP unit there, appeared before a Republican Platform subcommittee in Chicago, Illinois, to apprise them of threats, intimidations, reprisals and physical violence sit-in students faced in Memphis.

1960: At a New York NAACP luncheon in their honor, NAACP Executive Secretary Roy Wilkins is flanked by freedom fighters Joseph McNeil, one of the original four from the lunch-counter sit-in, and Carlotta Walls, one of the Little Rock Nine.

September 1960: NAACP brochure "The Meaning of the Sit-ins," by Roy Wilkins.

November 8, 1960: Seventy-five members of the Claflin College NAACP Youth Chapter marched at the Orangeburg, South Carolina, Confederate Memorial Square singing "John Brown's Body" and other Negro spirituals and patriotic songs in protest against the disenfranchisement of 3 million in the South.

1960: Members of the NAACP youth and college units inspect tenement housing in Central Harlem, New York, where they find defective plumbing, exposed electrical wires, inadequate heat, poor water pressure, unsuitable fire escapes and peeling plaster. They wage a campaign pressing Mayor Robert Wagner Jr. and Governor Nelson Rockefeller to improve conditions.

November 27, 1960: NAACP Miami Florida Branch President Father Theodore Gibson, who faced six months in jail for refusing to release the branch membership list to Florida officials, says the benediction for 1,030 people attending the $100-per-couple Fourth Annual NAACP Freedom Fund Dinner held in New York City. From left: Lena Horne, honoree, Dr. Algernon D. Black, Father Gibson, and Olympic track star Wilma Rudolph.

1960: NAACP leader Roy Wilkins greets Diane Karini (left) and Lucy Kago during a reception given by the NAACP Youth and College Division at New York's Belmont Plaza for 255 East African students. Excitedly happy, the students met more than six hundred NAACP youths, including sit-in leaders, and danced to a jazz combo.

1960s: NAACP Executive Director Roy Wilkins and his wife, Aminda (Minnie), share some quality time in their New York City apartment.

1960: Members of the Zeta Nu Chapter of Alpha Kappa Alpha sorority hold their membership plaque.

1961

• The NAACP Youth and College Division led the first sit-ins in the state of Mississippi; integrated forty-two new places of public accommodation in Oklahoma City, Oklahoma; ended discrimination in off-campus housing at Rutgers University; led a "selective buying" campaign in Durham, North Carolina, where more than one hundred new job opportunities were made available; and established active chapters at predominantly white institutions of higher learning in the South—Duke University, the University of North Carolina, and the University of Oklahoma.

• That June, Jim Peck, a white New Yorker, joined the first Freedom Rides in 1947 and again in 1961, detailing his experiences in the June/July 1961 issue of *The Crisis.* Peck was beaten and left unconscious. Approaching former President Harry S. Truman in a New York City park one morning, Peck introduced himself as "a Freedom Rider from the

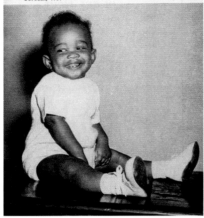

October 1961

north." Truman interrupted with, "Better stay up north, then."

• NAACP members voted to boycott an August Redskins-Rams game sponsored by the *Los Angeles Times* because of discriminatory hiring practices.

• On August 29, as chairman of the Leadership Conference on Civil Rights, Roy Wilkins and Conference Secretary Arnold Aronson presented a comprehensive sixty-page memorandum, "Federally-Supported Discrimination," to President John F. Kennedy, documenting federally supported racial discrimination and calling upon President Kennedy to "promulgate a general Federal Civil Rights Code governing the operation of the whole Executive branch of government."

• The memorandum further urged the president to "direct all departments and agencies of the Federal Government

1961: Delegates at the NAACP 52nd Annual Convention enjoy a line dance at one of the social events.

1961: Female youth delegates at the NAACP 52nd Annual Convention gather around Executive Secretary Roy Wilkins for autographs.

1961: NAACP Summerville Branch President Allen Yance and Memphis Branch President Jesse Turner inspect "Tent City" in Fayette County, Tennessee. These are the tent homes of Negroes who registered to vote November 8 and were driven from their homes as a result.

1961: NAACP youth are arrested for protesting the discrimination at Fairyland Park in Kansas City, Missouri.

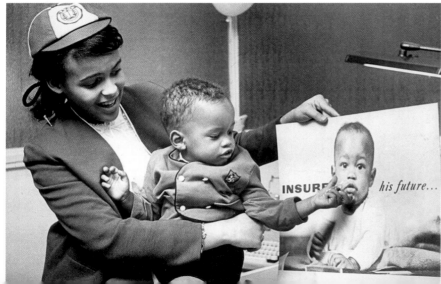

1962: NAACP Junior Life Membership Chair Adrienne Belafonte, twelve, with Robbie Bell, who is featured on an NAACP poster.

June 29, 1962: The Chester Pennsylvania, NAACP Youth Council picketing at the Great Leopard Skating Rink against its refusal to allow Negroes to skate any day of the week.

to assure non-discrimination" in all its activities, programs, institutions, and services.

• As Wilkins pushed for civil rights legislation and the first Freedom Ride bus was burned, Wilkins and Washington Bureau Director Clarence Mitchell Jr. met with U.S. attorney general Robert Kennedy to insist on federal protection for the riders. Not until Kennedy sent his assistant, John Seigenthaler, who was savagely beaten, to investigate did he really understand the seriousness of the situation.

• The U.S. government proposal for a "cooling-off" period for the Freedom Rides was rejected by the NAACP. Roy Wilkins stated, "American citizens have the right and duty to test the enforcement of the Constitution of the United States . . ."

1962

• In March, NAACP Washington Bureau Director Mitchell accused the Justice Department of failing to investigate the hate bombings of three black churches in Birmingham, Alabama, stating the department failed to perform adequately its duties as prescribed by the Civil Rights Act of 1960.

The CRISIS

AUGUST-SEPTEMBER, 1962   15¢

53rd ANNUAL CONVENTION
Gloster B. Current

EDUCATION AND POLITICS
Harry Golden

AMERICAN NEGRO IN COLLEGE, 1961-62

BRANCH AND COLLEGE NEWS

BOOK REVIEWS

August/September 1962

April 1962: NAACP officials investigate the murder of Corporal Roman Duckworth, a military policeman, by a Mississippi peace officer when he refused to move while seated on a Trailways bus on April 9, en route to his sick wife's bedside.

1962: NAACP convention delegates picket hotel discrimination in Atlanta, Georgia.

1962: NAACP convention delegates prepare for march against hotel discrimination in Atlanta, Georgia.

1962: Delegates to the NAACP 53rd Annual Convention in Atlanta, Georgia, picket downtown restaurants and hotels, which deny service to Negroes.

1963

• On September 30, as a result of a lawsuit by the NAACP Legal Defense Fund, James H. Meredith was admitted to the University of Mississippi as the first known Negro student at the university. United States marshals and troops were required to get him enrolled and to keep him from being ousted. Students and towns-people rioted, resulting in the death of a French news-man and an Oxford resident.

• In November, President Kennedy issued an executive order barring racial and religious discrimination in hous-ing built or purchased with federal aid and established the President's Commission on Equal Opportunity in Housing.

• The NAACP sued the Rochester, New York, school system for *de facto* segregation.

• The centennial of the Emancipation Proclamation was a year of hope and excitement for the Civil Rights movement. Membership in the NAACP increased, reaching a new high of 534,710. General income exceeded $1,000,000, thanks in large measure to a successful Life Membership campaign, which brought in $355,000.

• Two tragedies marred the year: Mississippi Field Director Medgar W. Evers was assassinated in Jackson on June 12. Five months later, on November 22, President Kennedy was assassinated in Dallas, Texas. Medgar Evers was posthumously awarded the 48th Spingarn Medal.

• The NAACP Washington Bureau led the fight for a comprehensive civil rights bill in Congress on June 19. President Kennedy intro-duced the bill and Roy Wilkins appeared twice before the House Judiciary Committee to testify on the need for such a strong measure.

• Four NAACP members were viciously beaten with chains, ax handles, and wrenches as they were dragged from their car in St. Augustine, Florida. Four KKK members were acquitted of the attack by an all-white jury.

• In the first week of his presidency, Lyndon Johnson invited Roy Wilkins to the White House for a personal conference on civil rights issues. Afterwards, Wilkins expressed confidence in Johnson's "commitment to civil rights."

• On August 27, Dr. W. E. B. Du Bois died in self-imposed exile in Accra, Ghana, just one day before the historic "March on Washington."

December 1963: *The Crisis* editor, Henry Lee Moon, prepares for the next edition.

December 13, 1963: Swedish ambassador to the United Nations Agda Russell chats with NAACP Executive Secretary Roy Wilkins and National Urban League Executive Director Whitney Young about civil rights in the U.S. at a reception in New York City's Park Sheraton Hotel.

1963: The NAACP's Pennsylvania Station New York City membership team pauses after its 10th annual drive.

RECEIVED MAY 6 1963

BU 4 B UDB106 NL PD UD NEW YORK NY MAY 3 1963
LEONARD H CARTER REGION IV NAACP OFFICE
    231 LINCOLN BLDG 18 AND VINE KSC
ARREST OF FREEDOM WALKERS AT ALABAMA STATE LINE TODAY AND CONTINUING
BRUTALITY, USE OF DOGS AND FIRE HOSES ON NEGRO DEMONSTRATORS
AND SPECTATORS IN BIRMINGHAM MAKE NECESSARY INTERCESSION OF
PRESIDENT AND JUSTICE DEPARTMENT TO INSURE FEDERAL GUARANTEE
OF CIVIL RIGHTS. WIRE PRESIDENT TO SPEAK OUT AND JUSTICE DEPARTMENT
TO INTERCEDE USING ALL POWER OF FEDERAL GOVERNMENT TO RESTORE
SANITY AND ORDER AND TO PROTECT THOSE WHO SEEK TO EXERCISE
THEIR CONSTITUTIONAL RIGHTS IN ALABAMA
    ROY WILKINS 20 WEST 40 ST
            728A CST

May 3, 1963: Telegram to NAACP Region IV Field Director Leonard Carter, notifying him of the arrest of Freedom Walkers at the Alabama state line and other brutalities on Negroes.

June 1963: Ten-year-old Jackson, Mississippi, youth tells an NAACP mass meeting of the brutality experienced while in jail as a result of his participating in street demonstrations. The youngster did an imitation of Mississippi Governor Ross Barnett, much to the delight of Lena Horne and Dick Gregory.

June 1963: Mississippi NAACP leader Medgar Evers, murdered just a few days after this photo was taken, listens to an NAACP youth demonstrator describe how he was beaten by police during a sit-in demonstration in Jackson, Mississippi.

June 1963: NAACP leaders Myrlie Evers, Henry Lee Moon, Charles Evers and Ruby Hurley at a press conference following the assassination of NAACP Mississippi Field Director Medgar Evers.

August 28, 1963: Director of Branch & Field Services Gloster Current, Bayard Rustin and NAACP Executive Secretary Roy Wilkins confer at the March on Washington for Jobs and Freedom.

1963: Widow Myrlie Evers addresses the NAACP convention in 1963, just weeks after her husband, Medgar, was assassinated on June 12.

1963: The NAACP marches against discrimination at the Association's 54th Annual Convention in Chicago, Illinois. From left to right: James K. Evers, Charles Evers, Rena Evers, Bishop Stephen Spottswood, Mayor Richard Daley, Roy Wilkins, and Arthur Spingarn.

July 1963: Delegates and friends of the NAACP 54th Annual Convention in Chicago, Illinois, march 125,000 strong on Independence Day.

1613 N. Glendale
Wichita 8, Kansas
August 15, 1963

RECEIVED AUG 1 6 1963

Mr. Leonard H. Carter
Field Secretary – Region 4
231 Line Building – 18th + Vine
Kansas City, Missouri

Dear Sir:

Mr. Chester Lewis has recommended that I write to you for details of the trip to Washington, D. C. for the march of August 28. My sister, Carol Markley, and I are planning to make the trip with the group, leaving by bus from Kansas City, if at all possible.

I would like to know specifically – in addition to any other information you think helpful – on what day, at what time and where should we meet to catch the buses; to whom and when must we send the $34 bus fare; whether or not we shall be able to share one small bag with a change of clothing for the day in Washington and some food; and at approximately what time the buses will return to Kansas City.

Thank you very much.

Sincerely,
(Miss) Marilyn Markley

August 15, 1963: Letter of inquiry about attending the 1963 March on Washington.

WE MARCH FOR JOBS FOR ALL NOW!

Washington Rabbis

WE MARCH FOR

NO U.S. DOUG TO HELP JIM CROW GROW

U.S. D

The CRISIS

OCTOBER, 1963   15¢

August 28, 1963: NAACP Executive Secretary Roy Wilkins with civil rights attorney Joseph Rauh, National Urban League President Whitney Young, AFL-CIO Vice President A. Philip Randolph, and UAW President Walter Reuther at the 1963 March on Washington for Jobs and Freedom.

• The NAACP was a cornerstone among organizations in the March on Washington for Jobs and Freedom, on August 28. In preparation for the massive demonstration where more than two hundred thousand participated, the Association mobilized its financial and human resources for what was to become the nation's greatest mass demonstration for civil rights.

1964

• On June 1, after four appeals to the U.S. Supreme Court in the case of *NAACP v. Alabama*, the NAACP ended efforts by southern states to cripple it by winning a unanimous decision that upset an injunction banning it from operating in Alabama. The Association had been barred from that state for eight years. This time, the high court ruled that the NAACP had a right to register in the state as a foreign corporation.

• The most outstanding gains in civil rights were legislative in contrast to earlier years when achievements were predominantly judicial or executive. The 1964 Civil Rights Act, enacted with the full support of the NAACP and signed by President Johnson on July 2, was the most comprehensive in the nation's history. Three days after President Johnson signed the act into law, an NAACP Board committee began

"You can kill a man but you can't kill an idea"

Mrs. Medgar W. Evers, widow of slain NAACP Mississippi State Field Secretary

KEEP THE IDEA OF FREEDOM ALIVE
JOIN NAACP

FILL OUT AND RETURN WITH YOUR CHECK OR MONEY ORDER TO: NAACP - 20 W. 40 ST. - NEW YORK, N.Y. 10018

I AM ENCLOSING $........ TO RENEW MY NAACP MEMBERSHIP.
I AM ENCLOSING $........ FOR ADDITIONAL NAACP MEMBERSHIPS (ATTACH LIST)
I AM ENCLOSING $........ AS A CONTRIBUTION TO THE FIGHTING FUND FOR FREEDOM.

NAME:
ADDRESS:
CITY & STATE:

(Minimum Annual Membership $2.00; with the Crisis, $3.50, $5.00, $10.00. Youth Membership, under 17, $.50;
17-21, $1.00; Life Membership $500.00, payable in annual installments of $50.00 or $100.00)

1964: NAACP membership advertisement featuring Myrlie Evers.

a tour of the South to test the act's public accommodations section.

• Other measures for which the NAACP successfully worked were the passage of the 24th Amendment to the Constitution, barring the poll tax as a requirement for voting in federal elections, and the Economic Opportunity Act, which was signed on August 24.

• Moving to shift the civil rights struggle from the streets to the ballot box, Wilkins announced that the NAACP would step up its drive to register black voters. This accelerated campaign, with the assistance of other organizations, registered a record total of six million black voters in time for the presidential election.

• The newest form of harassment against the NAACP was the damage suit. In Georgia, where this tactic began, a supermarket was awarded $85,000 in damages because the local branch had picketed and boycotted it.

• On June 21, three youth civil rights volunteers, James Chaney, Michael Schwerner, and Andrew Goodman, the latter two white, were beaten, shot, and buried. Among the nineteen suspects were the sheriff and the deputy sheriff of Neshoba County, Mississippi, but no convictions were obtained and charges were dismissed.

• Byron de la Beckwith's two trials for the murder of NAACP Field Secretary Medgar Evers ended in mistrials.

1964: NAACP leadership at a conference with President Lyndon B. Johnson at the White House.

May 1964: NAACP Executive Secretary Roy Wilkins chats with Langston Hughes at the NAACP Freedom Spectacular in New York City.

1964: Duke Ellington and NAACP Special Counsel Thurgood Marshall share a laugh at an event sponsored by Freedom House.

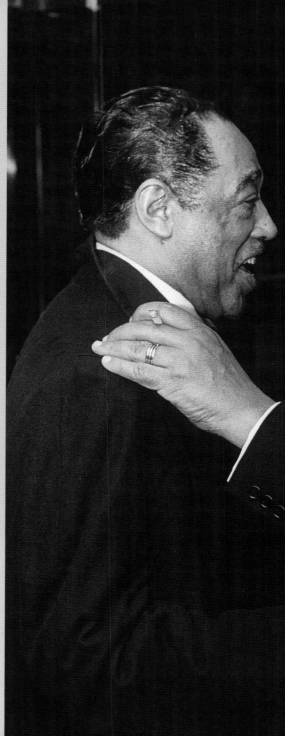

1964: Unidentified Baltimore, Maryland, youth and his dog cannot vote, but they do a great job of advising people to register to vote.

July 1964: Youth delegates to the NAACP 55th Annual Convention in Washington, D.C., prepare signs for a march on the Justice Department against the inhumane treatment of civil rights workers in Mississippi.

1964: Malcolm X (center) attending the NAACP 55th Annual Convention in Washington, D.C.

June 1964: Attorney General Robert F. Kennedy hears demands from NAACP delegates for U.S. intervention in Mississippi. Heading the delegation, which temporarily suspended sessions of the NAACP 55th Annual Convention, and who marched on the Department of Justice are NAACP Executive Secretary Roy Wilkins, Board Chairman Bishop Stephen G. Spottswood, Mrs. Medgar Evers, Mississippi Field Secretary Charles Evers, and Washington Bureau Director Clarence Mitchell, Jr.

- To protest discrimination in the auto industry, NAACP leaders threatened to carry out a nationwide selective buying campaign.
- The NAACP received its non-profit status tax deductible rating from the IRS and set up the Special Contribution Fund (SCF).

1965

- The NAACP played a vital role in the passage of another major civil rights law, the Voting Rights Act. President Johnson signed the act into law on August 6. But the passage of the act resulted from the effective lobbying of the NAACP Washington Bureau.
- In Alabama, Arkansas, Mississippi, and South Carolina, the NAACP helped 84,000 black voters to register. With such effective programs and the later presence of the federal examiners, who were provided under the Voting Rights Act, some 350,000 black voters were registered.
- In November, the homes of four Charlotte, North Carolina, civil rights leaders were bombed in the night, including the home of the NAACP's Kelly Alexander.
- The NAACP filed a suit in the California Superior Court seeking to invalidate Proposition 14, which repealed all laws mandating nondiscrimination in housing after a black man, Clifton Hill, was evicted because of his race.
- General Motors officials allowed the NAACP to review its personnel records to survey its progress in hiring salaried black personnel.
- The NAACP filed suit in Cincinnati, Ohio, against the school system, charging it practiced discrimination and segregation in its employment of black teachers and administrators. Also, the NAACP led a protest at Philadelphia's Girard College for its segregation practices.
- In Mississippi, NAACP leader George Metcalfe, who had been receiving threats as a result of his efforts to integrate the Armstrong Tire and Rubber Company cafeteria, was seriously injured by a bomb that destroyed his car.

March 1965

February 12, 1965: Mrs. Bernadine Whitmore, mother of George Whitmore, Jr., poses with attorneys: Norman Johnson and Ray H. Williams of NAACP Brooklyn New York Branch Legal Redress Committee; Stanley Reiben, chief defense attorney; and Arthur H. Miller, who are defending her son against murder.

1965: NAACP Dallas Texas Branch official conducts a successful drive to get people to pay their poll tax, which is required in that state in order to vote in local elections.

August 1965: NAACP Region IV Director Leonard Carter working with Watts riot victims in Los Angeles, California.

June 1965: Two weeks of demonstrations, which resulted in the arrest of thirteen persons protesting the discriminatory hiring policies of United Parcel Service in Hartford, Connecticut, ended when company officials agreed to the demands of civil rights groups led by the local NAACP branch and youth council. Among those jailed and fined for conducting a sit-in in front of a company truck: Gary Grimes (standing); NAACP Youth Council President Sylvia Govan (sitting), and Manny Williams (foreground).

1965: Members of NAACP New York City Youth Units demonstrate at the Federal Building on Foley Square to protest the denial of voting rights in Selma, Alabama. During the picketing, a six-person delegation met with U.S. Attorney General Robert Morganthau.

• California NAACP leader Ike Adams presented a six-point proposal to prevent more rioting in Watts in Los Angeles. A month later, NAACP attorney Leroy Clarke filed suit in the state supreme court asking that the prosecution of the 4,300 rioters be suspended until they were represented by legal counsel.

• The NAACP and LCCR partnered to draft legislation making it a federal crime to attack or kill a civil rights worker.

• NAACP Mississippi Field Director Charles Evers led a march of five hundred to the courthouse in Fayette, Mississippi, in the "Black Christmas" boycott against white stores in demand for the desegregation of public facilities and appointment of blacks to the police force.

1966

• On January 10, NAACP Hattiesburg, Mississippi, leader Vernon Dahmer was killed when his home was fire-bombed for making his store available for Negroes to pay their poll taxes. His wife died days later from the attack.

• The NAACP Voter Education Project accomplished additional marked successes in registering more black voters in the South. With the assistance of sixteen federal examiners, the Association helped 27,589 voters register in thirty-five Mississippi counties during the first five months of the year. An overall total of 163,000 were

January 1966: Newly elected NAACP President Kivie Kaplan with predecessor Arthur Spingarn. Kaplan, known for passing out "smile" cards to people he would meet, served as Life Membership chairman for thirteen years, increasing life memberships from 221 in 1953 to 18,210 at the end of 1965.

registered by the federal examiners themselves and other civil rights groups.

• As a result of the efforts of the NAACP and the Equal Employment Opportunity Commission, more than 1,500 Negro workers were promoted into hitherto all-white job classifications at the Newport News Shipbuilding and Dry Dock Company, one of the largest shipyards operated almost exclusively for the federal government.

• The NAACP Labor Department, under Director Herbert Hill, documented the patterns of discriminatory practices in the building, construction, and steel trade industries. In such cities as Cleveland and Cincinnati, Ohio, and Newark, New Jersey, the Association conducted public protests at federal construction sites where unions barred Negro workers from employment. The intervention of the Department of Justice at the Jefferson Memorial construction site in St. Louis, Missouri, marked the first time judicial enforcement of federal executive orders relating to government contract compliance was obtained.

• As a direct result of the NAACP efforts, more Negroes worked in the motion picture/television industry this year than ever before.

• Robert C. Weaver, former NAACP Board chairman, became the first member of his race to hold cabinet rank when President Johnson appointed him secretary of the Department of Housing and Urban Development (HUD).

• The NAACP Youth and College Division led a four-day, 100-mile

1966: NAACP Executive Director Roy Wilkins and Harlem NAACP Branch President Jeff Greenup address media during a "walking tour" on election day where they urged voters to support New York City's Civilian Police Complaint Review Board. Though rejected, the NAACP announced plans to aid citizens to process complaints of police misconduct.

October 29, 1966: Delegates to the Pennsylvania NAACP State Conference conducted a fair housing march to the steps of the Delaware County Courthouse. Pictured: Pittsburgh attorney Henry R. Smith Jr., state president; Tri-State NAACP Director Phillip H. Savage; journalist Bayard Rustin; Executive Director of the Delaware Valley Fair Housing Council Richard K. Taylor; and Alphonso Deal of Philadelphia.

January 1966: Soprano Leontyne Price is presented the 50th Spingarn Medal by the man who was responsible for her singing with the Metropolitan Opera Company, Rudolf Bing, Met General Manager, as NAACP Board Chairman Bishop Stephen Gill Spottswood looks on.

June 1966: Shown leaving New York to join the Mississippi civil rights march are (left to right): Jeff Greenup, Harlem New York NAACP Branch president; Gloster B. Current, NAACP director of branches and field administration, and Dr. Eugene T. Reed, NAACP New York State Conference President. On behalf of the state conference, Dr. Reed personally presented one hundred water canteens to the marchers at a rest stop near Batesville, Mississippi.

march from Oklahoma City to Lawton, Oklahoma, to protest the segregated amusement park Fairyland Park.

• The activities of the Kentucky Youth Council contributed to gaining the first fair employment measures below the Mason-Dixon Line.

• A significant victory was achieved in the case of *National Labor Relations Board v. Local 12,* United Rubber Workers where Negro plaintiffs, employees of the Goodyear Tire and Rubber Company, were denied promotions and transfer rights and were limited to segregated restroom, lunchroom, and recreational facilities. The U.S. Court of Appeals for the Fifth Circuit unanimously supported the NAACP's argument that the National Labor Relations Act was designed to give individual employees protection both against employer discrimination and union misuse of authority.

• Constance Baker Motley, former NAACP lawyer and Borough President of Manhattan, became the first black woman in the history of the United States to be named to a federal judgeship.

• In response to the slogan "Black Power," the NAACP joined with other civil rights organizations in an advertisement statement, "Crisis and Commitment," published in *The New York Times,* to reaffirm the organizations' commitment to integration as a goal and non-violence as a tactic.

1967

• In June, based on the findings of a two-man investigating team, which conducted a two-week tour of rural areas, the NAACP began its emergency relief program in Mississippi to provide food for starving black residents. Three centers were created in

June 1967: Some of the biggest names in Hollywood attend a luncheon in Beverly Hills, California, sponsored by the Association of Motion Picture and Television Producers, honoring NAACP Executive Director Roy Wilkins for the benefit of the NAACP Special Contribution Fund established in 1964 to provide tax-exempt programs of the NAACP. From left to right: actors Greg Morris, Gregory Peck, and Walter Pidgeon, Mr. Wilkins, NAACP Corporate Communications Director Walter McClane, Warner Brothers Studio Chairman Jack Warner, and Motion Picture Association of America President Jack Valenti. In his address, Wilkins stressed the importance of Hollywood in creating a favorable climate for racial progress in America.

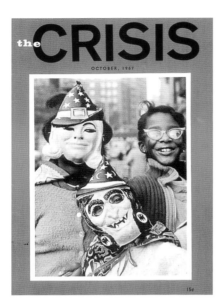

October 1967

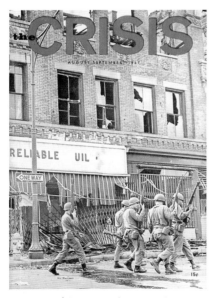

August/September 1967

July 1967: Rollie Banks, right, member of a two-man NAACP investigating team, questions a family on conditions in Mississippi during a 1,700-mile fact-finding tour of twelve counties in the state. Together with his teammate, Alex Waites, he reported to the NAACP 58th Annual Convention that hunger and lack of medical aid were so widespread that the counties should be declared a disaster area and receive massive federal aid.

1967: NAACP National Headquarters from 1967–1980: 1790 Broadway, New York City.

1967: Roy Wilkins holds a press conference at the NAACP's annual meeting in New York City.

the most impoverished areas of the state to distribute money for purchasing food stamps.

• On June 15, rioting, the rise of black militancy, and the continuing desegregation and discrimination fights led Roy Wilkins to issue a "Red Alert" to all NAACP branches, asking them to use all possible resources to head off another "long hot summer."

• On July 29, President Johnson named Roy Wilkins to the eleven-member National Advisory Commission on Civil Disorders to investigate the causes and consequences of the urban riots and to recommend remedial action.

• On August 30, the Senate confirmed President Johnson's nomination of Thurgood Marshall as associate justice of the U.S. Supreme Court, the first Negro to be named to the high court.

• In a significant decision supported by the NAACP affecting civil rights, *Loving v. Virginia,* the Supreme Court invalidated Virginia's anti-intermarriage law. The Court concluded that anti-miscegenation laws were racist and were enacted to perpetuate white supremacy.

1968

• Roy Wilkins was designated chairman of the U.S. delegation to the International Conference on Human Rights, which met in Tehran, Iran, under the auspices of the United Nations. Wilkins presented the American position on human rights to the convention.

• The passage of another major civil rights law, the Fair Housing Act, known as Title VIII of the 1968 Civil Rights Act, was achieved largely through the mastery efforts of Washington Bureau Director Clarence Mitchell Jr. The act climaxed a long, torturous struggle by civil rights forces to remove some of the most obvious practices of housing discrimination.

• The editorial "Time to Speak Up," in the November issue of *The Crisis,* was the most widely acclaimed, reprinted, and quoted NAACP item in recent years.

• The NAACP Labor Department formed the National Afro-American Builders Corporation, the first and only national consortium of Negro-owned building contractors, to help Negro contractors pool their financial resources in order to qualify for the rigid bonding requirements on construction projects.

• As a result of NAACP pressure and protests, the Office of Contract Compliance began to threaten disbarment procedures against companies that were clearly in violation of the executive order prohibiting racial discrimination in employment. After three years in existence, the office had completed only one hearing; at the end of 1968, seven cases were pending.

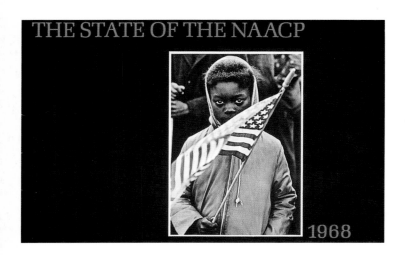

THE STATE OF THE NAACP

1968

1968: "The State of the NAACP/1968" by NAACP Executive Secretary Roy Wilkins.

the CRISIS

FEBRUARY, 1968

Du Bois Centennial

Dr. W. E. B. Du Bois
1868-1963

15¢

February 1968

the CRISIS

MAY, 1968

May 1968

April 1968

the CRISIS

APRIL, 1968

Dr. Martin Luther King, Jr.
1929-1968

1968: John A. Morsell, NAACP assistant executive director, and Robert Tindal, Detroit NAACP executive secretary, holding a press conference on the poor of Mississippi, Alabama and Detroit at the NAACP 59th Annual Convention.

1968: The NAACP's Roy Wilkins confers with CBS anchor Walter Cronkite shortly after Wilkins testified before the platform committee at the Democratic National Convention.

1968: NAACP delegates registering at the convention.

October 1969: These twenty-four San Fernando Valley State College students are on trial in the Superior Court of Los Angeles, California, charged with 1,730 felonies committed during a campus disturbance.

• In February, the NAACP Housing Department was reactivated with the appointment of William R. Morris as director.

• On March 1, the National Advisory Commission on Civil Disorders, of which Wilkins was a member, released its report. The Commission affirmed that white racism was the root cause of the nation's racial tensions and conflicts.

• On April 4, Dr. Martin Luther King Jr. was assassinated in Memphis, Tennessee. Rioting erupted after King's murder. In an effort to bring calm, Wilkins initiated a massive nationwide drive to avert further racial violence, sending action-program kits, including the National

Advisory Commission on Civil Disorders, to all branches. The plan included finding jobs for youth and the "hard-core" unemployed, fostering cooperation between blacks and law enforcement through the "Adopt A Cop" program, and the promotion of a "cool it" attitude.

• On June 6, Robert F. Kennedy was assassinated in Los Angeles, California, after winning the California primary for president.

• On August 1, President Johnson signed into law the Housing and Urban Development Act of 1968. Hailed as the most meaningful housing bill in the nation's history, it

October 1969: NAACP General Counsel Nathaniel R. Jones consults with Los Angeles lawyers retained by the NAACP for the defense of twenty-four San Fernando Valley State College students during a campus disturbance. From left: Loren Miller Jr., Halvor Thomas Miller Jr., Mr. Jones, and Morgan Moten.

provided for decent and affordable housing for lower-income families.

• Cecil Victor Sessum, one of twelve men charged with the 1966 murder of NAACP Hattiesburg, Mississippi Branch President Vernon Dahmer, was sentenced to life by an all-white jury.

• Two men were found guilty and sentenced to prison for their plot to assassinate Wilkins and National Urban League Director Whitney Young Jr.

• Founded during a meeting at the home of singer-actor Sammy Davis Jr., the NAACP Image Awards was created to honor individuals and projects that had demonstrated exemplary works by and for people of color.

• A *Fortune* magazine poll survey ranked the NAACP the top civil rights organization.

1969

• The momentum of the Civil Rights movement, which had slowed, picked up as the Nixon administration revealed its policies for the nation.

• President Nixon nominated Clement F. Haynsworth to the Supreme Court; the NAACP's efforts led to the rejection of his nomination by the Senate because of his racism. The fight against the Haynsworth nomination was led by Roy Wilkins and Clarence Mitchell Jr. in Washington, D.C. They successfully undertook the tedious task of persuading at least fifty-one senators that a vote for the president's nominee would not be in the best interest of the nation.

• The NAACP spearheaded the fight, which was similar to one forty years earlier that Executive Secretary Walter White had directed against Judge John H. Parker, whom President Hoover had nominated to the high court.

• The National Youth Mobilization Conference to Lower the Voting Age to Eighteen, which was sponsored by the NAACP Youth and College Division, was held in Washington, D.C., from April 21 to 22. More than two thousand delegates from 33 states and Canada participated.

• Julius Williams, a World War II veteran, was appointed NAACP director of armed services and veterans affairs.

• The Association launched, in 1969, the National Afro-American Builders Corporation to enable minority builders to obtain bonding and contracts. In its first year of operation alone, the corporation brought eighteen companies under its umbrella in eleven states.

• NAACP Washington Bureau Director Clarence Mitchell Jr. was named the 54th Spingarn Medalist.

November 1969

May 1969

April 1962: "The NAACP in Action" brochure.

We've just started...

The Crisis *Magazine continues to be one of the most outstanding journals in this country. As the publisher of the magazine for almost fifteen years, I know the heartbreaks, sorrows and joys of producing an outstanding literary contribution to all of America, but particularly Black Americans.*
I wish the NAACP and The Crisis *Magazine all the best and continued success.*

Benjamin L. Hooks
70th Spingarn Medalist

April 1969: Booklet on the words and hands of NAACP Executive Director Roy Wilkins.

1977: The Honorable C. Delores Tucker, secretary of the Commonwealth of Pennsylvania, chats with NAACP Life Members James Carter and Arnelle Highsmith of Hampton, Virginia, at the branch's annual Life Membership banquet, where Tucker was the guest speaker.

1970–1979

the NAACP is people

1970

• Barely two months after the Senate rejected Clement F. Haynsworth by a vote of fifty-five to forty-five because of his racist record, President Richard Nixon nominated another anti-black judge, G. Harrold Carswell of Florida, to the Supreme Court. The NAACP determinedly launched another attack to bar his confirmation. In April, the Senate rejected the Floridian by fifty-one to forty-five votes.

• The NAACP initiated and strengthened service programs while continuing its traditional battles. The National Afro-American Builders Corporation markedly helped its members gain nearly $29 million in surety bonding, thus enabling black construction companies to successfully bid on $378 million worth of construction.

• The NAACP approved the creation of the National Housing Development Corporation as a non-profit affiliate designed to assist local NAACP units to sponsor moderate and low-income housing. The Glen Cove, New York Branch became one of the first units to benefit from the program.

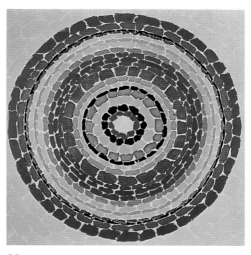

May 1970

• In another Long Island town (Oyster Bay, New York), the NAACP moved to demolish the latest barriers to equal housing opportunity for black families—restrictive zoning—with the preparation of a class-action suit against such zoning.

• The U.S. Department of Housing and Urban Development (HUD) released the first nationwide registry of minority construction contractors compiled by the NAACP.

• *The Crisis* changed its format from the pocket-sized issues that had prevailed since November 1949 to a larger format.

1978: NAACP membership brochure.

July 1970: NAACP Youth and College Director James Brown with youth members at the 61st Annual Convention.

"Our nation is moving toward two societies, one black, one white — separate and unequal...

"This deepening racial division is not inevitable. The movement apart can be reversed. Choice is still possible. Our principal task is to define that choice and to press for a national resolution."

REPORT OF THE NATIONAL ADVISORY COMMISSION ON CIVIL DISORDERS—March 1, 1968

ONE SOCIETY

61st NAACP ANNUAL CONVENTION

Cincinnati, Ohio
June 29-July 4, 1970

NATIONAL ASSOCIATION FOR THE ADVANCEMENT OF COLORED PEOPLE
1790 Broadway, New York, N.Y. 10019

• NAACP General Counsel Nathaniel R. Jones and Armed Services and Veterans Affairs Director Julius Williams visited the U.S. Air Force Base at Goose Bay, Nova Scotia, to investigate complaints of racism. Their investigation resulted in the dropping of unfounded charges against a group of black servicemen and the transfer of the commanding officer. At the end of the year, Jones, Williams, and another member of the legal department, Melvin Bolden, began preparation for similar investigations on U.S. bases in West Germany.

• The first NAACP day care center was opened by the Jamaica, New York Branch.

• The NAACP's Education Department continued its drive to have textbooks properly and efficiently include the many contributions by African Americans and other minorities and to have these textbooks integrated into the nation's school curriculums. The Association sponsored the publication of "American Majorities and Minorities: A Syllabus of United States History for Secondary Schools" and distributed listings of multicultural books that highlighted African American contributions to American life.

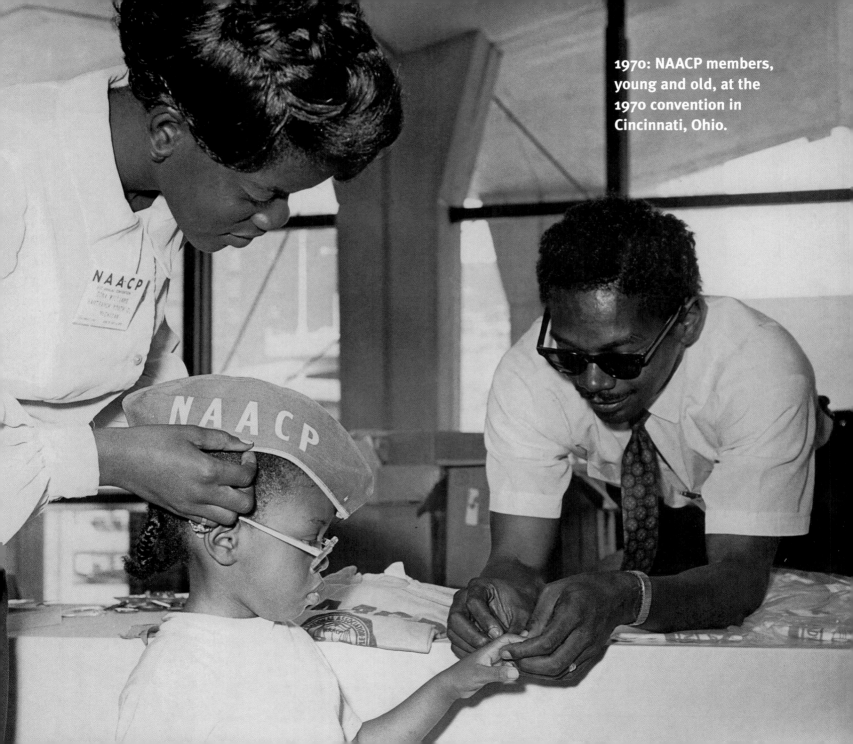

1970: NAACP members, young and old, at the 1970 convention in Cincinnati, Ohio.

1970: Members of the NAACP on a European housing tour.

1970: NAACP Executive Director Roy Wilkins at the Jamaica, New York NAACP Day Care Center.

1971

• Forty-five years after Clarence Darrow made his famous closing argument in the Ossian Sweet case in defense of a man's right to protect his home against mob attack, the NAACP again focused the civil rights spotlight on Detroit, Michigan. In the public school desegregation case that reached the Supreme Court in 1973, the NAACP exploded the myth that Northern-style segregation was merely a creature of natural forces. The NAACP contended that such residential segregation, which is characteristic of urban areas, resulted from deliberate governmental policy. United States District Judge Stephen J. Roth upheld the NAACP view.

• In Mississippi, the NAACP made national headlines when it went to the aid of striking pulpwood workers—white as well as black. The NAACP Southern Labor Office helped organize picket lines and provided technical assistance in the workers' struggle for higher wages. An NAACP contribution of more than $5,000 in strike benefits helped the men win a fair settlement.

• The NAACP Youth and College Division sent delegations to visit and interview prisoners on their needs as part of a Prison Visitation and Reform Program, waged a vigorous drug abuse education program, and developed a sickle cell education program.

• The Association waged a nationwide campaign to register the newly enfranchised eighteen-year-old voter.

• The NAACP stepped up its commitment to prison reform in the wake of the tragedy at the Attica Correctional Facility in New York.

• Based on investigations in West Germany by an NAACP team headed by General Counsel Nathaniel R. Jones, the NAACP published its comprehensive military justice report, "The Search for Military Justice," sparking legal and administrative reforms by the Department of Defense.

• While at the NAACP national convention in Minneapolis, Minnesota, the home of Chattanooga, Tennessee, Branch President James Mapp was bombed. In Anniston, Alabama, terrorists fired into the home of the Rev. J. S. Nettles, organizer of the Calhoun County Branch; charges came that the city, county, and FBI were involved.

• The NAACP urged the Justice Department to take action when twenty-eight-year-old Carnell Russ of Star City, Arkansas, a father of nine, was shot down inside a police station where he was taken to pay a fine.

June 1971

• The Association established the NAACP National Radio Network to inform people about the history and work of the NAACP.

• The NAACP brought suit against the state of California, charging that it failed to take action to curb discrimination within its governmental structure.

Your $10 gift can provide $400 worth of food for the hungry.

On the back roads of Mississippi, Alabama and other parts of the deep South, there are still many thousands of families facing slow starvation. Right now. Right here in the U.S.A.

Their diets are so inadequate that hunger and malnutrition have become part of their lives. Many children of tenant farmers and seasonal workers have actually never known what it is like *not* to be hungry.

The NAACP Emergency Relief Fund is now in its fourth year of collecting money to buy Food Stamps for the neediest of these families. Under the federally spon-

sored Food Stamp Plan, $1 buys as much as $40 or more in Food Stamps. Thus your $10 can mean $400 worth of urgently needed nourishment to help a family survive.

To contribute to this fund, please send as little or as much as you can to the NAACP Emergency Relief Fund. Contributions are tax-deductible.

Thank you

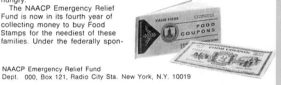

NAACP Emergency Relief Fund
Dept. 000, Box 121, Radio City Sta. New York, N.Y. 10019

1971: NAACP Youth Council booth at the International Black Expo.

1971: NAACP "Emergency Relief Fund" advertisement.

1971: NAACP Executive Director Roy Wilkins presents a Life Membership plaque to Oscar Smith of New York, who is handicapped and authorized the NAACP to use this photo for ads and posters to promote membership.

1971: One of the world's most renowned entertainers in the twenties, Ada "Bricktop" Smith Duconge presents her check to NAACP Executive Director Roy Wilkins for her Life Membership.

1971: NAACP Executive Director Roy Wilkins visiting a farmers market in Monrovia, Liberia, after heading U.S. delegation to the funeral of President William S. Tubman.

1971: Benjamin L. Hooks and wife, Frances, at NAACP "March Against Racism in South Africa."

1971: NAACP cheerleaders at the 62nd convention.

1972: NAACP Pride Center Director Haysteen Cain and NAACP Pride Youth Center (Waterbury, Connecticut) advisor Kay Wyrick present a portrait painted by Curtis Murray to NAACP Executive Director Roy Wilkins at the Association's Fellowship Dinner.

1972

• The Washington Bureau again played a crucial legislative role by pushing the passage of the Equal Employment Opportunity Act of 1972. Congress strengthened the Equal Employment Opportunity Commission (EEOC), a provision of the 1964 Civil Rights Act, by giving it power to seek legal enforcement of its findings. They also broadened coverage to forbid discrimination in federal, state, and local government agencies.

• The NAACP went to the defense of twenty-one black seamen charged with rioting aboard the U.S. Aircraft Carrier Kitty Hawk. Also, General Counsel Jones served as co-chairman with Lt. Gen. Claire Hutchin Jr. of the Joint Military Task Force on Justice. The task force submitted its comprehensive report to the Secretary of Defense on November 30.

• The NAACP was credited with the promotion of military officers and enlisted men and the increased number of blacks enrolled in ROTC programs.

• In Flint, Michigan, the school board named an elementary school after NAACP Executive Director Roy Wilkins.

• On July 6, the first NAACP prison branch was chartered at Lewisburg Federal Penitentiary in Pennsylvania.

• Executive Director Wilkins charged the Nixon Administration with thwarting school desegregation by exploiting the fear by whites of busing as an instrument in achieving school integration. The Administration was also charged with condemning millions of low-income families to continued misery in the slums by imposing an eighteen-month moratorium on federal assistance to meet their housing needs.

• The NAACP proved in federal court that Philadelphia, Pennsylvania, screened out black applicants but not white applicants, to the police department through background investigations.

• Along with eleven other organizations, the NAACP challenged discrimination in the area of home financing and urged the Federal Deposit Insurance Corporation (FDIC) to carefully scrutinize its lending practices to African Americans.

1972: NAACP Annual Report for 1972.

NAACP

ANNUAL
REPORT
1972

NATIONAL ASSOCIATION FOR THE ADVANCEMENT OF COLORED PEOPLE
1790 Broadway/New York, N.Y. 10019

July 6, 1972: NAACP Freedom Gala Program featuring entertainer Diahann Carroll.

1972: Report to the 63rd NAACP Annual Meeting "The NAACP in 1971: a review."

NAACP Freedom Gala

Sponsored by
THE CO-CHAIRMEN
OF THE
63rd NATIONAL
CONVENTION
COMMITTEE

MICHIGAN PALACE SUPPER CLUB
Thursday Evening, July 6, 1972

NAACP

The NAACP in 1971: a review

1972: Delegates at the NAACP 63rd Annual Convention in Detroit, Michigan.

1973

• The NAACP assumed the defense of twenty-three of the twenty-five Kitty Hawk sailors charged with rioting and disorderly conduct. When the trial of the last Kitty Hawk case ended in mid-April, only four of the twenty-three men facing courts-martial were convicted of rioting aboard ship. Eleven won significant reductions in their charges and eight others were acquitted of all charges.

• On June 12, the Sixth Circuit Court of Appeals, sitting *en banc,* affirmed District Judge Stephen J. Roth's findings that the Detroit School District was segregated and agreed that a remedy limited to the city only would be wholly inadequate. Thus, the Court of Appeals affirmed the propriety of considering relief extending beyond the geographic boundaries of Detroit. However, it vacated for procedural reasons the ruling on the proposed area and plan for desegregation in order to give the suburbs a chance to join in the suit.

1973: Myrlie Evers and NAACP Executive Director Roy Wilkins confer at the NAACP 64th Annual Convention.

• In New York City, NAACP Assistant General Counsel James I. Meyerson challenged the denial of temporary injunctions in Community School Districts 18 and 21 in Brooklyn by appealing the district court's ruling. Consequently, the court was ordered to try the District 21 case on its merits. Still unresolved was the question of appropriate remedy for District 18, which involved highly emotional issues in the Canarsie schools. Here, the NAACP was battling to have the school district accept black children from the Tilden Houses project.

• The record-long trial of a $3.5 million damage suit against the NAACP that grew out of a boycott against merchants in Port Gibson, Mississippi, appeared to be just past the halfway mark as the year ended. The boycott began on April 1, 1966, in Claiborne County and lasted for more than three years. The suit was potentially disastrous for the NAACP because of the amount of money involved.

• As a result of a long-standing NAACP lawsuit, a federal court ordered the U.S. Steel Corporation and the United Steelworkers of America, at Fairfield, Alabama, to

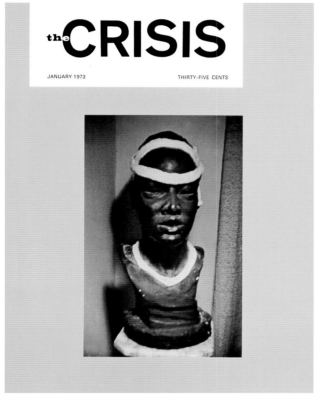

January 1973

June 1973

NEWS FROM

NAACP

3158 SEP17'73

NATIONAL ASSOCIATION FOR THE
ADVANCEMENT OF COLORED PEOPLE

1790 BROADWAY   NEW YORK, N. Y. 10019   212 245-2100
ROY WILKINS   HENRY LEE MOON
EXECUTIVE DIRECTOR   *DIRECTOR OF PUBLIC RELATIONS*

FOR RELEASE: UPON RECEIPT   September 15, 1973

BROOKLYN SCHOOL ORDERED
TO ADMIT 10 BLACK PUPILS

NEW YORK. -- Following a three-hour emergency hearing in the Federal District
Court in Brooklyn on Monday, September 10, the National Association for the Advancement of Colored People succeeded in winning an order for the admittance of 10 black
children into a nearby elementary school over the strong opposition of a white mob.

The case represented a significant, though partial, victory for the NAACP
which has been representing the children in a related school desegregation case.

They were from the Tilden Houses project in a heavily black section of the
borough. They were also part of a group of students from that project who were
barred from entering other predominantly white schools in another school district
in the Canarsie area.

Following the decision by Chief Judge Jacob Mishler, NAACP General Counsel
Nathaniel Jones said that the order "gives hope that Little Rock tactics will find
no permanent resting place here."

Continuing, he said that: "White obstructionists must learn that court orders
from northern judges cannot be flouted any more than those handed down by southern
judges. A few more examples of this kind of judicial firmness will go a long way
toward restoring respect for law and establishing order."

Because white parents had opposed the acceptance of the original Tilden Houses
children, in School District 18, the New York City Board of Education bowed to the
pressure and officially barred them from entering schools in that area.

Instead, the children were given the option of entering schools in Districts
20, 21 and 22. Judge Mishler himself had denied in August a NAACP request for an
injunction against the board's ruling.

So parents for the 10 kindergarten and elementary school children registered
them at Public School 251 in District 22, which they felt was the best of the al-
ternatives open to them. But when the children appeared at the school on the opening day of classes, an angry white mob prevented them from entering.

Led by Mr. Jones and James I. Meyerson, assistant counsel, the NAACP there-

September 15, 1973: NAACP press release announcing the NAACP's success at winning an order for admittance of ten black children into a Brooklyn, New York, elementary school.

eliminate discriminatory seniority lines of promotion and to replace them with a new plant-wide seniority structure. The court also ordered the systematic promotion of black workers and imposed goals and timetables for the hiring of blacks in hitherto all-white job classifications. Black workers received over $200,000 in compensation and other forms of relief for the many years of discrimination they endured.

• In another drawn-out legal battle, the Sixth Circuit Court of Appeals in Columbus, Ohio, issued a far-reaching decision in a case that was brought by the NAACP in 1966 against the Timken Roller Bearing Corporation and the United Steelworkers of America. Again, a federal court held that an entire class of black workers had been victimized by a systematic pattern of discrimination and were entitled to back pay. The court also ordered a substantial restructuring of seniority lines. In cases against Bethlehem Steel in Georgia, the scope of relief was extended to black workers in Title VII cases by expanding the definition of the affected class to include those who were furloughed because of discrimination.

1973: NAACP conducts a housing training Conference in Oklahoma City, Oklahoma.

1974

• On April 25, at the urgent request of the NAACP, Federal Judge Alfonso J. Zirpoli halted the highly controversial mass search by the San Francisco police for the so-called "Zebra Killer." Their search was based on vague profiles of one or more black men. Judge Zirpoli ruled that the police had violated the U.S. Constitution by stopping and questioning more than six hundred black men in their investigation of twelve random killings of white people and the wounding of six others.

• The U.S. Supreme Court gave the supporters of integration a sharp setback on July 25, when it ruled 5-4 that the NAACP had to prove that the Detroit suburbs themselves were guilty of segregatory acts before cross-district busing could be ordered. The NAACP, which brought the case, had contended that it was the state's responsibility to protect the Fourteenth Amendment rights of all citizens. Thus, because Michigan was given the sole responsibility of public education by its own constitution, the NAACP argued that the state was responsible for the segregation that was found to exist in Detroit public schools. The NAACP

1974: NAACP membership ad.

Bill Cosby says:

"Get in the Scene!"

JOIN ME AND 53,000 LIFE MEMBERS* OF THE NAACP

INDIVIDUALS & ORGANIZATIONS

NAACP LIFE MEMBERSHIP

Payable in ten installments of $50.00 per year. Full cost $500.00.

Make your $50.00 Check or Money Order payable to: NAACP Life Membership

Mail to:

BILL COSBY
NAACP
1790 Broadway
New York, New York 10019

Or to your local NAACP Branch

NATIONAL ASSOCIATION FOR THE ADVANCEMENT OF COLORED PEOPLE

position had been previously upheld by District Court Judge Philip Roth and the Sixth Circuit Court of Appeals.

• On July 30, the House followed up the anti-black temper of the nation by voting on the strongest anti-busing measure ever adopted by Congress. The action was earlier approved by the Senate in May as an amendment to the $25 billion bill providing federal aid to elementary and secondary education. The NAACP Washington Bureau waged a successful campaign that resulted in a compromise in the final bill with less stringent anti-busing provisions, which President Gerald Ford signed.

• Another threat to civil rights developed toward the end of the year when Maryland Republican Representative Marjorie Holt offered an amendment to an $8.6 billion House education money bill that would have ended the fund cutoff provisions of the 1964 Civil Rights Act. The NAACP Washington Bureau, with the support of the AFL-CIO, led the fight that defeated this amendment.

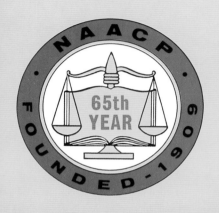

February 1974

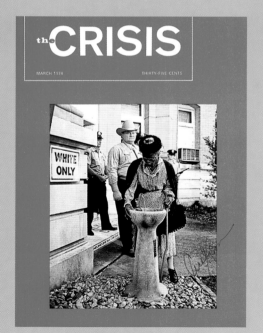

March 1974

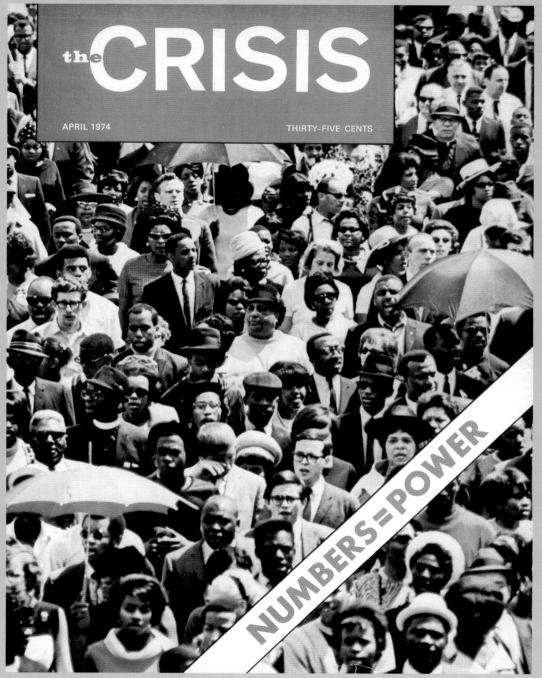

April 1974

October 1974

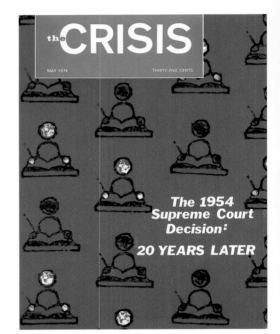

May 1974

December 1974

• Bombarded by intense pressure from white parents in New York City, Federal Judge Jack B. Weinstein softened his desegregation order for the Mark Twain Junior High School in the Coney Island section of Brooklyn. Judge Weinstein had ruled in January that Community School Board 21 and the New York City school chancellor had violated the Constitution by creating and maintaining a segregated school. Initially, he proposed dramatically firm remedies for correcting the racial imbalance. But, in July, he ordered the Central Board of Education and the local community school board to convert Mark Twain into a special school for gifted children as one way of attracting white students.

• The NAACP was represented by Assistant General Counsel James I. Meyerson in *Hart v. Community School Board*. Kenneth B. Clark and Dan Dodson, nationally recognized education experts, supported the NAACP's case.

• On June 21, U.S. District Judge W. Arthur Garrity Jr., in a case brought by the NAACP, ruled that Boston, Massachusetts, maintained a racially segregated school system and sternly ordered the city to eliminate "every form of racial segregation." The NAACP charged in its suit that the school committee had engaged in unconstitutional "deliberate racial segregation of pupils and teachers."

• In July, artist and former NAACP Public Relations Assistant Warren Marr became editor of *The Crisis*, reflecting his panoramic vision in text and graphics.

• As in Little Rock, Arkansas, in 1957, Boston, Massachusetts, commanded the full resources of the NAACP in the fall when public schools in the largely black areas of Roxbury and Mattapan, and the mostly white South Boston and Hyde Park, began the first phase of Judge W. Arthur Garrity's integration order. For several weeks, white opponents violently attacked black children both in the schools and on buses, launched boycotts of some schools, and otherwise demonstrated against the cross-district integration plan. NAACP Executive Director Roy Wilkins, General Counsel Jones, and Branch President Thomas Atkins led the NAACP's fight to ensure that the plan would not be scuttled or weakened and to obtain city, state, and federal protection for the children. On October 31, Judge Garrity issued his final ruling on the case. His guidelines, which called for a long-range desegregation plan, were a carbon copy of the NAACP's recommendations.

• On December 1, Bishop Stephen Gill Spottswood, chairman of the NAACP National Board, died at the age of seventy-seven at his home in Washington, D.C.

1975

• Following her election as chairman of the NAACP National Board of Directors, St. Louis, Missouri, attorney Margaret Bush Wilson explained to reporters that the question of her sex was irrelevant and immaterial. "My sex and my race are accidents of my birth," she said, and stated that she assumed she was elected because of her competence and professionalism.

• On January 22, in a letter to Lynn Townsend, chairman of the board of Chrysler Corporation, Wilkins noted that black unemployment was usually two to three times that of the national rate of unemployment.

• On January 28, the U.S. Senate adopted a resolution recognizing Roy Wilkins as "a statesman and master of power in the arena of civil rights, serving his fellowman with unassuming compassion and commitment to the religious ethic." The resolution was introduced by long-term ally of the NAACP Senator Hubert Humphrey (D) and Senators John G. Tower (R) and Lloyd M. Bentsen (D), both of Texas.

• Wilkins was named "American of the Year" by the American Religious Town Hall Meeting, Inc., a prominent interfaith organization with a nation-wide television network for spreading the gospel of brotherhood.

• On May 17, fifty thousand people gathered in Boston, Massachusetts, at an NAACP rally held in commemoration of the historic *Brown* decision outlawing separate but equal education and in support of efforts to desegregate the city's

the CRISIS

MARCH 1975   THIRTY-FIVE CENTS

March 1975

1975: NAACP Executive Director Roy Wilkins introduces Margaret Bush Wilson to the news media following her election as chairman of the NAACP National Board of Directors.

public schools. Demonstrators from across the country gathered at Fenway Stadium, where they started on a two-and-one-half mile march to the Boston Common.

• U.S. District Judge W. A. Garrity Jr. remained firm that Boston public schools conform to the requirements of the Fourteenth Amendment. A desegregation plan was adopted by Judge Garrity and ordered into effect in September. The plan included an "educational" compo-

nent to overcome the effects of segregation. With one exception, the plan promised to effectively desegregate schools in all sections of Boston. Known as Phase II, it also called for creation of biracial parent councils.

• Marking a change in the position of the Justice Department and several weeks before the opening of classes, the head of the department's civil rights division, Assistant Attorney General Stanley Pottinger, visited Boston to

1975: Attending the NAACP Annual Fellowship Dinner on January 7: NAACP Executive Director Roy Wilkins, NAACP Life Membership Committee Chairman Sammy Davis Jr., NAACP Membership Director Kivie Kaplan, Mississippi Field Director Charles Evers, and Milwaukee, Wisconsin Youth Council Advisor Father James Groppi.

1975: NAACP Washington Bureau Director Clarence Mitchell Jr. and NAACP Director of Development Mildred Roxborough make plans at the NAACP 66th Annual Convention. Also pictured: NAACP Convention Chair Dr. William Holman, standing.

coordinate the federal government's monitoring of the desegregation program.

• With the exception of South Boston High School, desegregation proceeded with comparative ease. The situation at South Boston High grew increasingly tense as opponents increased their resistance. Black students were harassed and attacked by white students. Teachers and state police on duty at the school provided little or no assistance to black students.

• The Detroit Michigan Branch of the NAACP appealed the desegregation plan that U.S. District Judge Robert DiMaschio had ordered into effect commencing January 26, 1976. The NAACP had sharply contended that the guidelines he issued in August were unconstitutional.

• During this year, the chief area of employment activity involved litigation on the historic discriminatory practices in the basic steel industry. Litigation was pressed against Bethlehem Steel and United States Steel in both New York and Alabama. The NAACP challenged the national consent decree in the case of *U.S. v. Allegheny-Ludlum Industries*. There was a settlement between the federal government and the nine largest steel producers in the nation.

• But, as a result of the NAACP challenge, the consent decree was reinterpreted to improve protection of sixty thousand black steelworkers. The NAACP had contended that the relief they would have received under the original consent decree was inadequate.

• The tragedy surrounding the brutal killing of Carnell Russ on May 31, 1971, was compounded when an all-white federal court jury in Pine Bluff, Arkansas, dismissed the damage lawsuit brought by the NAACP on behalf of Russ's widow and children. Russ was shot down in cold blood inside the Star City, Arkansas, police station when he went in to pay a fine for a minor traffic violation while his family waited outside in their car. The suit accused various police officials of denying Russ his civil rights through racial discrimination. The NAACP sued U.S. Attorney General Edward Levi in the U.S. district court in the District of Columbia over the failure of the FBI to investigate seriously the Carnell Russ police murder. The government filed a motion to dismiss the suit.

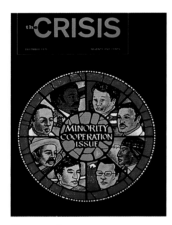

December 1975

• On August 6, President Ford signed H.R. 6219, amending and extending certain provisions of the 1965 Voting Rights Act, culminating a two-year effort by the Washington Bureau and cooperating organizations. The 1974 Act extended protection of the right to register and vote to non-English speaking groups, especially Hispanics.

• The NAACP expressed its concern for the jobless black worker by calling for the suspension of government regulations that resulted in the increase of car prices during the prevailing severe economic recession.

1976

- Roy Wilkins announced, following the January Board meeting, that he would retire as Executive Director on January 1, 1977. The date was later amended to July 31.

- In January, Dr. Montague Cobb, distinguished professor emeritus at Howard University, was elected the first black NAACP president.

- Wilkins and General Counsel Jones said that a Senate Intelligence Committee report confirmed the basic findings of the 1973 NAACP study "Search and Destroy." This study concluded that the FBI conspired with state and local law enforcement officials in Illinois to murder Black Panther leader Fred Hampton.

- On July 8, Wilkins was a guest at the reception of Her Royal Highness, Queen Elizabeth II, and Prince Philip, Duke of Edinburgh, at the British Embassy in Washington, D.C.

- Wilkins condemned the recent "mass killings" of demonstrating South Africans by police and urged that the U.S. government take appropriate diplomatic action and support effective sanctions against that country's government in order to bring an end to apartheid.

- Because African Americans considered the 1976 presidential election one of the most crucial, NAACP units across the nation worked to increase voter registration with a coalition of thirty-nine other organizations in "Operation Big Vote," coordinated by the Joint Center for Political Studies.

- On September 13, the NAACP National Board of Directors appointed Gloster B. Current administrator of the Association's internal structure so that Executive Director Roy Wilkins could concentrate on the Association's fund-raising.

1976: President Gerald Ford with NAACP Executive Director Roy Wilkins at the White House, September 3.

• On November 6, the NAACP National Board of Directors voted unanimously to accept the recommendation of the Search and Screening Committee that Benjamin Lawson Hooks be selected Executive Director of the NAACP. Dr. Hooks was to become Executive Director-designate in January and assume full duties upon the retirement of Executive Director Roy Wilkins on July 31, 1977.

• On November 29, with the help of the NAACP, Clarence (Willie) Norris, last of the "Scottsboro Boys," returned to Montgomery, Alabama, to receive his pardon for a rape conviction from the Alabama Pardons and Parole Board.

• Chairwoman Margaret Bush Wilson warned in a keynote address to the 65th NAACP Annual Convention in Memphis, Tennessee, that the veteran civil rights organization might find it necessary to oppose publicly any presidential candidate who trampled on the rights of black Americans, stating, "Black Americans are in no mood to sit silently by while those who would be our national leaders elected to uphold the constitutional rights of all people, flagrantly and deliberately trample on our rights."

• In December, the NAACP stepped up its investigation of racial incidents at the Marine Corps Camp Pendleton base in California, where the active presence of the Ku Klux Klan reportedly led to violence and the arrest of twelve black servicemen.

• Also in December, Wilson reported that the recently concluded African American conference in Lesotho, organized by the African-American Institute (an independent organization seeking to develop meaningful social and economic ties with Africa) was "most impressive" despite South Africa's refusal to grant visas to her and more than half of the high-ranking official U.S. delegation.

• The NAACP, as *amicus curiae* in the *Gautreaux v. Hills* case, hailed the historic U.S. Supreme Court's decision of April 20 that required federal corrective action to provide low-income housing in the suburbs of Chicago, Illinois. The Court found HUD guilty of violating the Constitution and Civil Rights laws.

• The NAACP was one of ten plaintiffs in a landmark lawsuit filed against the Federal Financial Regulatory Agencies to force the government to take action against lending institutions that discriminated in issuing home mortgage and repair loans.

• NAACP Housing Program Director William Morris testified before HUD on the problem of redlining.

1976: 67th Annual NAACP Convention "Save the Date" flyer.

• Over 51 percent of black families in rural areas lived in substandard or unfit housing. The Association worked to improve housing for blacks in rural areas with the assistance of the Housing Assistance Council; it also worked to equalize government benefits for blacks through the Farmers Home Administration.

• The NAACP report on "Minority Testing" was released on the 22nd anniversary of the *Brown* decision.

• The NAACP was ordered to pay the sum of $1.25 million for financial hardships inflicted on twelve white merchants in Port Gibson, Mississippi, during the successful boycott of white businesses in 1966.

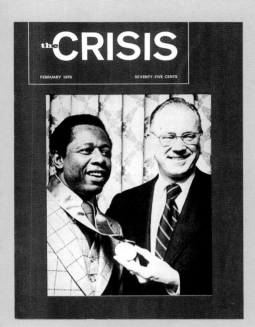

February 1976

October 1976

1977: Newly appointed NAACP Executive Director Benjamin L. Hooks contemplating the future of the NAACP.

1977

• The NAACP charged that the nation's school boards were failing to uphold educational standards in public schools and released a comprehensive report to assist local units in developing programs to bring about quality education in their communities.

• The NAACP extended its full support to U.N. Ambassador Andrew Young, who came under attack for his comments on racism and minority white rule in South Africa. In a telegram to Young, a copy of which was sent to President Jimmy Carter, NAACP Executive Director Roy Wilkins said that the ambassador was speaking the "brutal unvarnished truth about the role racism has played in shaping America's institutions and attitudes."

• NAACP Chairwoman Margaret Bush Wilson declared that the NAACP was "dismayed and disheartened" by President Carter's lack of support for the Hawkins-Humphrey Full Employment Bill.

• On June 28, against the background of high praise for his lifelong dedication to the causes of human justice and freedom, Roy Wilkins bade an emotional farewell from active leadership of the NAACP during the 68th Annual Convention at the St. Louis Gateway Convention Center.

• In September, the NAACP Board of Directors commended President Carter for bringing to an end fourteen years of negotiations on the Panama Canal and urged the Senate to ratify the treaty.

• NAACP General Counsel Nathaniel R. Jones expressed relief over the changes that were evident in a brief from the U.S. Department of Justice that was filed in a case challenging special admissions programs for minorities at the University of California Davis Medical School. The NAACP

June 1977

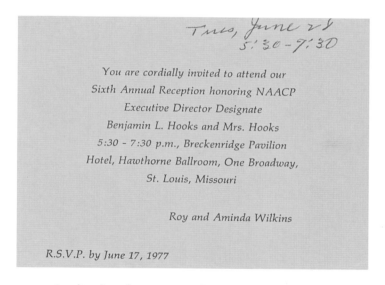

Tues, June 28
5:30 – 7:30

*You are cordially invited to attend our
Sixth Annual Reception honoring NAACP
Executive Director Designate
Benjamin L. Hooks and Mrs. Hooks
5:30 – 7:30 p.m., Breckenridge Pavilion
Hotel, Hawthorne Ballroom, One Broadway,
St. Louis, Missouri*

Roy and Aminda Wilkins

R.S.V.P. by June 17, 1977

1977: Invitation from outgoing NAACP Executive Director Roy Wilkins and wife, Minnie, for a reception in honor of the new Executive Director, Benjamin Hooks and his wife, Frances.

1977: NAACP staffer Earlene Bollin serenades staff at dinner.

previously had protested to the White House and the Justice Department that the Carter Administration's reported position in the Bakke case would have been harmful to future efforts to open up similar opportunities for minorities in such institutions as Davis.

• The NAACP joined local and national organizations in picketing the South African Consulate to protest the serious intensification of racial repression in that country. Carrying picket signs that said "South Africa Lift Ban on Black Newspapers" and "South Africa Release Political Prisoners," the NAACP staffers marched quietly for nearly two hours along New York's prestigious Park Avenue at 55th Street, where the consulate was located.

• In response to the worldwide petroleum crisis, the NAACP convened the first minority-run national energy conference, which opposed any artificial boost in energy prices designed to reduce demand. Speaking for its black and poor constituencies, the NAACP promulgated the first black energy policy statement, which supported economic growth and job creation. A permanent NAACP energy committee was created.

• NAACP attorneys persuaded Mississippi's Supreme Court to reverse a lower court libel judgment, which had awarded $240,000 to a state highway patrolman who was accused of racist behavior.

1977: NAACP "Freedom Seals" Poster.

1978

November 1978

• For a full generation, Hubert Horatio Humphrey was an indomitable foe of racial bigotry as well as a living symbol of human decency and fortitude. In recognition of his unflagging support in the epic civil rights battles that led to the enactment of the Civil Rights Acts and other legislation to improve the lives of the poor and oppressed, the NAACP awarded Senator Humphrey the first Walter White Award on January 8. Senator Humphrey, who died five days later, was represented by his sister, Francis Howard to receive the award.

• In January, the NAACP National Board of Directors adopted a far-reaching series of recommendations on Africa and called on the U.S. government to take stern action against South Africa to help bring down its system of apartheid.

• Dramatizing his concern for the plight of millions of blacks who were trapped in America's ghettos, Hooks led delegates to the expanded annual meeting weekend in a pilgrimage to Harlem, New York. There, in the multimillion-dollar state office building that represented a somewhat forgotten commitment to the rebuilding of America's best-known black community, NAACP leaders from across the nation prepared themselves for the continuation of the struggle.

Cabinet-level Appointees

January 1977

March 1978

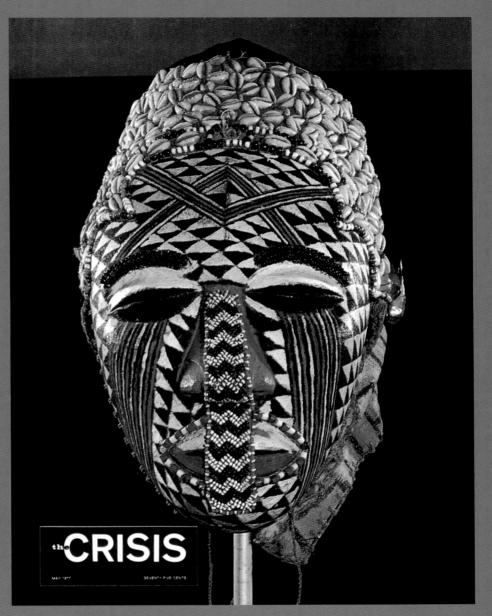

May 1977

March 1978: NAACP "March Against Racism in South Africa."

1978: *The Crisis* Special Report: "NAACP and Africa."

NAACP & AFRICA the **CRISIS**

APRIL 1978   SEVENTY-FIVE CENTS

• Also in January, signaling another new dimension in the NAACP's struggle for jobs, Chairwoman Wilson testified at a hearing of the Highway Traffic Safety Administration that proposed fuel economy rules for light trucks would hurt consumers and black workers and warned against regulations that would possibly result in Chrysler's closing its Detroit, Michigan, plants. Two months later, the administration announced that it was lowering its requirements. Chrysler Chairman John J. Riccardo told Wilson that this change would permit his company to reinstate the program for converting the assembly plant to light truck production, thus avoiding loss of jobs for blacks.

• NAACP Washington Bureau Director Clarence Mitchell Jr. led efforts to reorganize and consolidate federal civil rights enforcement programs in 1977, placing most of the authority within the Equal Employment Opportunity Commission. The NAACP's full support helped the president to sign the reorganization papers on schedule.

• On March 18, Likening the system of apartheid to the brutality of Nazi Germany, Hooks led a crowd of four thousand in a march across the street from Vanderbilt University in Nashville, Tennessee, to protest South Africa's participation in the Davis Cup tennis matches.

1978: NAACP 69th Annual Convention program.

1978: NAACP Religious Affairs Director Rev. J. C. Hope and Chairman Kelly Alexander raise funds at the 1978 NAACP convention.

1978: Frances Hooks and Dick Gregory at the NAACP 69th Annual Convention.

• In May, a Mobile, Alabama, jury found Charles Smith Jr., a black man, not guilty of killing a twenty-year-old white man. The case in the NAACP annals ranks with equal importance to the Ossian H. Sweet tragedy of 1925, where a black doctor was charged with murder.

• In July, Hooks spoke to the Republican semi-annual conference at the Detroit Plaza Hotel, telling them they must support persons who were both sensitive and committed to those programs necessary for realizing racial justice.

• President Carter approved an increase in import tariffs on high carbon ferrochrome, which was used in the manufacture of stainless steel. This was to a large extent a result of the urging of NAACP Executive Director Hooks. The action effectively limited imports from South Africa, as the Association had sought.

• The NAACP Board adopted a broad anti-apartheid program, including a demand for stern U.S. action against South Africa's racist policies.

• The Supreme Court reached a distressing decision on June 18 in the famous *Bakke* case, which overturned preferential minority admissions practices at the University of California Davis Law School. In the wake of this decision, the NAACP convened a Post-*Bakke* Symposium in Detroit consisting of civil rights lawyers and experts to deal with the fallout from the decision and to forge a new strategy for minority college admissions.

• Several hundred black political, civic, and professional leaders answered the NAACP's Call to Leadership Summit in Chicago to map new electoral and other strategies for the Civil Rights movement.

• To promote academic excellence and provide a forum for expression among high school students,

the NAACP established ACT-SO (Academic, Cultural, Technological, and Scientific Olympics), the brainchild of journalist Vernon Jarrett.

1978: NAACP Executive Director Benjamin L. Hooks at the 69th Annual Convention Youth Awards Banquet with speaker Julian Bond, Atlanta Branch President and Georgia state representative.

1978: NAACP ACT-SO founder Vernon Jarrett and NAACP Board Member Herm Willie with ACT-SO winners Scott Jenkins and Paula Ingram at the first ACT-SO competition at the NAACP 69th Annual Convention.

STATEMENT BY ROY WILKINS   MAY 31, 1978

The statement attributed to me by an unknown source in a national newspaper story is pure fantasy and a malicious lie. Every American citizen who has paid the least amount of attention to his newspaper, radio or television, knows that the late J. Edgar Hoover was unrelenting in his attempts to weaken and destroy the movement for civil rights in this country, and in his attempt to discredit Dr. Martin Luther King.

My record of loyalty to my people, to the 450,000 members of the NAACP and to the cause of individual and civil rights is open for everyone to see. At this stage in my life I do not think I have to defend it.

1978: NAACP Executive Director Roy Wilkins and A. Philip Randolph in their last public appearance together.

1978: Statement issued by NAACP Executive Director Emeritus Roy Wilkins regarding a publicized false statement attributed to him.

July 10, 1979: NAACP prayer vigil in Washington, D.C., against the Mottl Anti-busing Resolution.

1979

• The NAACP launched a major drive to defeat a proposed constitutional amendment to balance the budget; the amendment was regarded as injurious to all Americans.

• The NAACP charged that a suit filed by Sears Roebuck & Co. against ten federal agencies was not "raising valid issues." The giant merchandising company contended that conflicting government regulations were hampering the company in implementing affirmative action requirements to hire and promote minorities and women. On May 15, U.S. District Judge June Green dismissed the suit. She agreed with the U.S. Justice Department, which had opposed it, that Sears had failed to present a case that could be tried.

• Convinced that it had no alternative, the NAACP National Board of Directors adopted a resolution at its convention meeting in Louisville, Kentucky, revoking permission that had been granted the NAACP Legal Defense and Educational Fund, Inc., to use the "NAACP" initials.

• In May, the veteran civil rights organization was warmly welcomed by South Carolina Gov. Richard W. Riley during the commemoration of the 25th anniversary of the Supreme Court's *Brown v. Board of Education* judgment.

• During a special White House program in commemoration of the May 17 *Brown* decision, President Carter announced that he was appointing NAACP General Counsel Nathaniel R. Jones to the U.S. Court of Appeals for the Sixth Circuit.

• In July, Hooks called on black Americans to celebrate the "peculiar, unique genius of black folk" yearly on January 1, which would be designated "Jubilee Day" in observance of Abraham Lincoln's signing of the Emancipation Proclamation in 1863.

• On July 20, Dr. Hooks led a prayer vigil in Washington, D.C., against an amendment to the U.S. Constitution sponsored by Rep. Ronald Mottl of Ohio that would bar courts from ordering busing to achieve school desegregation. The amendment was subsequently defeated in the House.

December 1979

• Wilson and Hooks testified before the House Subcommittee on Africa in opposition to the lifting of sanctions against Rhodesia as being dangerously counterproductive. They centered the NAACP's opposition on the constitution—the foundation upon which Bishop Abel Muzorewa's government had been elected—which they felt gave the 4 percent white minority population lopsided control over the black majority.

• On August 14, Michigan Gov. William G. Milliken signed an NAACP-backed bill that Hooks regarded as a cornerstone in the Association's voter mobilization program. The bill deputized high school principals as voter registrars, empowering them to register graduating students.

• The NAACP won a major court victory in *Turner v. Marks*, whereby the court upheld NAACP charges that the

Clarence M. Mitchell, Jr.
"101st U.S. SENATOR"

68th
Birthday
Dinner

March 14, 1979: Program cover from the
Clarence M. Mitchell Jr. 68th Birthday
Dinner shows Mitchell greeted by
President Lyndon B. Johnson.

Eglin Air Force Base racially discriminated in its hiring and promotion practices. The $2 million judgment for damages to the black plaintiffs, in addition to the order to create one hundred new jobs and twenty-five promotions for black workers, sent a telling message to military installations at home and abroad to clean up their act.

• The NAACP launched its first national corporate campaign, chaired by William Ellinghaus, president of AT&T. Over the next fifteen years, corporate gifts exceeded $37 million.

• *The Crisis* dedicated the entire February 1979 issue to the fallout behind the Supreme Court's decision in *Bakke v. University of California.*

1979: Rev. M. D. McCollom presents the NAACP Thalhemier Award to the founder and treasurer emeritus of the South Carolina Conference, Levi G. Byrd, at the NAACP 70th Annual Convention.

I want to congratulate our NAACP on its one hundredth anniversary of pursuing justice for all people in America. I am the recipient of the 59th Spingarn Medal, and I have had the pleasure of presenting the award to the following recipients: Ms. Rosa L. Parks, the 64th recipient; Mayor Coleman Alexander Young, the 66th recipient; and Mr. Oliver W. Hill, the 90th recipient of the Spingarn Medal.

The NAACP has been the guardian for justice in America for these one hundred years, and I am proud to have played a role in its fight for freedom.

Honorable Damon J. Keith

59th Spingarn Medalist

1989: NAACP leads the charge at the "Silent March."

1980–1989

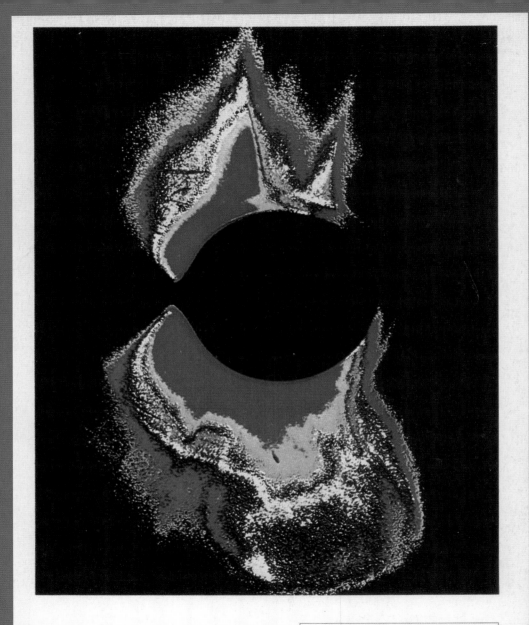

the CRISIS

MARCH 1980   SEVENTY-FIVE CENTS

March 1980

1980

• The NAACP vastly expanded voter registration and get-out-the-vote campaigns, registering forty-nine thousand in New York and forty thousand in North Carolina, while also gearing up to promote maximum black participation in the U.S. Census.

• The Law Enforcement Assistance Administration made a grant to the NAACP to analyze and monitor police use of deadly force in several southern and western states. Later in the year, to encourage, support, assist, and direct branch efforts to bring about policy change in the use of deadly force by police, the NAACP began the Police-Citizen Violence Project.

• The Supreme Court decided that the federal government did not have to finance most abortions for welfare recipients, which the NAACP considered a travesty against poor women.

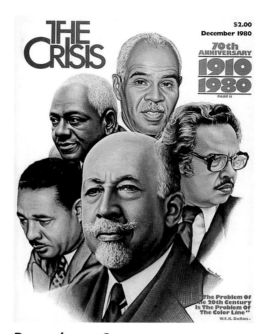

December 1980

• The NAACP applauded the Supreme Court's decision to uphold a federal law guaranteeing minority-owned businesses a 10 percent share of all federal public work grants.

• On December 17, 1979, Arthur McDuffie, a black insurance salesman who was driving his motorcycle on a suspended license due to mounting tickets, led Miami police on a high-speed chase. When McDuffie lost control of the motorcycle and police caught up with him, they beat him so savagely they cracked his skull, and he died days later. On May 17, 1980, the last of the officers to be charged was acquitted by an all-white jury and rioting broke out. The NAACP sent letters to the Justice Department asking that they

1980s: Jerry Guess, NAACP director of communications, greets Haitian President Jean Bertrand Aristide before he receives the NAACP's Walter White Award, as NAACP Executive Director Benjamin Hooks and TransAfrica CEO Randall Robinson look on.

1981: NAACP leaders: Washington Bureau Director Althea Simmons, Executive Director Benjamin Hooks, Youth Board Member Corwin Macklin, and Deputy Executive Director Charles Smith display a petition signed by NAACP members and citizens across the nation before presenting it to Congress at a Legislative Mobilization for extension of the 1965 Voting Rights Act.

1980: NAACP Chairman William Gibson receives a kiss from an NAACP member at the Association's 71st Annual Convention in Honolulu, Hawaii.

NAACP NEWS — NATIONAL ASSOCIATION FOR THE ADVANCEMENT OF COLORED PEOPLE

| 1790 BROADWAY | NEW YORK, N.Y. 10019 | 212 245-2100 |

Benjamin L. Hooks
EXECUTIVE DIRECTOR

Paul Brock
DIRECTOR OF PUBLIC RELATIONS

STATEMENT BY BENJAMIN L. HOOKS
EXECUTIVE DIRECTOR, NAACP
71ST ANNUAL CONVENTION
MIAMI BEACH, FLORIDA
JUNE 30, 1980

RONALD REAGAN

We deeply regret and deplore the decision today by Republican presidential candidate, Ronald Reagan, not to attend this 71st NAACP Annual Convention. Even more, we strongly deplore what will in fact deny black people here in Miami --- and across this nation --- the opportunity to hear Mr. Reagan on the issues that are of such vital interest to them.

We will not attempt to speculate on why Mr. Reagan found it unimportant to come to Miami. It is sufficient just to note that he found a week of play and recreation of higher priority.

One can only wonder whether this decision means he has "written off" the black vote. It would be tragic if this is the case.

-30-

June 30, 1980: A press release announcing the NAACP's displeasure at the decision of presidential candidate Ronald Reagan not to attend the Association's 71st Annual Convention.

monitor the trial. NAACP Executive Director Benjamin L. Hooks and an NAACP delegation arrived in Miami on May 18 and set up a crisis response center and, a few days later, an Urban Affairs office to monitor the actions and compliance of the federal, state, and local authorities with civil rights laws. The NAACP also committed monies to the redevelopment of the destroyed areas.

1981

• Representing the Boston, Massachusetts NAACP branch, NAACP attorneys won a major court victory on behalf of local minority police officers and firefighters. After a finding of racial discrimination, a federal judge ordered an extensive affirmative action program for police and fire departments.

• The NAACP launched the Fair Share Program to increase jobs and promotions for black workers. NAACP Executive Director Benjamin L. Hooks signed the first round of Fair Share agreements with

December 17, 1981: NAACP staffers Jean Fortune and Vilma Jenkins with actor Denzel Washington at the NAACP Staff Theatre Party at The Negro Ensemble Company.

Brown, Zettler, Friedman, Smith: A network of hatred in
Anatomy of a
Now celebrating its fifteenth anniversary, the Negro Ensemble Company is a survivor. Under its indomitable artistic director, Douglas Turner Ward, it has pre-
playwrights like Joseph A.
destructive complexity: a man full of pride and self-hatred, a fiercely perfectionist soldier who despises the men in his charge because their human individuality resists his need to mold them into soldiers measuring up to some impossible ideal.
Here is the "black rage" that psycholo-
the best black playwrights, Fuller takes
freshening our vision of reality. Like
ensemble performance from his terri

Edison Electric Institute and the
American Gas Association, followed
by Walt Disney Productions and
MGM–United Artists.

• Federal judges ruled for the
NAACP in major cases charging
school desegregation in Cleveland
and Columbus, Ohio. Substantial
remedies were ordered as the
NAACP legal department broadened
nationwide attacks on segregated
public schools outside the South.

• Hooks was elected chairman of
the Leadership Conference on Civil
Rights, a lobbying coalition com-

M E M O R A N D U M
August 28, 1981

TO: THE STAFF

FROM: Benjamin L. Hooks

Mrs. Roy Wilkins would be most grateful to any of us who would be blood
donors to the NYC Medical Center Blood Program. Such donations will help replace
the blood transfusions given to Mr. Wilkins.

For your information, listed are the Guidelines for Donors:

The age range for donation is 18 to 65 years of age. 17
with written parental permission.

Minimum weight is 110 pounds.

Persons who have had hepatitis, jaundice or malaria are not
eligible.

Persons with colds or sore throats are asked to wait until
one week after their symptoms have disappeared.

If you now have hay fever, asthma or any other allergy, or if
you are taking any medication, please notify us when making
your appointment.

You may eat and drink (non-alcoholic beverages) before donating
blood.

UNIVERSITY HOSPITAL DONOR SERVICE
Room HG-21
560 First Avenue
New York, New York 10016

To make an appointment call 340-5440, between the hours of 9:00 a.m.
and 5:00 p.m., Monday through Friday.

HOURS FOR DONATION

Monday, Wednesday and Friday   9:00 a.m.-5:30 p.m.
Tuesday and Thursday   10:00 a.m.-7:30 p.m.
Alternate Sundays   10:00 a.m.-3:30 p.m.

If you do plan to participate, please let us know as Mrs. Wilkins will be anxious
to acknowledge your contribution.

The doctors report that Mr. Wilkins' condition is critical but stable.
Contrary to news reports, his ailment was not coronary but is related to his
kidneys.

Cards or messages are welcome and may be sent to:

NEW YORK UNIVERSITY MEDICAL CENTER
ICU
550 First Avenue, New York, N. Y. 10016

1981: Memo from NAACP Executive Director Benjamin L. Hooks to staff.

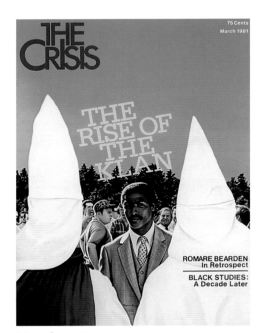

March 1981

posed of 152 national religious, labor, ethnic, and civil rights organizations founded in 1950 by Roy Wilkins, Walter White, Clarence Mitchell Jr., A. Philip Randolph, Bayard Rustin, and other civil rights leaders.

• A coalition led by the NAACP and Leadership Conference on Civil Rights won a congressional extension of the Voting Rights Act by vast margins. President Ronald Reagan reluctantly signed the veto-proof bill, which extended the act for twenty-five years and the overturned reactionary 1980 Supreme Court

December 1981

Service

ROY WILKINS

AUGUST 30, 1901   SEPTEMBER 8, 1981

EXECUTIVE DIRECTOR EMERITUS

National Association for the Advancement
of Colored People

Friday, September 11, 1981
11:00 A.M.

COMMUNITY CHURCH OF NEW YORK
40 EAST 35th STREET
NEW YORK CITY

September 11, 1981: Funeral program for former NAACP Executive Director Roy Wilkins.

1982: Dr. Annie Martin, New York branch president (seated to left), heads up a New York voter registration drive.

NEW YORK BRANCH N.A.A.C.P.

NEW YORK BRANCH N.A.A.C.P. Voter...Registration DRIVE

1982: NAACP Membership Director Janice Washington presents a Golden Heritage Life Membership Plaque to Julian Bond at the NAACP Atlanta Branch's Emancipation Day Program.

1982: Senator Edward Brooke presents the 1982 Spingarn Medal to Benjamin E. Mays.

decision requiring "intent" as proof in voting rights cases.

• The NAACP formally presented its 170-page report "Alternative Policies in the Public Interest for Economic Growth" to the Reagan Administration.

1982

• The NAACP locked horns with the Reagan Justice Department over the latter's attempt to award tax-exempt status to Bob Jones University, a racially segregated institution. In an expedited appeal, civil rights forces challenged the Justice Department decision upwards through federal courts until the U.S. Supreme Court, by eight to one, repudiated the Justice Department position and prohibited tax-exempt designation for Bob Jones University.

• The U.S. Supreme Court overruled a $1.25 million judgment against the NAACP imposed in 1976 in the 1966 Mississippi boycott case at Port Gibson.

• The Voting Rights Act of 1965 was renewed for another twenty-five years.

• The NAACP's Voter Registration Department signed up more than 850,000 new voters in an effort to draw a record turnout for the national election.

• In the case *Turner v. Marks*, the NAACP successfully challenged discriminatory employment and promotion policies at Elgin Air Force Base, resulting in a $2 million settlement and one hundred new jobs.

• In a Cleveland, Ohio, school desegregation case, the Association persuaded the district court to enter findings of liability against the state of Ohio and place the Cleveland school system in receivership under a court-appointed desegregation administrator.

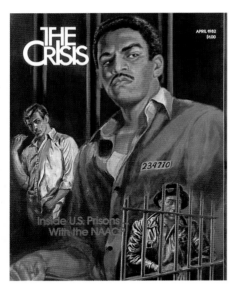

April 1982

• The Association was awarded a fifteen-month technical assistance grant by the Economic Development Administration (EDA) to establish the Minority Business Enterprise Economic Development/Technical Assistance Project to advocate on the national, state, and local levels for favorable legislation and corporate policies to increase and enhance employment and business opportunities for minorities.

1983

• After a long grassroots campaign, the NAACP and its allies succeeded in persuading Congress to enact the Martin Luther King Jr. Holiday Bill, which passed by a three to one margin in both houses, persuading a reluctant President Reagan to sign it.

• The NAACP advocated for greater physical access to public streets, buildings, businesses, and transport for the physically disabled and senior citizens. Congress enacted a groundbreaking bill.

• The NAACP stepped up the Fair Share program with thirteen agreements, including a $10 million pact with Georgia Power.

• After a lengthy study, the NAACP issued a hard-hitting report on the music recording industry. Entitled "The Discordant Sound of Music," the report documented widespread racial inequality throughout the industry and helped spark major changes industrywide, especially within the offices of the three major record labels.

• The NAACP and the St. Louis, Missouri, school system reached an agreement to desegregate city schools.

• The NAACP participated in the 20th anniversary of the "March on Washington."

August 1982

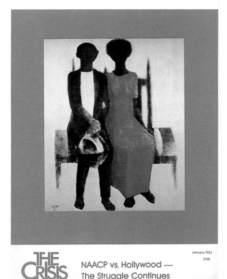

January 1983

1983: The Rev. Benjamin L. Hooks, NAACP Executive Director, outside his Detroit church with an NAACP delegation.

• In August and September, starting in Covington, Kentucky, and ending in Detroit, Michigan, the NAACP conducted a twenty-two-day Voter Registration/Education March, retracing the Underground Railroad route used by slaves.

• Federal District Judge Leonard D. Sands heard arguments in a lawsuit brought by the NAACP against Yonkers, New York, claiming that housing policies that intentionally fostered racial segregation directly resulted in segregated schools.

1983: NAACP Executive Director Benjamin L. Hooks and Voter Education Director Joe Madison lead a march against voter apathy in Detroit, Michigan.

August 1983

October 1983

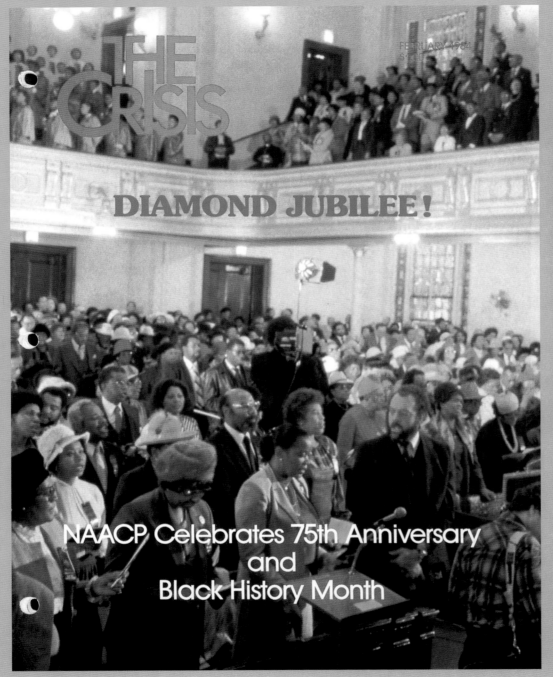

THE CRISIS

DIAMOND JUBILEE!

NAACP Celebrates 75th Anniversary
and
Black History Month

February 1984

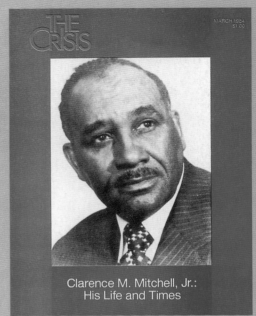

Clarence M. Mitchell, Jr.:
His Life and Times

March 1984

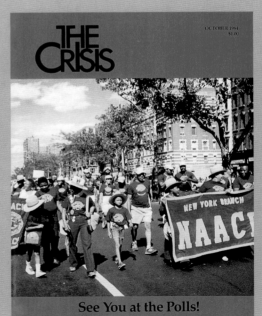

See You at the Polls!

October 1984

1984

• Several hundred scholars, social workers, child development experts, psychologists, and lay leaders met for three days to discuss and debate the problems, causes, and the possible solutions for the crisis in the black family at an NAACP/National Urban League-sponsored summit at Fisk University.

• The NAACP opposed the confirmation of Edwin Meese to become U.S. Attorney General and fought his efforts to repeal Executive Order 11246.

• To demonstrate the potency of black purchasing power, the NAACP organized its first Black Dollar Days by using only $2 bills and silver dollars for all purchases over a designated period.

1984: 75th Annual NAACP Convention ACT-SO ceremony. Pictured on left: Vernon Jarett, ACT-SO founder.

• Two years after he was wrongly convicted of armed robbery and sentenced to life imprisonment in Texas, Lenell Geter, a young black electrical engineer who maintained his innocence, was released from prison and then acquitted after NAACP attorneys successfully argued his appeal. The real perpetrator later confessed while in prison.

• Responding to the overwhelming tragedies stemming from the widespread famine in Africa, NAACP members raised $75,000 for famine relief.

• Concerned by the low college admissions rate for many young black people, the NAACP created a pilot project for its own SAT Test Preparation clinics in New York, Atlanta, and San Francisco. Dozens of NAACP branches subsequently conducted these clinics, which raised scores for black students on an average of fifty or more points.

1985: Executive Director Benjamin L. Hooks encouraged NAACP branches to intensify anti-apartheid demonstrations. Here, Hooks confers with Atlanta Mayor Andrew Young at an Atlanta, Georgia, protest.

1985

- The soaring dropout rate among black high school students convinced NAACP Executive Director Hooks to launch a national program, "Back to School/Stay in School." *The Reader's Digest* provided substantial program support for the first five years.

- Civil rights forces lobbied Congress to defeat the Helms-East "Courtstripping" Bill for the third and final time. The bill sought to strip the Supreme Court of jurisdiction over certain controversial constitutional issues including civil rights.

- After three years of battling with the Reagan-Meese Justice Department, the NAACP and Leadership Conference led the fight to defeat the nomination of William Bradford Reynolds as an associate attorney general. The Senate Judiciary Committee revealed for the first time that Reynolds used the fear of "quotas" as a smokescreen for the Justice Department's opposition to civil rights enforcement across the board.

- The City of Dearborn, Michigan, was sued by the NAACP after adopting an ordinance designed to exclude the children of black residents of neighboring Detroit—restricting the use of its parks to residents and guests.

1985: The coffin of apartheid is carried by (from top, left to right) Leonard Brown Jr., Carl Eggleston, L. Garnell Stamps, L. A. Franklin, Junius A. Haskins Jr., and Harvey Dickerson.

January 1985

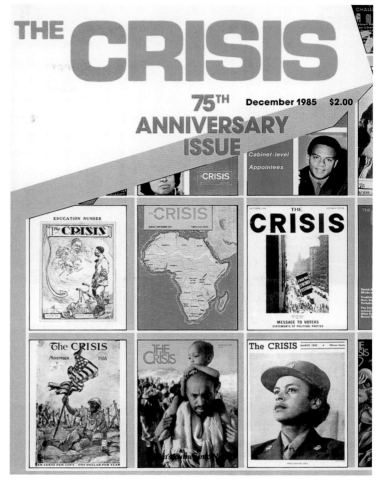

December 1985

• More than ten thousand New Yorkers jammed Fifth Avenue for a massive anti-apartheid rally sponsored by the NAACP and the City of New York; the rally ended with an ecumenical prayer service at St. Patrick's Cathedral.

• The NAACP's civil rights campaign to preserve the executive order on affirmative action was bolstered by support from many corporate CEOs who urged President Reagan not to change the order. Seventy U.S. senators and over two hundred representatives informed the president

1985: Dick Gregory addresses the NAACP 76th Convention as Executive Director Benjamin L. Hooks approves.

of their opposition to any change of the order, causing President Reagan to abandon the anti-civil rights measure.

• The NAACP blocked the nomination of Jeffrey Beauregard Sessions to serve as a federal judge in Alabama because of his views on race.

• Journalist Fred Beauford, who used an "activist" approach rather than a "reactionary" one to journalism, was named acting editor of *The Crisis*.

1986: NAACP Executive Director Benjamin L. Hooks prepares for the "NAACP March for Human Dignity in South Africa and at Home."

1986

• A concerted campaign led by the NAACP, senior citizens, organizations representing the disabled, and other civil rights forces produced a series of historic laws that prohibited age discrimination in employment, provided new disability protection, and introduced early intervention services for handicapped children. Some of these measures reversed retrogressive Supreme Court decisions that had been eroding disability rights.

• The NAACP joined a coalition to enact the Tax Reform Act of 1986, which removed six million poor Americans from tax rolls, increased the standard deduction for single heads of household, and raised the level for earned income credit.

• Civil rights groups led by the NAACP and Leadership Conference defeated the nomination of Jeffrey Zuckerman as general counsel of the U.S. Equal Employment Opportunity Commission.

• The NAACP sponsored a cross-continent "March for Human Dignity in South Africa and at Home." Starting in Los Angeles, California, NAACP members walked three thousand miles, concluding at the NAACP Annual Convention in Baltimore, Maryland.

• For the first time in NAACP history, the Association owned its headquarters when it relocated to Baltimore, Maryland.

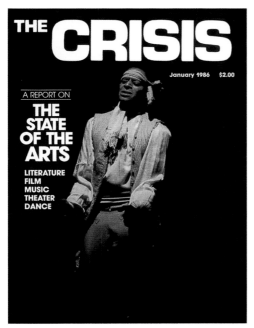

January 1986

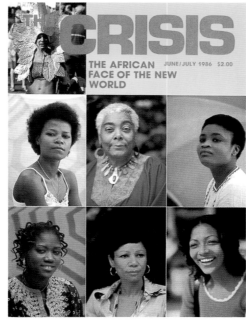

June/July 1986

February 1986

GOOD NEWS!

NATIONAL HEADQUARTERS AT THE TIME OF PURCHASE

ARTIST'S SKETCH OF BUILDING AFTER RENOVATION

1986: NAACP National Headquarters building in Baltimore, Maryland, at time of purchase and after renovations.

1986: Host committee for the NAACP National Headquarters move to Baltimore, Maryland, in 1986: C. Delores Tucker, Enolia McMillan, Juanita Jackson Mitchell, Raymond Haysbert, Joseph Lowery, Clarence Du Burns, and Emmett Burns.

NAACP Dedication Week • Oct. 16-19, 1986

DR. BENJAMIN L. HOOKS
Executive Director

WILLIAM E. POLLARD
Deputy Executive Director

JERRY M. GUESS
Executive Assistant

October 1986: NAACP program for the dedication of its new and first-owned headquarters in Baltimore, Maryland.

1986: The Rev. Jesse Jackson chats with Democratic congressional candidate Kweisi Mfume and NAACP Dedication Week Chairwoman C. Delores Tucker before speaking at a community rally in celebration of the NAACP's first-owned national headquarters.

1986: NAACP Mississippi State Field Director Cleve McDowell, the first African American to attend the University of Mississippi Law School, with employees and union workers at a catfish processing plant addressing unfair and unsafe labor practices.

1987

• With a new and enlarged foundation support, the NAACP filed thirty-two voting rights cases.

• The NAACP released its "Long Range Plan: The Year 2000 and Beyond," a blueprint for dealing with social issues as teenage pregnancy, female heads of households, crime, and substance abuse.

• In a precedent-setting move, the Boston Housing Authority agreed to settle a lawsuit brought by the NAACP charging racial discrimination in public housing. The Housing Authority agreed to pay about two thousand minority housing applicants a total of $3.1 million for either having steered them to minority projects or having discouraged their applications to predominantly white developments.

• NAACP attorneys won an acquittal for Cpl. Arnold Bracey, who was accused by military authorities of participating in a "Pay for Sex" scandal at the U.S. Embassy in Moscow. NAACP attorneys also won the reversal of conviction of U.S. Army Lt. Dennis Roy Butler, who was wrongly convicted of armed robbery and sentenced to seven years in prison.

• Midyear, the NAACP launched an all-out campaign to defeat Judge Robert Bork's nomination to the Supreme Court. The Senate vote (58-42) was the highest negative vote ever against a Supreme Court nominee.

• NAACP Executive Director Benjamin L. Hooks met with the commissioners of major league sports operations to secure pledges that they would include more minorities in the "front office."

• Responding to the loss of accreditation of black teachers, the NAACP devised a model test preparation clinic for the National Teacher's Exam (NTE). After a one-year trial in Maryland, the NTE clinics gradually spread to seven states, helping thousands of black education majors pass the exam.

• To combat the exorbitant jobless rate among black teenagers, the NAACP established a job readiness program to teach black youth job search skills.

• On the 25th anniversary of the use of federal troops to enforce integration of Little Rock's Central High, the NAACP reunited the Little Rock Nine and NAACP leader Daisy Bates at ceremonies at the Arkansas Capitol.

March 1987

• In an overwhelmingly bipartisan vote, both houses of Congress repudiated the Administration's curtailment of the Civil Rights Commission, including its loss of independence. Congress sharply cut the commission's budget and placed restrictions on its expenditures.

• Benjamin Hooks and Chairman William Gibson joined other civil rights leaders in a protest march through Forsythe County, Georgia—a KKK haven that prevented blacks from residing there.

1988

• The NAACP supported passage of the Civil Rights Restoration Act.

• Congress approved the NAACP-sponsored amendment to the Fair Housing Act of 1968.

• The ashes of Dorothy Parker were interred at the NAACP National Headquarters in a memorial garden. The Henry Lee Moon Library and Civil Rights Archives was also dedicated.

1987: NAACP's "Quest for Justice" brochure.

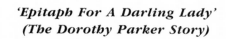

'Epitaph For A Darling Lady'
(The Dorothy Parker Story)

Published by
THE NATIONAL ASSOCIATION FOR
THE ADVANCEMENT OF COLORED PEOPLE
Baltimore, Maryland

1988: Literary genius Dorothy Parker left her estate to Martin Luther King Jr., and, in the event of his death, to the NAACP. In 1988, the NAACP asked that her ashes be buried in a memorial garden at the NAACP National Headquarters in Baltimore, Maryland.

1989

• After a series of Supreme Court decisions hostile to blacks and other minorities, especially the notorious *Richmond v. Croson* decision barring some minority set-aside measures, the NAACP and the Black Leadership Forum convened a conference called "The Present Crisis." Over two hundred representatives of minority, civil rights, women's, and other organizations developed a comprehensive package of strategies and tactics that local NAACP units and local governments used to bolster or preserve set-aside programs in their cities.

• A historic NAACP "Silent March" by one hundred thousand supporters in Washington, D.C., demanded congressional retrogressive decisions.

• The NAACP pushed for the enactment of the Fair Lending Act of 1989, which included tough measures against red-lining.

• The NAACP supported organized labor's successful drive to increase the minimum wage.

• In response to a study that showed African Americans were more likely to require organ transplants, the NAACP launched a nationwide outreach and educational campaign to encourage donorship.

• The NAACP responded to a riot in Virginia Beach, Virginia, involving African American students by offering legal help, investigating allegations by white business owners at the resort, and offering recommendations to avoid future conflicts.

• The NAACP and allies sharply clashed with President Reagan over the proposed 1990 Civil Rights Act, which Reagan opposed as a "quota" bill. Over 65 percent of congressional members supported the measure; however, Reagan vetoed it nevertheless.

• A mail bomb exploded in the Atlanta, Georgia, NAACP office. In Savannah, Georgia, civil rights attorney Robert E. Robinson was killed by a mail bomb.

One of my proudest moments was being appointed by Thurgood Marshall, upon Spottswood W. Robinson's recommendation, to be the registered agent for the NAACP's Legal Defense Fund, Inc. That appointment enabled me to meet and come to know the legal giants throughout this nation and witness firsthand their exemplary commitment to justice and equality in America. These esteemed individuals are far too numerous to mention; I would be unable to name all of them. Yet all of their efforts, along with countless others, provided the grist for the mill in terms of creating changes in our society of a lasting nature.

L. Douglas Wilder
74th Spingarn Medalist

February 1989

November 1989

January 1989

NORTH REGION
ACP
W YORK PENNSYLVANIA
NE
EW JERSEY DELAWARE
C

1989: NAACP Board Member Hazel Dukes leads the North-eastern Region delegates at the NAACP 89th Annual Convention.

1989: NAACP "Silent March on Washington" program.

THE NAACP SILENT MARCH
WASHINGTON, D.C.
SATURDAY, AUGUST 26, 1989

In response to the numerous requests received at NAACP National Headquarters, we have reprinted this brochure which encapsulates the efforts of the NAACP over the years and pays tribute to a few of the thousands who have dedicated their life's work to the struggle for freedom.
— Benjamin L. Hooks

NATIONAL OFFICERS

Dr. William F. Gibson
Chairman, Board of Directors

Enolia P. McMillan
President

Benjamin L. Hooks
Executive Director

Rev. Edward A. Hailes
Vice Chairman

VICE PRESIDENTS

Kelly Alexander, Jr.
John H. Gwynn, Jr.

Hazel N. Dukes
Dr. Charles H. Butler

Mrs. Rupert Richardson
Carl Breeding

WHY WE MARCH

We march because the Supreme Court in four 5-4 decisions has reversed civil rights gains and seems likely to do the same in other decisions still to come.

We march because we are fearful that the strides made over the past several decades will be reversed if these recent Supreme Court decisions are allowed to stand.

We march to make our voices heard in the corridors of the White House, in the halls of Congress, and across the land from the snow-capped peaks of Vermont to the sun-drenched shores of California.

We march because we have learned well from history that the price of freedom is eternal vigilance and unless we move on our own to protect what we have won at such great costs, we can look to no other quarter for help.

We march in silence to signal the depth of our concern and the real gravity and seriousness with which we view this moment in history.

We march to send a message to all people regardless of race, color, religion, sex or ethnic origin, that we will not and cannot acquiesce quietly as an uncaring Supreme Court majority dismantles court ruling after court ruling and turns its face toward the dark past and away from the present and the future.

We march because we are American citizens who believe in the Constitution and in the right to petition Congress for the redress of wrongs.

We march because we recognize that the decisions harm not only Black Americans, but erode the fundamental concept, so laboriously wrought, that this great nation in its own best interests, must set right the wrongs of the past.

Finally, we march proudly in the footsteps of our brave sisters and brothers from another age who marched 72 years ago in silent witness against lynching, discrimination, segregation and racism. For us not to march at this point in time would be a grave disservice to them.

LITANY FOR AUGUST 26
SILENT MARCH ON WASHINGTON

Leader: Why do we march?
Response: We march for justice!
Leader: We march to call the conscience of the nation to act to undo wrong.

We march to call upon the Congress of the United States to pass laws to clearly end economic discrimination against black and minority Americans and women.
Response: We march for economic parity.
Leader: We march to urge Richard Thornburgh, the Attorney General of the United States, to tell the truth about the damaging effects of recent Supreme Court decisions.
Response: Tell the truth, Mr. Thornburgh! Tell the truth!

1989: Dr. Benjamin L. Hooks, NAACP Executive Director, addresses the more than one hundred thousand participants in the NAACP's "Silent March on Washington, D.C." in August.

July 1990: Douglas Wilder receives the
75th Spingarn Medal. Surrounding him
are NAACP Board Member Percy Sutton,
Executive Director Benjamin L. Hooks,
Rev. Jesse Jackson, and NAACP Chairman
William Gibson.

1990–1999

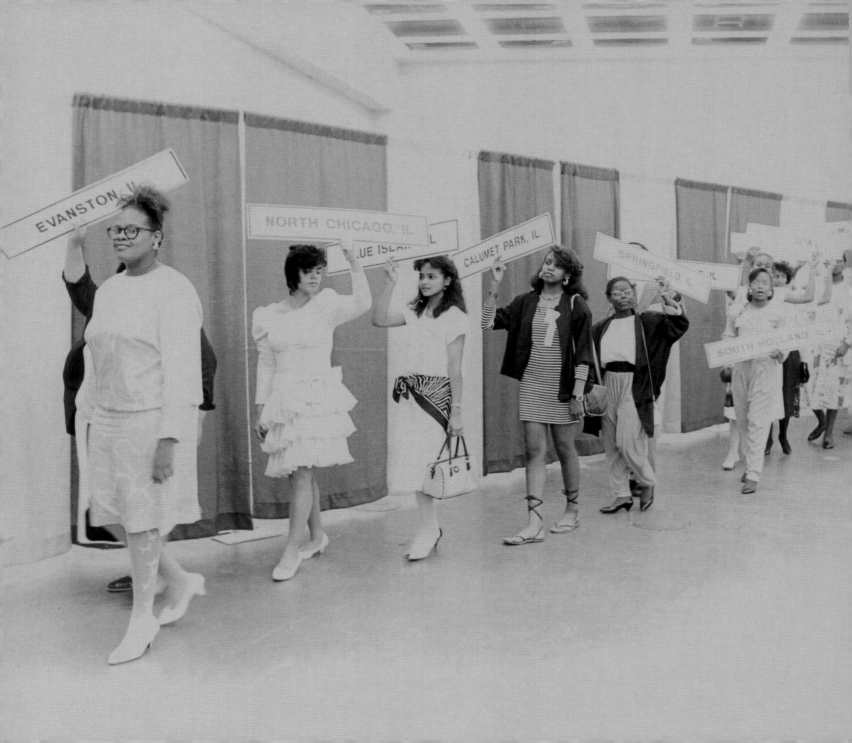

1990

- In response to a series of anti-black statements by Japanese leaders, NAACP Executive Director Benjamin L. Hooks launched a thirty-day program of protest demonstrations outside the Japanese Embassy in Washington, D.C. Japanese diplomats agreed to open negotiations.

- The NAACP joined over one hundred African American organizations to form the National Association of Black Organizations (NABO) to deal with social and economic issues faced by blacks.

- NAACP units began a massive campaign to maximize the 1990 census count of African Americans.

- Faced with an epidemic of racist incidents on college campuses, the NAACP Youth and College Division convened the first conference on campus racism, where representatives of thirty-five colleges met at the University of South Carolina (Columbia) to craft strategies to combat racism.

- NAACP branches registered 450,000 new voters nationwide.

- The NAACP protested the site of the PGA Open, Shoal Creek Golf Club, which barred African Americans. The resulting pressure compelled the club to end its color bar; other golf clubs followed suit after a threat of sizable monetary losses in the event that they were barred from hosting professional golf matches.

- Based on his record on affirmative action, the NAACP unsuccessfully opposed Judge David Souter's nomination to the U.S. Supreme Court.

July 1990: NAACP youth delegates from Illinois march into a meeting at the 1990 convention in Los Angeles, California.

1990: Pictured at the NAACP 81st Convention in Los Angeles, California, are NAACP Special Contribution Fund Trustee Laura Blackburne, Board Member Julian Bond and his wife, Pam Horowitz, and Frances Hooks.

July 1990: C. Delores Tucker, Frances Hooks, Mildred Bond Roxborough and philanthropist Patricia Kluge (second from left) who served as co-chair of the NAACP 75th Diamond Jubilee dinner.

1990–1992: NAACP Civil Rights Report Card for the 102nd Congress.

NAACP
CIVIL RIGHTS REPORT CARD
THE 102ND CONGRESS

1990 - 1992

THE CRISIS

OCTOBER 1991 $2.00

EDUCATING BLACK BOYS:
Are All Male Schools The Answer?

October 1991

1991

• After a bitter two-year battle, the NAACP and its allies overcame the Reagan Administration's "quota" ploy when a large congressional majority passed a Civil Rights Act similar to the one vetoed by President George Bush in 1990. This time, however, the grassroots clout of the NAACP, combined with the lobbyist skills of its Washington Bureau and other civil rights organizations, persuaded enough Republican senators to support the "new" version so that Bush could be overridden if he decided to veto. Instead, Bush declared the 1991 version was not a "quota" Bill and signed it. The 1991 Act overturned eight retrogressive Supreme Court decisions (in the past no Bill had reversed more than one at a time), making it easier for victims of discrimination to get into court and to prove discrimination. The act provided, for the first time, for women to obtain compensatory and punitive damages for discrimination. The same coverage was provided for the disabled and some religious minorities. The new law also covered Congressional employees.

• Another amendment by arch-reactionary Senator Jesse Helms to prohibit affirmative action remedies was defeated by the Senate with votes from moderate Republicans.

• Following the stunning victory in the Republican gubernatorial primary by former Klansman and neo-Nazi David Duke, the NAACP Louisiana State Conference, with broad national support, launched an unprecedented voter registration and Get-Out-The-Vote campaign. Black voters, who comprised 31 percent of the state vote, turned out in historic numbers—76.3 percent—to defeat Duke.

• The NAACP defeated the nomination of federal judge Kenneth L. Ryskamp to the Circuit Court of Appeals because of his views and record on race.

• With substantial support from private foundations, the NAACP launched its massive Redistricting Project in twenty-three states. Using state-of-the-art computer hardware and programs together with census data, the Redistricting Team (combining the Association's Legal and Voter Departments) inaugurated an all-out assault on old district lines—local, state, and congressional. With an unprecedented degree of success, local NAACP Units and State Conferences, working closely with black elected officials and candidates, pressed state legislatures for changes that would maximize black representation. In addition to the election of thirty-nine black members of Congress (including members from fourteen newly drawn districts) and the first female African American in the U.S. Senate, the newly devised districts resulted in the election of hundreds of new state, county, city, and school board electoral victories for black men and women, significantly changing the political face of the nation. The Redistricting Project began targeting recalcitrant states, towns, and counties for court challenges in 1992.

• The chronic failures within the public school system to educate the majority of black children, and the growing dissatisfaction with the quality of inner-city and rural education for black youngsters, compelled the NAACP to convene an education summit in Little Rock, Arkansas. Two dozen educators and experts joined over one hundred local and state education activists within the Association to discuss and debate new priorities at the First Daisy Bates Education Summit. A permanent advisory committee was established, headed by Federal Judge Robert L. Carter, one of the NAACP's lead attorneys who argued the 1954 *Brown* case.

• Hollywood was jolted by the NAACP's release of its landmark study of the status of African Americans in the film and television industries. Titled "Out of Focus," the NAACP report charged that blacks were systematically left out of behind-the-camera and front office jobs, even where films or TV shows exploited black superstars.

• Following an exhaustive study of Judge Clarence Thomas's record and philosophy (including a face-to-face meeting), the NAACP Board on July 31 voted unanimously (with one abstention) to oppose the confirmation of Thomas to the U.S. Supreme Court to succeed Justice Thurgood Marshall.

• In response to the police beating of Los Angeles motorist Rodney King, the NAACP conducted a series of hearings into police conduct toward African Americans in Norfolk, Miami, Houston, Los Angeles, St. Louis, and Indianapolis.

1992

• Newly signed agreements brought the number of Fair Share Signatories to seventy, the highest in the program's history.

• The NAACP with NationsBank established a pilot program to promote community development lending. NationsBank committed $10 billion for loans over ten years and $1 million a year for five Community Development Resource Centers (CDRC) to provide consumer and business education and counseling, economic development advocacy, public/private partnerships, affordable housing, and consumer lending.

• The NAACP's Military and Veterans Affairs Department parlayed with the Pentagon to minimize the impact of downsizing armed forces on black personnel, while holding hearings in Europe to record the grievances of blacks serving there. The NAACP arranged for Civil Rights Commission chairman Arthur Fletcher to hear complaints of discrimination.

• Ben and Frances Hooks led an NAACP delegation to Guantanamo Bay, Cuba, with relief supplies for Haitian refugees denied admission to the United States. In September, nearly one hundred civil rights activists, organized by the NAACP, were jailed for acts of civil disobedience in front of the White House in protest of the

1992: NAACP staff: General Counsel Dennis C. Hayes; Director of Programs John J. Johnson; Director of Branch and Field Services William Penn; and Region Two Director Paula Brown Edme are part of a hearing panel listening to black soldiers in Germany talk about racism in the armed forces.

U.S. policy towards Haiti. Led by NAACP Board Chairman William Gibson and CEO Ben Hooks, the activists included tennis star Arthur Ashe, TransAfrica President Randall Robinson, labor leader William Lucy, and entrepreneur Percy Sutton.

February 1992

• Following the acquittal of four policemen for the brutal beating of Rodney King a year earlier, vast civil disorders rocked Los Angeles, California, causing record death and destruction. Hooks met with California Governor Pete Wilson, Los Angeles Mayor Thomas Bradley, and local authorities and then convened meetings with local NAACP branch leaders to craft short-term and long-term solutions. Hooks and NAACP leaders led a march for "Dignity and Justice" in Sacramento to the state capitol, to demand reforms, including support for a civilian review process in Los Angeles.

• The NAACP hosted its first national health summit and began plans to create a national health department. The first booklet on AIDS aimed at teenagers was published.

• Hooks made an appeal to African Americans to buy cars manufactured in the U.S., noting that the industry had traditionally been a major employer of minorities.

April 1992: NAACP Executive Director Benjamin L. Hooks and wife, Frances, at the ceremony renaming streets around NAACP National Headquarters. Mt. Hope Drive was renamed Ben L. Hooks Drive.

NAACP Director of Communications Jerry Guess unveils the Ben L. Hooks Street sign.

CONGRATULATIONS!!
WE SAY THANKS
TO YOU
DR. BENJAMIN HOOKS

BEN L. HOOKS DR.

<4800

MT. HOPE DR.

<5700

METRO DR.

May 7, 1992: NAACP heads a march in the California state capitol of Sacramento to protest police brutality in the Los Angeles, California, beating of motorist Rodney King.

JUSTICE,
JUSTICE,
SHALT THOU
PURSUE!

September 9, 1992: NAACP Executive Director Ben L. Hooks (right), along with tennis champion Arthur Ashe and NAACP Chairman William Gibson, leads a march on the Capitol against the discriminatory Haitian policy.

• NAACP branches responded to Dr. Hooks's appeal to provide aid to victims of Hurricane Andrew. A relief office was established in the Miami area, where the greatest damage was recorded. The NAACP also provided aid for victims in Louisiana and South Carolina.

• As a result of unequal levels of funding, the NAACP filed suit in Maryland, charging inferior quality of public education was provided to African American children.

• The city of Yonkers, New York, was pressed by the NAACP to fulfill a court order for housing desegregation through scatter site placement of low and moderate income units.

• In 1915, the NAACP found itself in a battle against the showing of the racist film *Birth of a Nation*. Seventy-seven years later, NAACP leaders were beginning yet another protest against the film when the Library of Congress selected the film for inclusion on the prestigious National Film Registry.

• The ACT-SO competition was aired for the first time on ABC-TV.

1993

• Florida NAACP officials called on federal and state agencies on January 1 to investigate the hate crime against thirty-one-year-old New York stockbroker Christopher Wilson, who had traveled to Central Florida for the New Year's Day Hall of Fame football game. Three white men robbed Wilson, doused him with gasoline, and set him ablaze.

• In February, the NAACP demanded that the Clinton Administration immediately admit 267 Haitian refugees held at the U.S. Naval Base at Guantanamo Bay, Cuba; in June, the Association demanded that Clinton rescind the Bush Administration's executive order barring Haitian refugees from America's shores.

• In March, the NAACP National Headquarters was officially dedicated as the Benjamin L. Hooks Building.

• NAACP Executive Director Rev. Dr. Benjamin L. Hooks retired and was succeeded by civil rights activist Benjamin Chavis, the youngest Executive Director ever. One of Chavis's first efforts was to travel to a housing project to "get to the heart of the issue," stating that in economically deprived areas, youth often go from childhood to adulthood with no adolescence because of the economic demands.

• The NAACP supported President Bill Clinton's nomination of Lani Guinier for his cabinet and continued this support when she was attacked for her legal journal writings.

• In June, the NAACP held a conference on the "Environment and the Health of Americans of African Descent."

• The NAACP released a statement in June regarding the *Shaw v. Barr* Supreme Court decision, stating, "The NAACP is deeply saddened by the Supreme Court's woeful redistricting decision which gives the shape of electoral districts primacy over the historic struggle of African Americans to obtain a meaningful right to vote."

• The NAACP announced opposition to the North American Free Trade Agreement (NAFTA).

• During the summer, three suspicious fires damaged NAACP offices: San Francisco, California, on the 8th; Tacoma, Washington, on the 20th; and Sacramento, California, on the 27th.

• In light of new evidence concerning the innocence of Gary Graham, Dr. Chavis flew to Austin, Texas, in

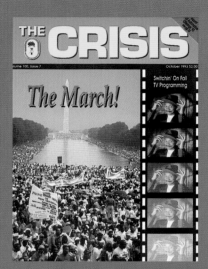

October 1993

April/May 1993

Fall Edition 1993 · A Publication of the NAACP Labor Department

Womack Named Chair of NAACP Labor Committee

Richard Womack, Director of the AFL-CIO Department of Civil Rights, was recently named Chairman of the NAACP National Board of Directors Labor Committee.

In making the appointment, NAACP Board Chairman William F. Gibson noted Womack's many years of work with the labor and civil rights communities, and particularly his dedication and support for the work of the NAACP.

Mark Stepp of Detroit, Michigan, was named Vice Chairman of the Committee. Other members are: Owen Bieber, Johnny Henderson, William Lucy, Doris Alexander, Turner Robert McGlocklin, Kevin McWhorter, Barbara Van Blake, Ernest Lofton, Joe Davis, Hon. Charles V. Johnson, Robert White, Robert E. Starr, John Sturdivant, Earlie Robinson, Tom Turner, Clayola Brown, William Pollard, Joseph E. Madison, Miss Sheila Williams, Ed Lewis, Earle Robinson and Mrs. Annie B. Martin.

NAACP OPPOSES NAFTA

Over 500 delegates crowded meeting room at NAACP Convention to hear presentation on North American Free Trade Agreement during the Labor Workshop.

The NAACP announced its opposition to the final ratification of the North American Free Trade Agreement (NAFTA) "in its present form," and called upon the Clinton Administration to pursue economic strategies for the United States which maximize the productivity of the nation's total potential workforce. The action was taken in an "emergency resolution" adopted by delegates to the NAACP's 84th Annual Convention in Indianapolis, Indiana (resolution p. 4).

The NAACP's opposition to NAFTA is based largely on concern for the agreement's potentially negative impact on African American and other workers in the projected loss to Mexico of industrial, agricultural and manufacturing jobs. Moreover, the continuing high level of unemployment in the African American community — which could be exacerbated by NAFTA-related job loss — renders the accord problematic. The absence of adequate education, job training and minority business initiatives associated with NAFTA were also consid-

(Continued on page 3)

1993: NAACP Labor Department newsletter, *The Force*, fall edition, 1993.

August to make a last-minute appeal to Governor Ann Richards to stay his execution for murder.

• On August 28, NAACP Chairman William Gibson, Chavis, Coretta Scott King, Walter Fauntroy, and AFL-CIO's Lane Kirkland joined together to organize the 30th Anniversary March on Washington for Economic Democracy.

• The NAACP received a $2 million commitment from the estate of the late Reginald F. Lewis to establish the NAACP Reginald F. Lewis Memorial Endowment.

• President Clinton named Dr. Chavis to the twenty-five-member President's Council on Sustainable Development to help develop U.S. policies that would encourage economic growth, job creation, and environmental protection.

• The NAACP filed a lawsuit against the city of East Haven, Connecticut, for employment discrimination after the town rejected an NAACP employment proposal designed to produce a work force reflecting the availability of qualified African Americans.

• The NAACP and the National Kidney Foundation joined forces to fight kidney disease in African Americans.

• Surrounding charges of discrimination against African Americans, Flagstar Corporation signed a $1 billion Fair Share Agreement with the NAACP, committing to hire 325 black managers and develop fifty-three black franchises, as well as investing in advertising, marketing, and professional services provided by African Americans.

1993: NAACP 30th anniversary March on Washington; at right, Chairman William Gibson, Executive Director Benjamin Chavis, and Chavis's wife, Martha.

• In a historic event, Nelson Mandela joined the NAACP at the 84th Annual Convention in Indianapolis, Indiana, where he received the W. E. B. Du Bois International award.

• After the Rodney King police beating, the NAACP held a series of public hearings into

police misconduct in six troubled cities: Houston, Texas; Los Angeles, California; St. Louis, Missouri; Norfolk, Virginia; Miami, Florida; and Indianapolis, Indiana. In conjunction with the Criminal Justice Institute of Harvard Law School and the William Trotter Institute of the University of Massachusetts, they combined the findings into a report called "Beyond the Rodney King Story," and called for police departments to "be part of the community they serve."

• The NAACP began the 1993 "Freedom Rides" with scores of activists, many of whom were college-age youth, traveling by bus from the South to New York City conducting "Get Out To Vote" registration and education drives.

• In October, the NAACP Board of Directors and Trustees met for the first time outside of the United States, holding its quarterly meeting in Nassau, Bahamas.

• The NAACP met with AT&T Corporation to express outrage over a cartoon that depicted a gorilla as a caller from Africa.

• The NAACP continued the fight with a protest march against the white town of Hemingway, South Carolina, which was attempting to secede from a predominantly black county.

• In November, the NAACP urged Congress to refocus Superfund, the Environmental Protection Agency's thirteen-year-old hazardous waste cleanup program.

• The NAACP and the League of United Latin American Citizens (LULAC) filed a petition asking the Federal Communications Commission (FCC) to deny the application of QVC Network for the purchase of Paramount Communications because of alleged noncompliance with the FCC's affirmative action and equal employment opportunity rules by TCI, Inc. (QVC's major partner in the deal).

• In December, twenty-four hours following the guilty verdict in the Detroit, Michigan, police beating death of motorist Malice Green, the NAACP Detroit Branch received several death threats.

• Dr. Chavis, who coined the term "environmental racism," spoke on PBS series *Earthkeeping*. Chavis called "environmental racism" a life-and-death issue and spearheaded the NAACP's movement to end it, alleging that a disproportionate number of minority communities were targeted for hazardous, toxic waste sites. He stated that "environmental racism" was an attempt to exclude people of color from decisions on public policy. The NAACP organized Branches to speak out on the issue and advocated for reform of the Superfund legislation.

• After a four-month investigation, the NAACP Montgomery, Maryland Branch attacked major insurer GEICO for redlining and employment discrimination against African Americans.

1994

• Chavis supported the idea that the NAACP focus more on economic empowerment to ensure a strong economic infrastructure for the African American community and other communities of color.

• In February, justice was served when Byron de la Beckwith was convicted of the 1963 murder of NAACP Field Secretary Medgar Evers.

• On March 8, the NAACP took aim at President Clinton's proposed "National Information Superhighway" and created an NAACP Telecommunications Task Force of Board members and industry leaders to ensure that

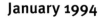

January 1994

November/December 1994

African Americans were participants in the ownership, management, and total employment package.

• The NAACP issued a statement vehemently opposing the selection of controversial nationally syndicated talk show host Rush Limbaugh, who had repeatedly attacked African Americans, as the spokesperson for the Florida Citrus Commission.

• On April 24, the NAACP conducted a voter education teleconference in seventeen cities across the U.S. to prepare South African citizens residing in the U.S. and

NAACP volunteers for participation in the special South African elections on April 26.

• Through the NAACP Community Development Resource Centers (CDRC), the Association established the Youth Entrepreneurial Institute to sharpen business acumen and launch enterprises for students ages fourteen to eighteen.

• In May, the NAACP and other organizations sponsored a youth summit to seek workable solutions to the drugs and violence in their communities.

• NAACP leadership led fifteen thousand chanting "SOS, Save Our Schools!" in a "March On Jackson" in support of Jake Ayers in the *Ayers v. Fordice* case that supported equal funding of all state-supported Historically Black Colleges and Universities (HBCUs) and in opposition to the proposal of merging or closing any of them.

• The NAACP publicly condemned the words, lyrics, and images that degraded, disrespected, and denigrated African American women with obscenities and vulgarities of the vilest nature in hip-hop culture and rap music. The Association sponsored a forum to address the issue.

• On June 12-13, the NAACP convened a meeting of black leaders across the country at National Headquarters for the National African American Leadership Summit. The summit addressed the development and implementation of effective strategies for African American economic development, youth and community development, and moral and spiritual renewal.

• The NAACP applauded the U.S. Department of Justice for filing a civil rights lawsuit against the Randolph County, Alabama, school district alleging continuing violations of previous court orders to desegregate its school system.

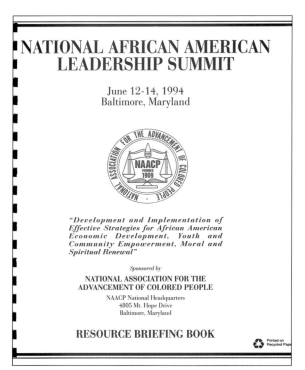

NATIONAL AFRICAN AMERICAN LEADERSHIP SUMMIT

June 12-14, 1994
Baltimore, Maryland

"Development and Implementation of Effective Strategies for African American Economic Development, Youth and Community Empowerment, Moral and Spiritual Renewal"

Sponsored by
NATIONAL ASSOCIATION FOR THE ADVANCEMENT OF COLORED PEOPLE
NAACP National Headquarters
4805 Mt. Hope Drive
Baltimore, Maryland

RESOURCE BRIEFING BOOK

Printed on Recycled Paper

June 1994: NAACP holds the National African American Leadership Summit, bringing together over fifty leaders of black organizations to address civil rights issues.

• The NAACP worked with blood donor centers to recruit black blood donors, led a "guns for toys" campaign, and made efforts to integrate Wall Street.

• The NAACP called on Congress to pass national health care reform legislation that would include "universal coverage" and universal access to necessary health care services for Americans.

• In July, the NAACP released a report called "African American Appointments to the Federal Courts" that called for an increased vigilance in support of racial and gender diversity in judicial appointments.

• Chavis reached out to young African Americans who wanted to be a part of the Civil Rights movement through such media outlets as MTV and radio stations, playing an NAACP theme song, "Come Back Home to the NAACP." He also worked with Run DMC to mobilize youth voters.

• On August 20, NAACP Chairman William Gibson issued a statement ending the tenure of Dr. Benjamin Chavis as NAACP Executive Director and named the interim management team of Earl Shinhoster and Fred Rasheed as senior administrators.

• On September 29, the NAACP Board convened a meeting with public relations professionals and corporate executives that resulted in the development of a national campaign theme, "Imagine an America Without the NAACP."

• Due to economic conditions, NAACP national staff were furloughed and the Board of Directors worked vigorously, asking that each donate or raise $5,000 within two weeks to increase the Association's revenue stream to resume full-speed operations. An emergency relief fund was established to help staff in need.

• The NAACP celebrated Nelson Mandela's triumph in the South Africa presidential election.

• The NAACP was outraged over Colonial Williamsburg's reenactment of a slave auction in an effort to educate the public about the horrors of slavery.

• In December, NAACP leadership adopted a reorganization plan that brought back many of its furloughed staff.

1995

• On January 16, the NAACP joined with the Minority Business Enterprise Legal Defense and Education Fund to demonstrate at the U.S. Supreme Court to bring attention to the *Adarand v. Pena* case regarding minority set-asides.

• On February 18, Myrlie Evers-Williams, the wife of slain civil rights leader and NAACP Field Director Medgar Evers, was elected chairwoman of the NAACP National Board of Directors. Within four days of her election, Evers-Williams lost her new husband, Walter Edward Williams, to cancer.

• The NAACP Board supported the confirmation of Dr. Henry W. Foster to serve as the U.S. Surgeon General.

• After reports of white supremacist activities at Fort Bragg, North Carolina, the NAACP appointed a state task force on "Community and Military Response to White Supremacist Activity in and Around Military Bases" and was credited by the FBI as being extremely helpful in the investigation.

• The NAACP Western Region Sports Committee, headed by former NFL Hall of Famer Jim Brown, formed a community partnership called Athletes Committed to Kids (ACK) focused on teaming professional athletes with inner-city youth to develop life management skills.

• On April 19, the NAACP rallied on the steps of the U.S. Supreme Court in support of minority congressional districts.

• The NAACP scored a victory when President Clinton vetoed the "welfare reform" legislation passed by Congress. The Association continued to oppose congressional efforts to cut Medicare and Medicaid expenditures.

• The NAACP suffered a setback when President Clinton declined to veto a sentencing Bill involving crack versus cocaine. Under current law, the penalty for crack was harsher, and the majority of convicted crack dealers were African American. The NAACP supported the position of the United States Sentencing Commission, recommending that the penalties between crack and powder cocaine be equalized at the current penalty levels set for powder cocaine.

• On December 9, Maryland Congressman Kweisi Mfume was elected president and CEO of the NAACP. He presented his five-point plan, which focused on protection of civil rights and civil liberties, voter empowerment, educational excellence, economic empowerment, and youth.

1996: ACT-SO contestants display their works at the NAACP 87th Annual Convention in Charlotte, North Carolina.

1996

- The Louisiana State Conference held the largest demonstration march, "March on the Governor's Mansion," in Louisiana history with more than twenty-five thousand people marching in protest to Governor Mike Foster's executive order terminating affirmative action programs.
- The Youth and College Department formed a coalition with "Rock the Vote" and "Black Youth Vote" to strategize on voter registration at black colleges.
- The NAACP Southern California area Branches partnered with Congresswoman Maxine Waters to request an investigation into the alleged connection between the CIA, Nicaraguan Contras, and the explosion of crack cocaine in our communities as exposed by journalist Gary Webb.
- The Youth and College Department partnered with the National Alliance of African American Athletes and the Princeton Review to provide SAT preparation for students called "SAT-PreGame!"
- *The Crisis* magazine suspended publication to reorganize.
- Due to the efforts of Chairwoman Myrlie Evers-Williams, the NAACP ended the year with assets totaling $2.4 million and eliminated all debt from previous years.
- The NAACP investigated the taped racial slurs by managers at the Texaco Corporation.
- During 1995 and into this year, there were over one hundred African American church arson fires, mainly in the Southeast. The NAACP established the NAACP Church Fire Project to assist these churches.
- The NAACP, along with the Criminal Justice Institute, released "Beyond the Rodney King Story: An Investigation of Police Misconduct in Minority Communities."

1996: Actor Jim Brown with NAACP Image Award Founder Maggie Hathaway (right) at the Association's 1996 convention.

- In two landmark cases, *Bush v. Vera* and *Shaw v. Hunt*, the U.S. Supreme Court ruled that using race as a factor in the creation of congressional districts is unconstitutional.

1997

- After Chairman Evers-Williams laid the groundwork, President and CEO Kweisi Mfume was able to capitalize on

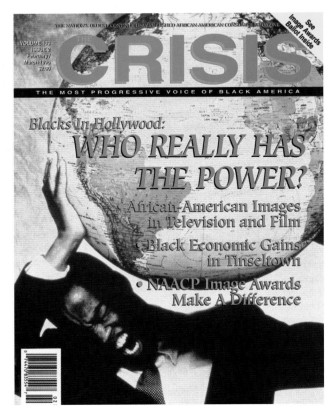

February/March 1996

her efforts and again close the year with increased assets. Mfume launched a major nationwide endowment drive to protect the future of the NAACP.

- *The Crisis* magazine resumed publication.

- The NAACP held a protest and rally in front of the Justice Department, calling on the president and attorney general to withhold federal dollars to jurisdictions that continued to have recurring incidences of alleged police brutality.

- On March 21, a kickoff rally was held in Brooklyn, New York, for the NAACP Youth and College Division launch of the "Stop the Violence, Start to Love" campaign in the wake of the violent deaths of rappers Christopher Wallace (Biggie Smalls) and Tupac Shakur and Ennis Cosby, son of Bill Cosby. Rallies were also held in Los Angeles, California, and Hollywood, Florida. The campaign commenced with a National Day of Non-Violence on April 4, the anniversary of the assassination of Martin Luther King Jr.

- Chinese government officials sponsored a delegation of ten social work officers from China to NAACP Region I to learn more about the plight of African Americans and other minorities.

- *The Tonight Show*'s Jay Leno and Music Director Kevin Eubanks partnered with the NAACP to form the NAACP Leno/Eubanks Scholarship to provide African American students with special needs assistance and/or to further their education in the music industry.

- The NAACP requested an investigation into the October 1994 death of a nineteen-year-old African American male found hung in Urbana, Missouri, citing the questionable manner in which the initial investigation was handled. Local law enforcement and the district FBI failed to respond to the request from the local branch.

- The NAACP joined with the A. Philip Randolph Institute, Amtrak, Simon and Schuster Publishers, labor unions, and other sponsors to promote a cross-country whistle stop tour to Pullman,

1997: NAACP President and CEO Kweisi Mfume and Board Chair Myrlie Evers-Williams cut the ribbon at the opening of the 88th Annual Convention Commerce and Industry Show in Pittsburgh, Pennsylvania.

Illinois, known as the "Pullman Blues Tour," highlighting the African American railroad passenger train employee spanning 1868-1968.

• On April 13, in one of the largest union drives in the United States, Director of Programs John J. Johnson represented the NAACP in joining with the United Farm Workers, AFL-CIO, and other labor, civil rights, and environmental groups at the California "March for Fairness" to improve the lives and working conditions of twenty thousand California strawberry workers.

• On July 17, in light of sexual harassment allegations among military personnel, the NAACP Armed Services and Veterans Affairs Division held a hearing, under the direction of General Counsel Dennis C. Hayes, at the 88th Annual Convention in Pittsburgh, Pennsylvania. A report, "The Continuing Search for Military Justice—Fifty Years Later," followed.

• The NAACP fought against California's Proposition 209, which would strike down affirmative action; however, the Supreme Court upheld the proposition. Despite the defeat in California, the Association fought with Houstonians against a similar Bill, Proposition A. By a margin of 55-45 percent, affirmative action was preserved in the state of Texas.

• The NAACP convened a race summit at the Medgar Evers Institute to discuss the future of race relations in the U.S.

• To address economic empowerment, the NAACP launched the Economic Reciprocity Initiative (ERI) as an arm to the Fair Share Program. The first consumer guide and report card focused on the hotel industry.

• The NAACP, along with People For The American Way, formed the Partnership for Public Education cam-paign as a vehicle to build support for public schools at the grassroots level. Together they fought and won against school vouchers funded by tax dollars.

• The NAACP denounced the *Merriam-Webster's Collegiate Dictionary* definition of "nigger" as "a black person," eventually forcing them to amend this definition.

• The National ACT-SO program was made available in syndication for broadcast across the nation.

• The NAACP Education Department joined President Clinton's "America Reads Campaign" aimed at ensuring that each child can read well and independently by the end of third grade. They also worked with the "I Am Your Child" campaign, dedicated to making childhood development a top national priority.

1998

• NAACP Chairwoman Myrlie Evers-Williams stepped down, and former Georgia state legislator, civil rights activist, TV host, and professor Julian Bond was elected chairman.

• Roger Wood Wilkins, a Pulitzer Prize–winning journalist and nephew of former NAACP Executive Director Roy Wilkins, was named chairman and publisher of The Crisis Publishing Company Inc.

• In the wake of the brutal and heinous slaying of James Byrd Jr., a black man who was tied to a truck by his legs, by three white men with alleged ties to hate groups, and dragged for miles to his death, the NAACP worked to ensure justice and racial reconciliation. President and CEO Kweisi Mfume called for a national day of mourning.

• Former Ku Klux Klan Imperial Wizard Sam Bowers was found guilty of Vernon Dahmer's murder and sentenced to life. Dahmer was murdered in January 1966 for allowing blacks to pay their $2 poll tax at his store.

• In May, the NAACP petitioned the Senate to oppose the Santorum Amendment, which would prevent the Department of Defense from using price credits to assist minority- and women-owned businesses.

• NAACP Region VII Women in the NAACP (WIN) Coordinator Sylvia Williams led an emergency national, regional, and state action team to Bayview, Virginia, to expose the subhuman and demoralizing conditions African Americans were forced to live in on the eastern shore of Virginia, bringing media attention to the plight of these impoverished people. The NAACP team demanded and won assistance from the Department of Housing and Urban Development (HUD), State of Virginia Housing and Public Works, and the U.S. Department of Agriculture.

• In September, the NAACP Youth and College Department mobilized youth members to participate in the historic Million Youth Movement in Atlanta, Georgia.

1998: NAACP President and CEO Kweisi Mfume leads an affirmative action protest at the Capitol Building in Washington, D.C.

• The NAACP led a highly publicized demonstration on October 5 in front of the U.S. Supreme Court on its shameful record in hiring minority law clerks. President and CEO Kweisi Mfume and staff were arrested during the demonstration.

• From November 30 to December 4, the NAACP Youth and College Department organized a national phone and fax protest demanding a meeting with Chief Justice William Rehnquist to address the Supreme Court's poor record in hiring women and minority law clerks. The impact of the "technology protest" was evident when operators began to divert calls to their answering service.

• The NAACP launched an aggressive voter education, registration, and participation campaign in Washington State to defeat the anti–affirmative action Initiative 200.

• The Association publicly petitioned Texas Attorney General Dan Morales to appeal the latest decree in the landmark Hopwood Case, which struck down the affirmative action program at the University of Texas School of Law.

• The Association released "NAACP 50 Year Anniversary Report on Executive Order 9981 and Its Impact on Race Relations in the United States," citing continued unequal opportunity within the military.

• The NAACP Maryland State Conference joined with the American Civil Liberties Union in a class-action lawsuit by African Americans who were unlawfully and

1998: NAACP Chairwoman Myrlie Evers-Williams shares a laugh with newly elected Board Chair Julian Bond before the press conference announcement.

unreasonably stopped by Maryland State Police along Interstate 95.

• As a result of the NAACP Programs Department continued dialogue with the Department of Agriculture, the Office of Rural Development Outreach was established to help NAACP Branches become more effective advocates for the black farmer.

• The Washington Bureau worked successfully to dwarf attempts by Congressman Steven Horn (R-CA) to pass a very restrictive Bill that would have created much easier opportunities for local elected officials to purge African Americans from their voting rosters, the Voter Eligibility Verification Act of 1997 (H.R. 1428). The Bureau also

July 1998: NAACP Board Member Willa Holden with President Bill Clinton at the NAACP 89th Convention in Atlanta, Georgia.

1998: Erykah Badu receives an Image Award for Outstanding Female Artist at the 1998 NAACP Image Awards.

successfully strategized with the Department of Justice and White House representatives to oppose the Juvenile Crime Control Act of 1997, which would eliminate racial safeguards in the juvenile justice system while federalizing local community school expulsion practices.

• The NAACP signed an unprecedented agreement with the Small Business Administration to assist in delivering $1.4 billion worth of loan assistance to African American businesses.

• The NAACP, along with other leaders, launched the "New Century Alliance for Social Security," an educational campaign organized around a "Statement of Principles for Social Security's Future" endorsed by 170 prominent leaders.

• As a result of the dramatic increase of HIV and AIDS in minority communities, the NAACP declared a state of emergency and called on Congress and President Bill Clinton to include funding in the Omnibus Bill for prevention and treatment.

• A legislative priority for the NAACP was the "Commission to Study Reparation Proposals for African Americans Act." However, the Bill went another year without even the benefit of hearings. The Bill would acknowledge the fundamental injustice, cruelty, brutality, and inhumanity of slavery in the United States and the thirteen colonies between 1619 and 1865.

• The United States Information Agency (USIA) sponsored two officials, Dr. Adriaan Botha and Mr. Ando Donkers, from the Constitutional Affairs Directorate of South Africa, to visit the NAACP as part of their research regarding the rights of cultural, ethnic, religious, and linguistic communities and minorities in the United States in relation to the South African situation.

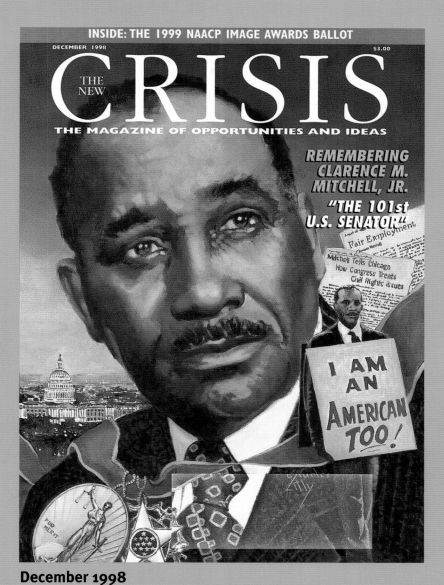

December 1998

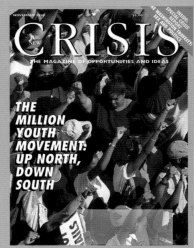

November 1998

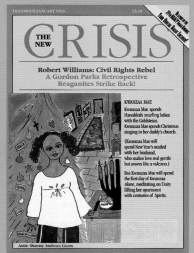

December/January 1998

1999: NAACP Board Member Richard Womack and Director of Programs John J. Johnson present the Benjamin L. Hooks "Keeper of the Flame" award to Jim Daniel at the 90th Annual Convention in New York City.

July 1999: Attorney Johnnie Cochran receives a huge greeting from 84th Spingarn Medal Recipient, Publisher Earl Graves.

July 1999: The Graves family attentively watches as patriarch Earl Graves Sr. receives the NAACP 84th Spingarn Medal.

1999

• In January, the NAACP and Fannie Mae announced a five-year partnership to provide expanded mortgage financing, homeownership counseling, and information to help at least twenty thousand underserved and minority families. A partnership was also formed with Freddie Mac, the largest commitment Freddie Mac has ever made to boost minority home ownership.

• Washington Bureau Director Hilary Shelton testified on March 2 on behalf of the Association before U.S. District Judge Paul Friedman on the proposed settlement for minority farmers. Shelton highlighted the need for the USDA to guarantee and direct loans and that the $50,000 per farmer settlement was inadequate compensation for the years of discrimination. Judge Friedman ordered the USDA back to the negotiating table.

• On March 22, in the wake of the proliferation of police brutality, the NAACP called for action from President Bill Clinton and Attorney General Janet Reno. The delayed response prompted the NAACP to meet with Reno and present a definitive plan of action.

• Due to the epidemic proportions of violence, especially against youth, the NAACP Youth and College Division called on young people to recognize a National Day of Nonviolence on April 4, Easter Sunday.

• The NAACP returned to Riverside, California, on June 7 for a march and rally to protest the district attorney's decision not to prosecute the police officers who fatally shot Tyisha Miller, who was asleep in her car. After NAACP pressure, the Riverside police chief announced his intent to fire the four responsible officers. Many Riverside police officers shaved their heads

March 1999: NAACP Director of Programs John Johnson listens as author Carroll Case shows on the map where the massacre of Negro soldiers took place at Camp Van Dorn in Mississippi.

(like skinheads) as a show of support for the fired officers.

• On June 9, NAACP President and CEO Kweisi Mfume attended a U.S. Justice Department "Conference on Strengthening Police-Community Relationships," where President Clinton announced the signing of a presidential order for federal law enforcement officials to collect data on people they stop or arrest. However, the NAACP continued to push for its three-point plan: (1) withhold federal law enforcement dollars from police departments with excessively high numbers of complaints; (2) federally fund the Crime Control Act; and (3) establish effective police accountability review boards. Also, the Washington Bureau director testified before the House Judiciary Committee and Congressional Black Caucus on the problem of police misconduct among people of color.

• In a letter to President Clinton, Mfume requested pardons for the forty-nine remaining sailors of the Port Chicago incident, where fifty African American soldiers assigned to load munitions witnessed a munitions ship explosion that killed 320 people of which nearly two thirds were black soldiers. White soldiers were granted leave, but the black soldiers were ordered back to work; they refused and were tried for mutiny and sentenced to fifteen years' imprisonment.

• The NAACP's persistence paid off as Rosa Parks was awarded the Congressional Medal of Honor on June 15.

• On July 16, the NAACP filed a class-action lawsuit in the U.S. District Court of New York against the gun

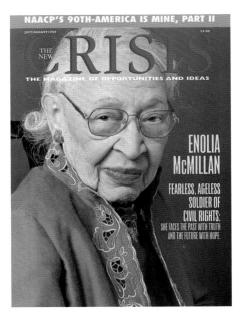

July/August 1999

manufacturing industry, naming 110 gun manufacturers as defendants. This landmark litigation sought to force the firearms industry to use more responsible distribution practices over their inherently dangerous products. The NAACP charged that safety was a civil rights issue, if not a human rights issue. According to a 1992 report by the American Medical Association (AMA), firearm homicide was the leading cause of death among African American males between fifteen and nineteen years of age. On October 29, the Association filed a second and separate lawsuit against a class of firearms distributors.

• In September, Women in the NAACP (WIN) helped the town of Princeville, North Carolina, the nation's first town incorporated by freed slaves after the Civil War, to heal and rebuild from Hurricane Floyd. WIN sent truckloads of clothing, medical supplies, and food.

• On October 5, the NAACP announced its class-action lawsuit against Cracker Barrel Old Country Stores. The suit was originally filed July 30 in the U.S. District Court of Rome, Georgia, based on the company's history of widespread discrimination against African Americans in hiring, firing, pay, promotions, and terms and conditions of employment.

• The Florida State Conference of NAACP Branches filed a lawsuit against the City of Daytona, Florida, for its proposed discriminatory traffic control pattern plan for the Black College Reunion weekend. The NAACP legal

July 1999: NAACP Chairman Julian Bond, Vice President Al Gore, and Chairman Emeritus Myrlie Evers-Williams have the full attention of President and CEO Kweisi Mfume during convention activities.

1999: Students who participated in the NAACP Reginald F. Lewis Youth Entrepreneurial Institute.

1999: NAACP President and CEO Kweisi Mfume and Loida Lewis, chair of the Reginald F. Lewis Foundation, sign an agreement to fund the NAACP Youth Entrepreneurial Institute (YEI) summer program.

As the voice of American civil rights, the NAACP rightly takes its place in history as the No. 1 strike force in our continuing struggle. As its flagship publication, **The Crisis,** celebrates its 100th anniversary, I'm proud to offer my sincere appreciation to the publication which continues to provoke our thought, challenge our complacency, and move us ever forward. As recipient of the NAACP's 84th Spingarn Medal, I can think of no greater satisfaction than knowing that BLACK ENTER-PRISE has benefited from and may continue in this great publishing tradition.

Earl G. Graves Sr.

84th Spingarn Medalist

- The NAACP criticized the National Rifle Association (NRA) for a racially stereotyped television commercial.
- On October 21, NAACP Washington Bureau Director Hilary Shelton testified before a House Subcommittee to express the Association's strong support of H.R. 906, the Civic Participation and Rehabilitation Act of 1999, legislation introduced by Congressman John Conyers Jr. (D-MI) that would restore federal voting rights to ex-felony offenders.
- The NAACP Washington Bureau joined in a Capitol Hill press conference to condemn Florida governor Jeb Bush's proposal to eliminate equal opportunity programs in Florida.
- The NAACP launched an intensive campaign to preserve the Community Reinvestment Act (CRA), a 1977 act requiring financial institutions to invest in the communities in which they are located.
- According to records, the 1990 census missed 8.4 million people and double-counted 4.4 million; people of color, children, and the urban and rural poor were often missed. The NAACP worked to make sure the 2000 census included as many Americans as possible.
- The NAACP pushed for the increase of the federal minimum wage from $5.15 to $6.15 an hour.
- The NAACP endorsed the following legislation: Hate Crimes Prevention Act of 1999 that would expand the definition of a hate crime as one that is perpetrated against a person because of the victim's gender, disability, or sexual orientation; H.R. 125 Bill that would establish a clearinghouse within the Federal Communications Commission to monitor the portrayal of ethnic minorities in television and on the radio; H.R.

department filed a lawsuit against the Adam's Mark Hotel for discriminatory treatment of individuals that stayed or visited the hotel during this weekend. Discrimination against black patrons included their being forced to wear orange wristbands, denial of valet parking by hotel workers, and their being ordered to prepay for their entire weekend stay.

1618 Bill that would eliminate mandatory minimum prison sentences for
small-time drug users.

• On November 3, an NAACP press
conference exposed New York City cab
drivers' refusal to pick up black men
hailing cabs.

• After the Department of Defense
released its Armed Forces Equal
Opportunity Survey to the public on
November 22, the NAACP Director of
Programs met at the Pentagon on
December 14 to improve race relations
and recommended they work with the
NAACP to organize an effective system
to monitor and track discrimination
complaints.

• The Sudan crisis called the
NAACP to demand action from the
United Nations to expose and condemn
the National Islamic Front (NIF) and order a cease and
desist in its slavery practice. The Association also called on
the president of the United States to intensify and expand
U.S. diplomatic and economic pressure on the NIF government to promote peace and develop a strategy to abolish
slavery in Sudan.

• During August 1998, the NAACP was made aware of
allegations that occurred in 1943 regarding 1,227 African
American soldiers of the 364th Infantry who were mur-
dered by military police at Camp Van Dorn in Mississippi.
The NAACP asked the U.S. Army to investigate these
charges, which were published in Carroll Case's book *The
Slaughter: An American Atrocity*. On November 9, Lieutenant
Colonel Graul of the United States Army Center for

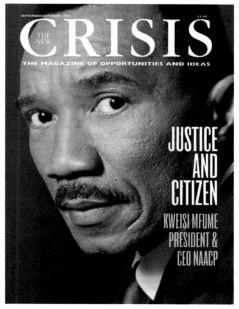

September/October 1999

Military History briefed the NAACP on
its report based on research from the
National Archives and Library of
Congress; it found no evidence to
support the allegations.

• The NAACP had been hampered
by the National Archives refusal to
release ten boxes of declassified secret
and top-secret intelligence reports.
Only after a formal written request
under the Freedom of Information Act
was access granted. NAACP Programs
Director John J. Johnson led a delegation to the site to investigate. The
NAACP called upon Attorney General
Janet Reno to investigate.

July 2007: NAACP Chairman Julian Bond leads the march and burial of the "N Word" at the 98th Annual Convention in Detroit, Michigan.

STOP

2000-2008

THE "N" WORD

GONE FOREVER

DON'T HATE ASSOCIATE

WWW.NAACP.ORG

(866) 63-NAACP

2001:
NAACP
membership
piece.

2000

- NAACP branches were reporting a large amount of police abuse, misconduct, and racial profiling cases across the nation. These included Staten Island, New York, where police grabbed three youth as they listened to music in a mostly white area where one of the youth lived; Mississippi, where two NAACP "Get Out the Vote" volunteers were killed; New York City, where unarmed Amadou Diallo was killed by police; Riverside, California, where Tyisha Miller was shot and killed by police as she slept in her car; and again in New York City, where an unarmed Haitian named Patrick Dorismond was shot and killed by police.

- In February, as a result of months of work by the NAACP, legislation titled "Law Enforcement Trust and Integrity Act of 2000" was introduced by Congressman John Conyers. The legislation was a comprehensive approach at identifying and curbing police misconduct.

- On March 7, the NAACP led approximately fifty thousand protesters to pack the Florida state capitol grounds in Tallahassee, demanding that Governor Jeb Bush end his "One Florida" initiative that was a scheme to end affirmative action in Florida.

- On November 29, the NAACP convened a daylong public hearing in Los Angeles, California, to address improving diversity in network television operations. Subsequent press conferences were held to sign television diversity network agreements with NBC, ABC, CBS, and FOX.

- Over forty-seven thousand people converged on Columbia, South Carolina, on January 17 for a march and rally to protest the Confederate battle flag flying over the state capitol. The NAACP joined with religious and other organizations to say in one united voice, "Take the flag down!"

- On September 15, the "Earl T. Shinhoster Voter Empowerment Bus Tour" kicked off in Atlanta, Georgia. The tour visited fifty southern cities to positively impact voter registration, education, and participation.

- In November, the NAACP Voter Empowerment Initiative helped the National Voter Fund to turn out more African American voters at the polls than ever before in the history

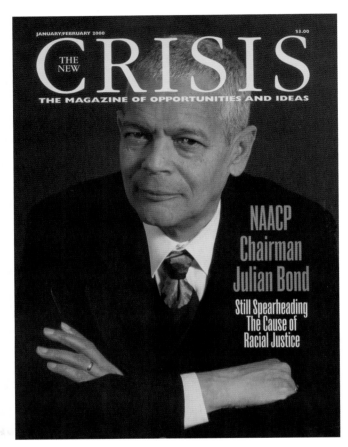

January/February 2000

of the nation. After receiving hundreds of complaints from minority voters in Florida, the Association convened a public hearing in Miami, Florida, to give disenfranchised voters the opportunity to present testimonies of voter irregularity. The hearing transcript was forwarded to the U.S. attorney general for investigation; however, the attorney general failed to act. In December, the NAACP called on the civil rights community to join in a "Count Every Vote: Make Every Vote Count" rally in Miami to protest the voter irregularities.

March/April 2000

• The NAACP Washington Bureau worked with groups to oppose the death penalty and promote a new study just released by the U.S. Justice Department that showed race as an important factor in determining death sentencing.

2000: NAACP staff and volunteers at the NAACP National Headquarters on Mt. Hope Drive during the twenty-four-hour monitoring of the 2000 presidential election.

2001

• On January 10, the NAACP along with other organizations filed a class-action lawsuit against the Florida Secretary of State Katherine Harris; the Director of Florida Division of Elections Clay Roberts; and Georgia Corporation Database Technologies to restore justice to thousands of black and other voters who were denied the right to have their vote counted on November 7, 2000.

• On George Bush's inauguration day, January 20, the Association participated in the "Fairness and Democracy, A Day of Moral Outrage: Count the Vote" rally in Tallahassee, Florida, to draw attention to the thousands of disenfranchised voters from the November 2000 presidential election and call for voter reform.

• The NAACP released its Reapportionment and Redistricting Manual.

• The NAACP Prison Project was reactivated under the leadership of Andrea Brown and continued to provide

July 2001: NAACP Chairman Julian Bond takes a moment to straighten the tie on his wax figure on display, courtesy of the Great Blacks in Wax Museum, at the annual convention in New Orleans, Louisiana.

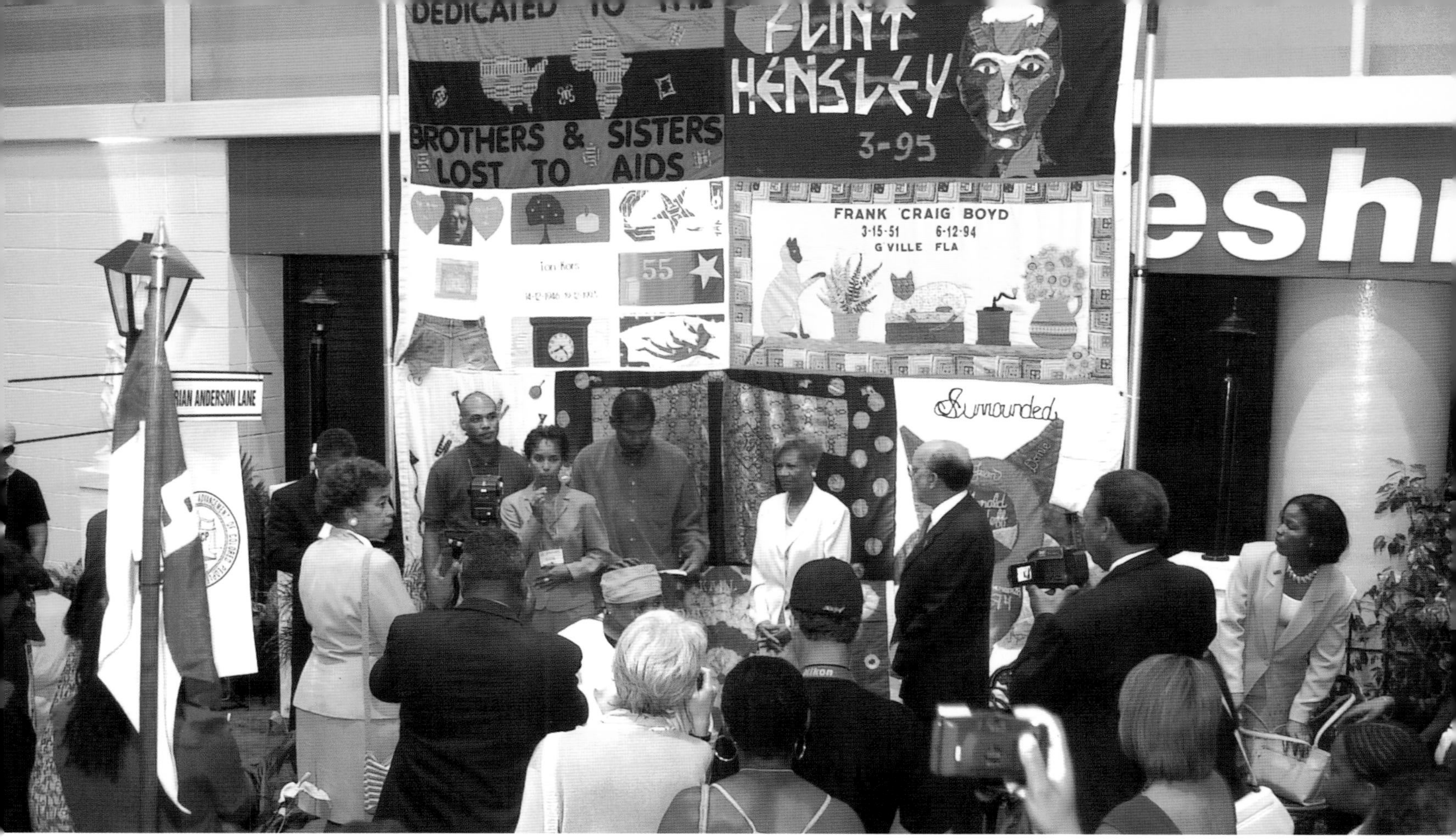
BROTHERS & SISTERS
LOST TO AIDS
HENSLEY
3-95
FRANK 'CRAIG' BOYD
3-15-51 6-12-94
G VILLE FLA
RIAN ANDERSON LANE
Surrounded

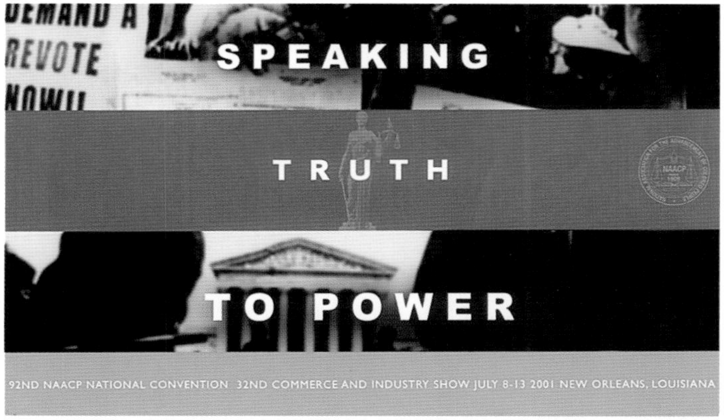
SPEAKING
TRUTH
TO POWER
92ND NAACP NATIONAL CONVENTION 32ND COMMERCE AND INDUSTRY SHOW JULY 8-13 2001 NEW ORLEANS, LOUISIANA

July 2001: The AIDS quilt, dedicated to those who lost their lives to HIV/AIDS, was placed on display as part of the health initiative of the NAACP during the New Orleans convention in 2001.

2001: NAACP 92nd Annual Convention program.

REAPPORTIONMENT AND REDISTRICTING MANUAL
" Drawing Truth and Power from Redistricting Lines "

2001: The NAACP releases the reapportionment and redistricting manual "Drawing Truth and Power from Redistricting Lines."

INSIDE: NAACP 2002 IMAGE AWARDS BALLOT

Black and Arab Relations in Detroit ■ Consumer Racial Profiling

The New **CRISIS**

NOVEMBER/DECEMBER 2001/$3.00

"BLACK PATRIOTISM is far more complex than flying Old Glory and singing "God Bless America" — or going to war, for that matter."

thecrisismagazine.com

November/December 2001

2001: NAACP Get-Out-The-Vote (GOTV) bus in Morgan City, Louisiana.

2001: NAACP GOTV truck dedicated to the memory of Interim Executive Director Earl T. Shinhoster, killed in a tragic car accident in 2000.

support for "The Civic Participation and Rehabilitation Act of 1999" (H.R. 906).

• On March 14, the NAACP Portland State University College Chapter held a racial profiling town hall meeting after an elderly woman, who committed a traffic violation, was pulled from her car by her head and rendered unconscious by a local police official. Despite a confession by the officer, an all-white jury concluded that no excessive force was used.

• On August 15, after a ten-year gap, the NAACP released an updated report on the film and television industry, "Out of Focus, Out of Sync, Take 2," with the original report having been released under former Executive Director Benjamin L. Hooks in 1991. The report encompassed an eighteen-month compilation of facts investigating the lack of diversity and opportunity for people of color in the industry and outlined actions to be taken, such as boycott, if progress was not made.

• NAACP Washington Bureau Director Hilary Shelton, Board Member Rev. Amos Brown, and WIN Director Thelma Daley represented the NAACP in August at the United Nations World Conference Against Racism, Racial Discrimination, Xenophobia and Related Intolerance (WCAR) in Durbin, South Africa.

• The NAACP renewed its call for a boycott of the Adam's Mark hotel chain because of discrimination. On August 10, the Association made its first round of protests at Adam's Mark headquarters, and, the following day, the Branch and Field Services Department led volunteers and supporters on an impressive demonstration protesting simultaneously at each of the twenty-four hotels around the country. Over a dozen organizations, including the United States Tennis Association, honored the boycott by canceling contracts with the hotel chain. The hotel filed a countersuit against the NAACP alleging defamation and interference with contractual relations and requested an end to the boycott.

• On August 21, the NAACP joined with People for the American Way, the Eastman Kodak Company, and the Advertising Council to launch a grassroots campaign, "Success in Schools Equals Success in Life," aimed at encouraging African American and Latino parents to become more involved in their children's schools.

• The NAACP investigated the lending and underwriting practices of Associated Financial Services, which the U.S. Department of Justice and Federal Trade Commission found to be discriminatory against African Americans.

• The NAACP Voter Empowerment Division released a report titled "Tried and Tested: Lift Every Voice and Vote, An Impact Analysis of the NAACP Southern States Voter Empowerment Project 2000."

• The programs director, John J. Johnson, addressed the national secretaries of state on civic engagement and discussed the widespread voting rights abuses and disenfranchisement.

• The NAACP Education Department issued a nationwide "Call For Action In Education" to the U.S. Secretary of Education Rod Paige; NAACP units were asked to identify the most egregious racial education barriers and challenge their state agencies to submit a five-year Education Equity Plan to the NAACP outlining the steps to be taken to reduce the disparities.

2002

• The Youth and College Department launched the first "National Take Affirmative Action Day" as a way to recruit, retain, and admit minority students to institutions of higher learning.

• NAACP President and CEO Kweisi Mfume led a National Board and staff delegation, along with officials from the Black Farmers Association, on a goodwill and trade mission to Havana, Cuba. The mission was designed to: improve trade relations and enable black U.S. farmers to export to Cuba; establish gender and cultural ties between WIN and Cuban women; and study the successes of the Cuban universal healthcare system.

• On May 15, almost a year to the day after Mfume testified in its favor, the "Notification and Federal Employee Anti-discrimination and Retaliation Act of 2001" was signed into law, thus protecting federal employees and whistleblowers against discrimination.

• On August 28, the Washington Bureau joined with the Washington-based Justice Policy Institute (JPI) to announce the results of their study "Cellblocks or Classrooms," which provided an in-depth analysis of the fiscal trade-off between spending on prisons versus education and reported that colleges and universities have lost budget battles to the nation's growing prison system.

• On September 8–10, the Washington Bureau hosted the National Legislative Mobilization Conference to help

2002: Brothers from the Alpha Phi Alpha fraternity in South Carolina join the NAACP in a mock funeral for the confederate flag and burial of voter apathy.

NAACP leadership become active participants in the legislative process and gain insight into issues affecting minorities. Capitol Hill felt the pressure as over six hundred NAACP members descended on their senators and representatives to impress upon them the NAACP congressional civil rights agenda.

• In October, the NAACP's work paid off as the Help America Vote Act (HAVA) and the Sudan Peace Act were signed into law. The HAVA Act set uniform minimum standards for federal elections, and the Sudan Act addressed the human rights violations in Sudan.

93rd Annual NAACP Convention ▪ July 6-11, 2002

The New

CRISIS

JULY/AUGUST 2002/$3.00

CRIME & PUNISHMENT

Restorative Justice: Beyond Punishment, Repairing the Community

U.S. Supreme Court Rules on Death Penalty, Will Review Three Strikes Law

Plus

Election 2002: What's at Stake for African Americans?

When it comes to denial of the vote to former felons, and Census-based redistricting and federal funding, largely white communities are profiting from mostly minority prisoners

Political Prisoners

thecrisismagazine.com

July/August 2002

July 2002: NAACP President and CEO Kweisi Mfume shares a laugh with a Sojourner Truth reenactor at the 93rd Annual Convention in Houston, Texas.

• A legislative victory the NAACP worked to achieve was the juvenile justice provisions that addressed Disproportionate Minority Confinement (DMC), requiring states to address and reduce the disproportionate number of ethnic youth who were confined in prison or who came in contact with the juvenile justice system.

• The NAACP, working with other organizations, began an attack on predatory lending through a letter to Comptroller of the United States John Hawke.

• The NAACP Voter Empowerment Tour Bus traveled thirty thousand miles over 150 days, visiting 192 cities in fifteen states and Washington, D.C., hosting "Rap the Vote" rallies at colleges and universities.

• The NAACP, the first African American organization to participate in the Kentucky Derby Pegasus Parade, entered a sixty-five-foot float honoring African American jockeys and earned the highest honor, the Sweepstakes Award.

• The Prison Project received a grant from the Ford Foundation for a national public education campaign aimed at teaching ex-offenders their voting rights. Also, to impact the juvenile justice system, the Prison Project collaborated with the Youth and College Department to develop The Phoenix Institute. This program reached youth in detention centers, engaging them in the political process and preparing them for future leadership.

• On election day 2002, the NAACP implemented the most advanced election-day tracking system available anywhere, Aristotle, which allowed the Association to properly record the information on any voter denied the right to vote.

2003

• The Youth and College Department partnered with the SEIU Labor Union to provide employment and economic educational resources and with the Families Against Mandatory Minimums (FAMM) to help the

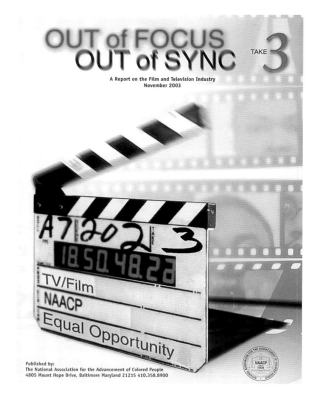

The NAACP released an update on the television and motion picture industry's diversity efforts with "Out of Focus, Out of Sync, Take 3." The report revealed that the four major networks made incremental increases in the hiring of African Americans for on-air roles; however, such progress had not been made behind the camera in the hiring and promotion of writers, producers, directors, and executives.

2003: NAACP Washington Bureau Chief Hilary Shelton and President/CEO Kweisi Mfume hold a press conference to discuss the unfinished business of the 107th Congress.

chapters fight against unfair mandatory minimum drug sentencing laws.

• During Memorial Day weekend for the past twenty-four years, African American bikers descended on the town of Atlantic Beach, South Carolina, for "Black Bike Week." Complaints were made that the black bikers encountered markedly different conditions than their mostly white counterparts attending the Harley Week held one week earlier. The Yachtsman Resort Hotel required Black Bike Week guests to sign a thirty-four-rule guest contract, pre-pay their entire stay, and submit photo identification before their stay, among other discriminatory acts. The NAACP filed suit and won a groundbreaking settlement in the amount of $1.2 million.

• The NAACP Texas State Conference won a stay of execution for Frances Newton, a woman on death row who

2003: NAACP voter registration drive in Texas.

maintained her innocence in the 1988 murder of her husband and children. Evidence in the case was found uncataloged and mislabeled in a warehouse, and DNA testing was possibly contaminated.

• Through a public battle that included campus protests, Catholic University student William Jawando successfully fought the university to start an NAACP college chapter.

• On April 1, while the Supreme Court was contemplating two cases, *Gratz v. Bollinger, et al.* and *Grutter v. Bollinger et al.*, that challenged affirmative action at the University of Michigan, the NAACP joined with By Any Means Necessary (BAMN), the coalition to Defend Affirmative Action & Integration, Fight For Equality, and other civil rights groups to converge on the steps of the U.S. Supreme Court to protest this assault on affirmative action.

• On June 4, the Youth and College Department joined over ten thousand people in front of New York City Hall in Russell Simmon's "Countdown to Fairness Rally," which urged politicians to repeal the discriminatory Rockefeller Drug Laws.

• Through a grant from the Kellogg's Corporate Citizenship Fund, the Legal Department developed the NAACP Law Fellow Program to give students with at least one year of law school the opportunity to work at the National Headquarters and Washington Bureau for a summer.

• In October, NAACP President and CEO Kweisi Mfume expressed outrage over the names of two new products: "Pimp Juice" sports drink and the board game "Ghettopoly," which depicted African American males brandishing semi-automatic weapons and black women as "hoes." The object of the game was to buy stolen property and get the "whole neighborhood addicted to crack."

2003: NAACP Vice Chair Roslyn Brock is fashionable in pink as she greets attendees to the WIN fashion show at the annual convention in Miami, Florida. WIN Director Thelma Daley and WIN Region VII Sylvia Williams look on.

• On October 25, the NAACP mourned the death of George Frye, to whom much of the pictorial history of the NAACP was attributed for twenty-six years.

• General Counsel Dennis C. Hayes represented the NAACP in Paris, France, at a conference convened by two African French organizations—Conseil Representatif des Associations Noires de France (CRAN) and Cap Div, Cercle d'Action pour la Promotion de la Diversite en France—to address the state of blacks in France.

• The NAACP California State Conference was successful in its efforts to defeat Proposition 54, which would have prohibited the state from identifying its residents by race, ethnicity, color, or national origin.

• The NAACP Legal Department prepared a letter of clemency on behalf of Ohio death row inmate Jerome Campbell, whose sentence was commuted from death to life without the possibility of parole. Campbell was accused of a stabbing death, but DNA evidence later showed the blood on his tennis shoe was his own, as he had stated, and not that of the murder victim.

• The NAACP Legal Department worked to oppose landfill operations in two African American communities: Tallapoosa, Alabama, and Mobile, Arizona.

2004

• The release of two films on the murder of Emmett Till revealed new evidence that pushed the NAACP and others to call upon the Justice Department to reopen the case.

• NAACP Chairman Julian Bond made remarks at the Association's 95th annual convention condemning the administration policies of President George W. Bush.

July 2003: At the 94th Annual Convention, *The Crisis* Chairman and Publisher Roger Wilkins stands by the wax figure (courtesy of Great Blacks in Wax) of his uncle, Roy Wilkins, NAACP Executive Director from 1955–1977 and editor of *The Crisis* from 1934–1949.

July 2004: Jane White Viazzi, daughter of former Executive Secretary Walter White, at the unveiling of wax figures of Thurgood Marshall and White at the NAACP 95th Annual Convention in Philadelphia, Pennsylvania.

2003: NAACP President and CEO Kweisi Mfume shares a stage moment with Image Awards host Cedric the "Entertainer."

convened education leaders to address disparities in accessing education;

- "From Brown, Bakke, to Bollinger: The Legal and Legislative Battle to Increase Access and Retention in Higher Education" to increase minority student enrollment in colleges;
- "NAACP Education Summit of the States: Assessing the Price, Identifying the Promise and Mapping the Course for Progress," to develop ways to fulfill the *Brown* decision;
- *Brown v. Board of Education* 50th Anniversary Commemorative Awards Gala;
- "Brown 50 Years and Beyond: Promise and Progress," a plenary session at the July convention.

Bond's remarks led the Internal Revenue Service (IRS) to question the Association's status as a 501(C)(3) corporation and call for an audit. The NAACP saw the request as a chilling political ploy to deter its voter registration activities.

- The NAACP coordinated a nationwide commemoration of the 50th anniversary of the *Brown v. Board of Education* decision from January to July. Activities included:

  - *A tribute to Brown Attorneys,* panel discussions which recognized Robert Carter, Constance Baker Motley, and Oliver Hill;
  - "From the Courtroom to the Classroom: The Role of Teacher Quality in Closing the Achievement Gap," which

- In November, the Association partnered with Pax Christi USA, the national Catholic peace movement, in a nonpartisan, nongovernmental effort to bring international election observers to the United States to monitor the presidential election.

2005

- On January 15, the NAACP mobilized in support of a march and rally that drew over eight thousand to protest the fatal shooting of an unarmed African American, Kenneth Walker, by a white sheriff in Columbus, Georgia. From Georgia, the group moved to Columbia, South Carolina, on January 17 to lend support for a march and rally at the South Carolina State Capitol to protest the flying of the Confederate flag.

• NAACP Vice Chairwoman Roslyn Brock led the charge to recruit the next generation of leaders by establishing the NAACP Leadership 500 Summit, geared to individuals ages thirty to fifty to help shape the future direction of social justice advocacy efforts.

• The February 6 shooting of thirteen-year-old Devin Brown by Los Angeles, California, police officers was one of several police shootings that spurred NAACP

2005: NAACP Board members Madie Robinson, Rev. Theresa Dear, Hazel Dukes and Vice Chair Roslyn Brock march to "Keep the Vote Alive."

officials to hold public hearings and release a report with recommendations for policy and legislative changes.

• The NAACP Georgia State Conference opposed the new voter ID bill signed into law that stated a social security card or birth certificate would no longer be accepted as identification at voting polls. Photo identification, such as a driver's license, would be the only acceptable form of ID.

• With a strong policy of opposition to the death penalty, the NAACP was involved in the high-profile campaign that sought clemency for former gang leader and children's author Stanley "Tookie" Williams, who had helped broker a gang truce between the Bloods and the Crips.

• In May, the NAACP declared victory with the Senate decision to repeal the Florida Class Size Reduction Amendment and commended the NAACP Florida State Conference, National Education Committee, and National Advocacy and Policy Committee for their successful efforts in their nationwide movement against the amendment.

• In June, Interim President and CEO Dennis Hayes called on the Mexican government to immediately cease printing and distributing a postage stamp that bore an offensive cartoon character with black skin and thick lips known as Memin Pinguin and his mother, who resembled an early version of Aunt Jemima.

• In June, forty-one days to the date after James Chaney, Andrew Goodman, and Michael Schwerner were brutally killed in Mississippi, the NAACP supported the manslaughter conviction of former KKK leader Edgar Ray Killen in the 1964 death of the three civil rights workers.

• On August 6, the Youth and College Department joined over fifteen thousand participants in the "Keep the Vote Alive" march from the federal courthouse to a rally at Herndon Stadium on the campus of Morehouse College in

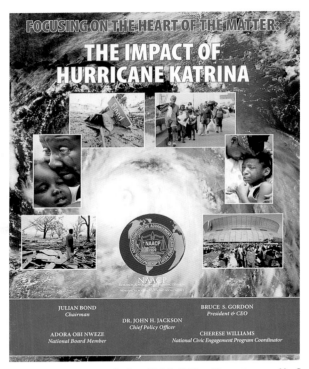

2006: As part of the NAACP's disaster relief efforts, the NAACP releases a report on Hurricane Katrina: "Focusing on the Heart of the Matter: The Impact of Hurricane Katrina."

Atlanta, Georgia, to keep intact the Voting Rights Act's key provisions set to expire in 2007.

• In August, former Verizon executive Bruce Gordon became the NAACP's new president and CEO.

• In August, under the leadership of WIN Coordinator Thelma Daley, following a formal invitation from the Benin government, a small delegation including Chief Policy Officer John Jackson traveled to participate in Benin's reconciliation and development celebration and the opening of the NAACP school and community center in Yawa, Benin—the only educational facility within ten miles.

• In September, while America watched with horror the devastation left by Hurricane Katrina that battered the coasts of Louisiana, Mississippi, and Alabama, NAACP officials were assembling an extensive disaster relief effort. The Association was the first organization to ship items into Gulfport and Biloxi, Mississippi, and set up disaster relief command centers at various branches.

• The NAACP filed an amicus brief in support of death row inmate Vernon Evans on grounds that supplemental studies of Baltimore County Attorney's Office demonstrated the county singled out black defendants from similarly situated white defendants to receive the death penalty.

2006

• The NAACP worked closely with drug companies and senior advocate groups to provide enrollment training to seniors on the new Medicare Part D plan that had even those in the medical field baffled.

• In January, through the work of the Florida State Conference of Branches, Florida's voucher program (which used public funds to educate students at private schools) was terminated by the Florida Supreme Court.

- In March, the Eastern Shoshone of Wyoming became the first Native American tribe to take an NAACP corporate membership.

- On April 20, the NAACP filed an amicus brief in the matter of *ACLU v. National Security Agency, et al.* and a similar case challenging the constitutionality of the National Security Agency's (NSA) program to intercept vast quantities of international telephone and internet communication of innocent Americans without court approval. On August 17, the court granted Plaintiff's Motion for Partial Summary Judgment and held the NSA's spying program violated the Separation of Powers Doctrine, the First and Fourth amendments of the United States Constitution, and statutory law.

- On July 7, the NAACP Legal Department, along with the Washington Bureau, held a public hearing on Capitol Hill to address the U.S. Department of Justice's failure to fulfill its mandate to enforce civil rights laws.

- In July 19, during the NAACP 97th Annual Convention in Washington, D.C., nearly two thousand members marched and converged on Capitol Hill to make scheduled visits to their representatives as part of the campaign "Storming the Hill/Taking the Hill" aimed at winning passage of the Voting Rights Act and to address other national concerns.

- After five invitations and five rejections to address the NAACP at its annual convention, President George Bush accepted the sixth invitation and addressed the NAACP Convention in the nation's capitol.

> I, along with many others, am absolutely thrilled that the NAACP and **The Crisis** magazine have reached this momentous point in history. The combined efforts of the NAACP and **The Crisis** magazine have certainly resulted in numerous opportunities for all people not only throughout this nation, but throughout the world. I do not feel that I could have realized the many achievements that I have been fortunate to participate in, without the hard work derived from these entities and the sacrifices made by the members. I am, at the same time, grateful and very proud of the NAACP and **The Crisis** magazine.
>
> *Benjamin S. Carson, M.D.*
> *91st Spingarn Medalist*

- Citing inequities in the education of low-income and minority students, the NAACP launched a national campaign, "Equity Matters," that focused on four areas: funding; teacher quality; class size; and access to a college-bound curriculum.

- The NAACP rallied in the state of Michigan with

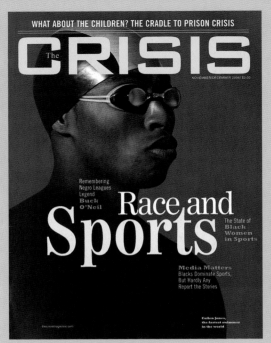

2006: NAACP Leadership—Bruce Gordon, Roslyn Brock and Julian Bond, perform HIV-AIDS testing at the NAACP's 97th Annual Convention in Washington, D.C.

November/December 2006

July 2006:The 97th Annual Convention began with a delegation of over two hundred NAACP members who traveled on historical trains, provided by CSX, to Harpers Ferry, W. Virginia to lay the "Great Tablet" at Storer College seventy-four years after W.E.B. Du Bois led a delegation there in 1932 but was turned away.

2006: The NAACP Youth and College units make a strong statement at the "Solidarity March for Justice and Change" in New York City in response to the police shooting death of Sean Bell.

"Operation Save Affirmative Action" to defeat Ward Connelly's attempts to end affirmative action.

• At the start of the NAACP Annual Convention in July in Washington, D.C., Chairman Julian Bond and President and CEO Bruce Gordon led a delegation of over two hundred NAACP members on historical trains provided by CSX Corporation, including the "NAACP/A. Philip Randolph Freedom Train," to finally lay the "Great Tablet,"seventy-four years later, at Storer College in Harpers Ferry, West Virginia.

• Fifty-two years after the U.S. Supreme Court ruled that school segregation was unconstitutional, the Nebraska state legislature approved a bill to divide Omaha public schools into racially identifiable districts; this led the NAACP to partner with the NAACP Legal Defense Fund to file a lawsuit to challenge the bill that would go into effect July 2008.

• In July, the NAACP honored Alabama attorney Fred Gray with the William Robert Ming Advocacy Award. Gray represented Rosa Parks in her 1955 bus boycott and the Tuskegee Syphilis Study class-action lawsuits against the federal government.

• In August, the NAACP partnered with the National Association of Home Builders (NAHB) to issue a report, "Building on a Dream," that focused on the state of minority housing, barriers to housing, and policy recommendations to address affordable housing for the minority community.

• On August 9, the IRS ruled that the NAACP did not violate tax laws or commit undue political intervention based on Chairman Bond's remarks at the 2004 annual convention.

• In September, the NAACP joined with other humanitarian and civil rights groups at rallies in front of the White House and in New York City as part of a continuing campaign to stop the genocide in the Darfur region of the Sudan.

• On December 4, the Youth and College Department mobilized over two thousand to rally at the U.S. Supreme Court as opening oral arguments were heard in two monumental cases: *Meredith V. Jefferson County Public Schools* and *Parents Involved in Community Schools v. Seattle School District*. The petitioners' lawsuits sought to have the court bar race-conscious measures used by school districts to promote racial integration and equal opportunity.

2007

• On January 11, the shooting death of incoming Westlake, Louisiana, mayor Gerald Washington and intimidation of the mayor of Greenwood, Louisiana, led the NAACP to request the U.S. Department of Justice take necessary steps to protect African American mayors from intimidation and death threats.

• In January, NAACP Washington Branch President Lorraine Miller became the first African American appointed clerk of the U.S. House of Representatives.

• In February, the NAACP denounced racist comments published in the local San Francisco newspaper *AsianWeek* by columnist Kenneth Eng. In the article, Eng, who had called himself an "Asian supremacist" in past writings, listed reasons to discriminate against and hate blacks.

• In February, Attorney General Alberto R. Gonzales and FBI Director Robert S. Mueller III joined the NAACP, National Urban League, and the Southern Poverty Law Center to announce new partnerships aimed at the Civil Rights-Era Cold Case Initiative. The NAACP supported the FBI's intent to reinvestigate "cold" civil rights cases, citing the Lloyd Gaines case, *Gaines v. Canada,* in which a young African American man sued to gain admission to the University of Missouri Law School. The case went to the U.S. Supreme Court, where he won. Gaines then disappeared one March night in 1939, never to be found.

• On March 2, the NAACP Image Awards, hosted by LL Cool J, was televised live for the first time in its thirty-eight-year history. The NAACP and the ONE Campaign announced an unprecedented new alliance at the 38th NAACP Image Awards, joining together for the first time in a life-saving partnership in the

December 2007: In the heart of New York's financial district, known as Wall Street, Interim NAACP President & CEO Dennis Hayes addresses a crowd at a rally calling for action against the mortgage foreclosure crisis that has crippled America.

fight against global AIDS and extreme poverty in Africa and the world's poorest countries.

• In March, NAACP President and CEO Bruce Gordon resigned.

• The NAACP legislative report card gave the 109th Congress an "F" on civil rights matters.

• The International Affairs Department met with the Zimbabwe ambassador to address police brutality. At the

ambassador's request, the NAACP sent a letter to the United Nations Security Council asking that the UN peace keeping mission (MONUC) in the Democratic Republic of the Congo be re-mandated.

• In July, in the midday heat of Detroit, Michigan, thousands of NAACP members and hip hop artists gathered at the Hart Plaza amphitheater for a funeral to bury the "N" word.

• The NAACP Florida State Conference vehemently opposed the seating of an all-white jury in the case of Martin Lee Anderson, a black fourteen-year-old who died at the Florida Bay County Boot Camp after a severe beating by camp officials. All the accused in this death-penalty trial were acquitted.

• In July, the NAACP filed suit in federal court, in the first known lawsuit that challenged lending practices on a broad scale, against fourteen of the country's largest lenders, alleging systematic, institutionalized racism in sub-prime home mortgage lending.

• Earlier in the year, the NAACP testified before the Senate Financial Services Committee and called for a moratorium on foreclosures resulting from sub-prime lending. That fall, the NAACP joined with other groups at "Save Our Homes: Restructure Loans, Not Repossess Homes" rallies on New York's Wall Street and at HUD headquarters in Washington, D.C.

• The NAACP Washington Bureau worked with Congress on the reauthorization and expansion of the Head Start program, a reauthorization that did not include the controversial and NAACP-opposed "Charitable Choice" provision.

• The NAACP, in partnership with the Money Management Institute, launched the Gateway to Leadership Program that arranged summer internships at leading financial firms for undergraduate students from America's Historically Black Colleges and Universities (HBCUs).

• In August, former *Washington Post* Deputy Book Editor Jabari Asim joined *The Crisis* as editor-in-chief.

• As part of the NAACP Centennial activities, the NAACP partnered with Starbucks to host a series of civil rights schools, bringing together renowned historians, scholars, and social scientists to discuss the NAACP's past, present, and future. The schools were held at UCLA, NYU, Howard University, and Harvard University.

• In September, the NAACP coordinated a demonstration against the sentencing of Mychal Bell, one of the "Jena 6." Thousands converged on Jena, Louisiana, and the LaSalle Parish Courthouse on September 20 as defendant Bell was sentenced for his role in an altercation with a classmate following a series of racial incidents after three nooses were hung in a tree at the local high school.

• In November, the Civic Engagement and Youth and College Divisions rolled out the "Vote Hard" campaign, an aggressive plan for increasing voter registration and participation of young voters between the ages of eighteen and thirty-five.

> *My grandmother, Cora Calhoun Horne, made me a lifetime member of the NAACP when I was two years old. Twenty years later, Walter White was a major mentor and "godfather" of my career. I consider the NAACP to be like family.*
>
> **Lena Horne**
> *68th Spingarn Medalist*

September 2007: Interim NAACP President & CEO Dennis C. Hayes leads the march to "Free the Jena 6."

• The NAACP North Carolina State Conference continued to produce significant results as prosecutors stated that twenty-one-year-old James Johnson would not face murder charges in connection with the death of a white female classmate following their 2004 graduation from a high school in Wilson.

• The NAACP filed a racial discrimination lawsuit against Friendly's Restaurant for discriminating against African Americans by closing the Myrtle Beach, South Carolina, Ocean Boulevard location during every Black Bike Week from 2000 through 2005.

• Because of an increase in reports of violence and overly aggressive prosecution against African American youth by law enforcement officials, the NAACP declared a "State of Emergency" requiring immediate action by local and state authorities as well as the U.S. Department of Justice and the U.S. Congress.

2008

• The NAACP expressed outrage at the verdict issued by New York State Supreme Court Justice Arthur J. Cooperman in the police shooting death of Sean Bell. The Association demanded that the U.S. Department of Justice's Civil Rights Division launch a thorough investigation.

• The NAACP was instrumental in working with the diverse, bi-partisan coalition of elected officials and organizations responsible for facilitating passage of the historic legislation, *Second Chance Act of 2007*. The act would provide essential resources to assist local communities to help decrease prisoner recidivism and ease ex-offender reentry obstacles throughout the country.

• Through the generous support of the Ford Foundation and contributions from Global Justice, Inc., the NAACP Youth and College Department created "Young, Black & Secure," a nationwide Social Security empowerment initiative.

• NAACP leaders were distressed by the dismissal verdict rendered by Circuit Court Judge Michael M. Galloway in the death of Isaiah Simmons III at the hands of adults who sought to discipline him at an alternative juvenile justice facility in Carroll County, Maryland. The NAACP called on the U.S. Department of Justice to investigate.

• NAACP Chairman Julian Bond and Teamsters General President Jim Hoffa asked Major League Baseball (MLB) to intervene with the exclusive on-field cap manufacturer, New Era Cap, and were successful in ending racial discrimination and worker rights violations at the company's distribution center in Mobile, Alabama. The NAACP released its investigative report, "Racial Discrimination, Repression and Retaliation at New Era Cap."

• At the May meeting, the NAACP Board of Directors selected Benjamin Todd Jealous as the new president and CEO. His tenure began in September.

May 17, 2008: The NAACP Board of Directors names Benjamin Todd Jealous NAACP President & CEO Designate.

A century ago, a small, multi-ethnic group of dreamers gathered in a New York City apartment and committed to rid the nation of lynch mobs. Three decades later, they succeeded.

Today, their political descendants—the activists of the NAACP—number in the hundreds of thousands and are active in every state, several continents, and on the worldwide web.

From ending Jim Crow to desegregating global corporations to leveling the political playing field, as the NAACP has grown, so has our track record of success.

With this book, we invite you to join us in celebrating these victories and in recommitting to our ongoing work to transform the world by making the dream and promise of America real for all families.

Benjamin Todd Jealous
NAACP President and CEO

Appendix A

NAACP Board of Directors

Julian Bond (Washington, DC),
Chairman

Roslyn M. Brock (Elkridge, MD),
Vice-Chair

Benjamin Todd Jealous, (Baltimore,
MD), President & CEO

Jesse Turner Jr. (Memphis, TN),
Treasurer

Angela Ciccolo (Baltimore, MD),
Interim General Counsel/
Secretary

Carolyn Coleman (Pleasant Garden,
NC), Assistant Secretary

Myrlie Evers-Williams,
Chairman Emeritus

Benjamin L. Hooks, Executive
Director Emeritus

Daisy Bates*, Director Emeritus

Dr. Eugene T. Reed*,
Director Emeritus

Ashley Anderson, Beaumont, TX

Rev. Wendell Anthony, Detroit, MI

Ophelia Averitt, Akron, OH

Hon. Fred L. Banks, Jr., Jackson, MI

Gary Bledsoe, Austin, TX

Karen Boykin-Towns, New York, NY

Cora Breckenridge, Elkhart, IN

Amos Brown, San Francisco, CA

Clayola Brown, Washington, DC

Willie L. Brown, Jr.,
San Francisco, CA

Jessica Butler, Harrisburg, PA

Bishop Clarence Carr, Marietta, GA

Donald Cash, Landover, MD

William E. Cofield, Frankfort, KY

James W. Crowell III, Biloxi, MS

Harold Crumpton, St. Louis, MO

Rev. Theresa A. Dear, Bartlett, IL

Hazel Dukes, New York, NY

Christopher Edley, Jr., Berkeley, CA

Willis Edwards, Los Angeles, CA

Katherine T. Egland, Gulfport, MS

Scott X. Esdaile, Hamden, CT

Myrlie Evers-Williams, Pomona, CA

Michael Fleming (Youth),
Morgantown, WV

James Gallman, Aiken, SC

James E. Ghee, Farmville, VA

David Goatley, Washington, DC

Bishop William H. Graves,
Memphis, TN

General Holiefield, Detroit, MI

Alice Huffman, Sacramento, CA

Frank A. Humphrey, Madison, WI

Leonard James, III, Fairfax, VA

Derrick Johnson, Jackson, MS

Ernest Johnson, Baton Rouge, LA

Shayla A. King (Youth),
Chicago, IL

Oluyemi Kuku (Youth),
Northridge, CA

William Lucy, Washington, DC

Robert Lydia, Dallas, TX

Annie B. Martin, New York, NY

Kameron Middlebrook (Youth),
Des Moines, IA

Lorraine Miller, Washington, DC

Jerome W. Mondesire,
Philadelphia, PA

Michael Nelson, Detroit, MI

Appendix B

NAACP Chairmen

William English Walling
Chairman of National Negro
Committee
1909

Charles Edward Russell
Acting Chairman of National
Negro Committee

Oswald Garrison Villard
Temporary Chairman of National
Negro Committee

William English Walling
Chairman of Executive
Committee, NAACP
May 1910–January 1911

Oswald Garrison Villard
Chairman of Executive
Committee, NAACP
January 1911–June 20, 1912
Chairman of Board of Directors,
NAACP
June 20, 1912–January 1914

Joel E. Spingarn
Chairman of Board of Directors,
NAACP
January 1914–January 6, 1919

Mary White Ovington
Acting Chairman of Board of
Directors, NAACP
May 14, 1917–November 1, 1918
Chairman of Board of Directors,
NAACP
January 6, 1919–1934

Dr. Louis T. Wright
Chairman of Board of Directors,
NAACP
1934–1953

Dr. Channing H. Tobias
Chairman of Board of Directors,
NAACP
1953–1960

Dr. Robert C. Weaver
Chairman of Board of Directors,
NAACP
1960–1961

Bishop Stephen Gill Spottswood
Chairman of Board of Directors,
NAACP
1961–1975

Margaret Bush Wilson
Chairman of Board of Directors,
NAACP
1975–1983

Kelly M. Alexander, Sr.
Chairman of Board of Directors,
NAACP
1983–1985

William F. Gibson
Chairman of Board of Directors,
NAACP
1985–1995

Myrlie Evers Williams
Chairman of Board of Directors,
NAACP
1995–1998

Julian Bond
Chairman of Board of Directors,
NAACP
1998–Present

NAACP Executive Secretaries, Presidents and CEOS

Frances Blascoer
Executive Secretary
February 1910–March 7, 1911

Mary White Ovington
Executive Secretary
May 16, 1911–June 4, 1912

Mary Childs Nerney
Executive Secretary
June 1, 1912–January 3, 1916

Mary White Ovington
Acting Executive Secretary
January 10, 1916–February 15, 1916

Royal Freeman Nash
Executive Secretary
February 15, 1916–September 1, 1917

James Weldon Johnson
Acting Executive Secretary
May 14, 1917–January 1, 1918

John R. Shillady
Executive Secretary
January 1, 1918–May 10, 1920

James Weldon Johnson
Acting Executive Secretary
September 13, 2920–
December 13, 1920

Executive Secretary
December 13, 1920–January 1931

Walter White
Executive Secretary
January 1931–April 1955

Roy Wilkins
Executive Director
April 1955–August 1977

Dr. Benjamin L. Hooks
Executive Director & CEO
August 1977–May 1993

Benjamin F. Chavis, Jr.
Executive Director & CEO
May 1993–August 1994

Earl T. Shinhoster
Acting Executive Director & CEO
September 1994–January 1996

Kweisi Mfume
President & CEO
February 1996–December 2004

Dennis C. Hayes
Interim President & CEO
January 2005–July 2005

Bruce S. Gordon
President & CEO
August 2005–March 2007

Dennis C. Hayes
Interim President & CEO
March 2007–September 2008

Benjamin T. Jealous
September 2008–Present

The Crisis Editors

William Edward Burghardt Du Bois
1910–1934

Roy Wilkins
1934–1949

James W. Ivy
1950–1966

Henry Lee Moon
1966–1974

Warren Marr II
1974–1980

Chester Higgins, Sr.
1981–1983

Maybell Ward
1984–1985

Fred Beauford
1985–1992

Garland Thompson
1992–1994

Denise Crittendon
1994–1995

Gentry W. Trotter
1995–1996

Paul Ruffins
1997–1998

Ida Lewis
1998–2000

Victoria Valentine
2001–2007

Jabari Asim
2007–Present

Appendix C

NAACP Branches by State

Region I

Alaska, 4

Arizona, 10

California, 76

Hawaii, 1

Idaho, 3

Nevada, 6

Oregon, 4

Utah, 5

Washington, 8

Region II

Connecticut, 26

Delaware, 10

Maine, 4

Massachusetts, 22

New Hampshire, 6

New Jersey, 54

New York, 97

Pennsylvania, 72

Rhode Island, 5

Vermont, 0

NAACP Regional Offices

(AE – Germany), 3

Region III

Illinois, 41

Indiana, 39

Kentucky, 41

Michigan, 48

Ohio, 65

Wisconsin, 12

West Virginia, 18

(AE – Germany), 1

Region IV

Colorado, 10

Iowa, 19

Kansas, 29

Minnesota, 13

Missouri, 38

Montana, 0

Nebraska, 6

North Dakota, 0

South Dakota, 1

Wyoming, 4

Region V

Alabama, 55

Florida, 90

Georgia, 125

Mississippi, 84

North Carolina, 121

South Carolina, 88

Tennessee, 47

Region VI

Arkansas, 36

Louisiana, 59

New Mexico, 16

Oklahoma, 22

Texas, 76

Region VII

Washington D.C., 8

Maryland, 48

Virginia, 119

Appendix D

NAACP General Counsels

Moorfield Storey, Arthur Spingarn:
Co-Chairs National Legal
Committee

Clarence Darrow: Member National
Legal Committee

Charles Hamilton Houston

Thurgood Marshall

Robert L. Carter

Matthew Perry *

Nathaniel R. Jones

Theodore Berry *

Thomas I. Atkins

Herbert Henderson *

Grover Hankins

Herbert Henderson*

Dennis C. Hayes

Angela Ciccolo *

* Interim

U.S. Supreme Court Cases Argued by the NAACP

1910: *Franklin v. State of South Carolina*

1915: *Guinn v. United States (aka the Grandfather Clause Case)*

1917: *Buchanan v. Warley* (aka Louisville Segregation Case)

1923: *Moore v. Dempsey (aka Elaine, Arkansas Cases)*

1926: *Corrigan v. Buckley*

1927: *Nixon v. Herndon* (aka First Texas Primary Case and the Second Texas Primary case)

1927: *Harmon v. Tyler*

1930: *City of Richmond v. Deans*

1932: *Nixon v. Condon*

1935: *Hollins v. Oklahoma*

1936: *Brown v. Mississippi* (aka the Brown, Ellington and Shields cases)

1936: *Murray v. University of Maryland* (aka Murray v. Pearson)

1938: *Gaines v. Canada*

1938: *Hale v. Kentucky*

1939: *Lane v. Wilson*

1940: *Chambers v. Florida*

1940: *White v. Texas*

1940: *Hansberry v. Lee*

1940: *Canty v. Alabama*

1942: *Hill v. Texas*

1942: *Ward v. State of Texas*

1943: *United States v. Adams, Bordenave & Mitchell*

1944: *Lyons v. Oklahoma*

1944: *Smith v. Allwright*

1946: *Morgan v. Commonwealth of Virginia*

1947: *Patton v. Mississippi*

1948: *Shelley v. Kraemer*

1948: *Sipuel v. Board of Regents of the University of Oklahoma*

1948: *Fisher v. Hurst*, 333 U.S. 147, decided February 16, 1948

1948: *Lee v. Mississippi*

1948: *Taylor v. Alabama*

1949: *Watts v. Indiana*

1950: *McLaurin v. Oklahoma*

1950: *Sweatt v. Painter*

1950: *Henderson v. United States*

1950: *Rice v. Arnold*

1951: *Shepherd v. Florida*

1952: *Gray v. University of Tennessee*

1953: *Barrows v. Jackson*

1953: *Burns v. Wilson*

1954: *Brown v. Board of Education*

1954: *Hawkins v. Board of Control*

1954: *Tureaud v. Board of Supervisors*

1954: *Muir v. Louisville Park Theatrical Assn.*

1954: *Reaves v. Alabama*

1955: *Lucy v. Adams*

1955: *Brown v. Board of Education*

1955: *Mayor and City Council of Baltimore v. Dawson*

1955: *Holmes v. Atlanta*

1956: *Frazier v. University of North Carolina*

1956: *Hawkins v. Board of Control*

1956: *Flemming v. South Carolina Electric & Gas Co.*

1956: *Gayle v. Browder*

1957: *Fikes v. Alabama*

1957: *Bryan v. Austin*

1958: *Evers v. Dwyer*

1958: *NAACP v. Alabama*

1959: *Patterson v. NAACP*

1960: *Boynton v. Virginia*

1960: *Bates v. City of Little Rock*

1960: *Gomillion v. Lightfoot*

1961: *Louisiana ex rel. Gremillion v. National Ass'n for the Advancement of Colored People*

1961: *NAACP v. Gallion*

1963: *NAACP v. Button*

1963: *Gibson v. Florida Legislative Investigation Committee*

1964: *National Ass'n for Advancement of Colored People v. Alabama ex rel. Richmond Flowers*

1964: *NAACP v. Webb's City, Inc.*

1964: *Griffin v. Prince Edward County*

1964: *NAACP v. Alabama*

1966: *South Carolina v. Katzenbach*

1966: *NAACP v. Overstreet*

1967: *Loving v. Virginia*

1969: *Hunter v. Erickson*

1970: *Or v. Mitchell*

1972: *Furman v. Georgia*

1972: *Aikens v. California*

1972: *Love v. Pullman Co.*

1973: *Lumpkin v. Meskill*

1973: *NAACP v. New York*

1974: *Holmes v. Laird*

1974: *Milliken v. Bradley*

1974: *DeFunis v. Odegaard*

1974: *Emporium Capwell Co. v. West Addition Community Organization*

1975: *Oliver v. Kalamazoo School Board*

1975: *Goss v. Lopez*

1976: *National Ass'n for Advancement of Colored People v. Federal Power Commission*

1976: *Pasadena City Board of Education v. Spangler*

1976: *Runyon v. McCrary*

1977: *Bradley v. Milliken*

1977: *Brinkman v. Dayton Board of Education*

1978: *Regents of University of California v. Bakke*

1979: *Penick v. Columbus School Board*

1979: *Cannon v. University of Chicago*

1979: *Fullilove v. Klutznick*

1979: *Estes v. Metropolitan Branch of Dallas NAACP*

1979: *Brinkman v. Dayton Board of Education*

1979: *United Steelworkers v. Weber*

1980: *Reed v. Rhodes*

1982: *N. A. A. C. P. v. Claiborne Hardware Co.*

1985: *N.A.A.C.P. v. Hampton County Election Commission*

1988: *Town of Huntington, N.Y. v. Huntington Branch, N.A.A.C.P.*

1990: *Spallone v. United States*

Appendix E

Spingarn Medalists

1915: Ernest E. Just (biologist)

1916: Colonel Charles Young (U.S. Army)

1917: Harry T. Burleigh (composer, pianist, singer)

1918: William Stanley Braithwaite (poet, editor, literary critic)

1919: Archibald H. Grimke (U.S. Consul, president of the American Negro Academy, president of the D. C. Branch of the NAACP)

1920: William E. B. Du Bois (author, founder of NAACP)

1921: Charles S. Gilpin (actor)

1922: Mary B. Talbert (president, National Association of Colored Women)

1923: George Washington Carver (botanist)

1924: Roland Hayes (singer, soloist with the Boston Symphony Orchestra)

1925: James Weldon Johnson (poet, Executive Secretary of the NAACP)

1926: Carter G. Woodson (historian and founder of the Association for the Study of Negro Life and History, editor of *Negro Orators and Their Orations*)

1927: Anthony Overton (businessman, president of the Victory Life Insurance Company)

1928: Charles W. Chesnutt (author)

1929: Mordecai W. Johnson (educator)

1930: Henry A. Hunt (high school principal)

1931: Richard B. Harrison (actor)

1932: Robert Russa Moton (principal of Tuskegee Institute)

1933: Max Yergan (missionary)

1934: William T. B. Williams (dean of Tuskegee Institute)

1935: Mary McLeod Bethune (educator and activist)

1936: John Hope (educator)

1937: Walter F. White (Executive Secretary of the NAACP)

1938: No award given

1939: Marian Anderson (opera singer)

1940: Louis T. Wright (surgeon)

1941: Richard N. Wright (author)

1942: A. Philip Randolph (labor leader)

1943: William H. Hastie (jurist and educator)

1944: Charles R. Drew (physician)

1945: Paul Robeson (singer, actor)

1946: Thurgood Marshall (lawyer and later Solicitor General and Supreme Court justice)

1947: Percy L. Julian (research chemist)

1948: Channing Heggie Tobias (participant on the President's Committee on Civil Rights)

1949: Ralph J. Bunche (diplomat and Nobel laureate, 1950)

1950: Charles Hamilton Houston (Chairman, NAACP Legal Committee)

1951: Mabel Keaton Staupers (leader of the National Association of Colored Graduate Nurses)

1952: Harry T. Moore (NAACP leader, martyr in the "crusade for freedom")

1953: Paul R. Williams (architect)

1954 Theodore K. Lawless (physician, educator, philanthropist)

1955: Carl J. Murphy (editor, publisher, civic leader)

1956: Jack R. Robinson (athlete)

1957: Martin Luther King, Jr. (activist and minister)

1958: Daisy Bates and the Little Rock Nine (desegregation activists)

1959: Edward "Duke" Ellington (composer and pianist)

1960: J. Langston Hughes (poet and playwright)

1961: Kenneth B. Clark (professor of Psychology at CCNY)

1962: Robert C. Weaver (Administrator of Housing and Home Finance Agency)

1963: Medgar W. Evers (martyr in the civil rights movement in Mississippi)

1964: Roy Wilkins (Executive Director of the NAACP)

1965: Leontyne Price (Metropolitan Opera star)

1966: John Harold Johnson (founder and president of Johnson Publishing Co.)

1967: Edward W. Brooke III (first Negro to win popular election to the U.S. Senate)

1968: Sammy Davis, Jr. (entertainer)

1969: Clarence M. Mitchell Jr. (NAACP regional director, civil rights lobbyist)

1970: Jacob Lawrence (painter)

1971: Leon Howard Sullivan (clergyman, activist)

1972: Gordon Parks (photographer, writer, filmmaker, composer)

1973: Wilson C. Riles (educator)

1974: Damon J. Keith (jurist)

1975: Henry L. Aaron (athlete)

1976: Alvin Ailey Jr. (choreographer and dancer)

1977: Alexander P. Haley (author)

1978: Andrew Young (diplomat, civil rights activist, minister)

1979: Rosa L. Parks (activist)

1980: Rayford W. Logan (educator, historian, author)

1981: Coleman A. Young (politician)

1982: Benjamin Mays (educator, civil rights activist, president of Morehouse College)

1983: Lena Horne (singer)

1984: Thomas Bradley (mayor of Los Angeles)

1985: William H. Cosby Jr. (entertainer, author and educator)

1986: Benjamin Hooks (Executive Director of the NAACP)

1987: Percy Sutton (public servant, businessman, community leader)

1988: Frederick Douglass Patterson (educator, veterinarian, visionary, humanitarian)

1989: Jesse L. Jackson (civil rights activist and presidential candidate)

1990: L. Douglas Wilder (public servant)

1991: General Colin L. Powell (public servant)

1992: Barbara C. Jordan
(public servant)

1993: Dorothy I. Height
(president of the National Council
of Negro Women)

1994: Maya Angelou (author)

1995: John Hope Franklin
(historian, educator)

1996: Aloyisus Leon Higginbotham Jr.
(jurist, public servant)

1997: Carl T. Rowan (journalist)

1998: Myrlie Evers-Williams
(civil rights activist, Chairman of
the NAACP)

1999: Earl G. Graves
(chairman of *Black Enterprise Magazine*)

2000: Oprah Winfrey
(actress and philanthropist)

2001: Vernon E. Jordan Jr.
(public servant)

2002: John Lewis
(civil rights activist and
member of Congress)

2003: Constance Baker Motley
(federal court judge, Senator)

2004: Robert L. Carter
(federal court judge, cofounder of
National Conference of Black
Lawyers)

2005: Oliver W. Hill
(civil rights lawyer)

2006: Benjamin Carson
(neurosurgeon)

2007: John Conyers (congressman)

NAACP National Conventions

1910 New York, New York

1911 Boston, Massachusetts

1912 Chicago, Illinois

1913 Philadelphia, Pennsylvania

1914 Baltimore, Maryland

1915 New York, New York

1916 Boston, Massachusetts

1917 Washington, DC

1918 Providence, Rhode Island

1919 Cleveland, Ohio

1920 Atlanta, Georgia

1921 Detroit, Michigan

1922 Newark, New Jersey

1923 Kansas City, Missouri

1924 Philadelphia, Pennsylvania

1925 Denver, Colorado

1926 Chicago, Illinois

1927 Indianapolis, Indiana

1928 Los Angeles, California

1929 Cleveland, Ohio

1930 Springfield, Massachusetts

1931 Pittsburgh, Pennsylvania

1932 Washington, DC

1933 Chicago, Illinois

1934 Oklahoma City, Oklahoma

1935 St. Louis, Missouri

1936 Baltimore, Maryland

1937 Detroit, Michigan

1938 Columbus, Ohio

1939 Richmond, Virginia

1940 Philadelphia, Pennsylvania

1941 Houston, Texas

1942 Los Angeles, California

1943 Detroit, Michigan

1944 Chicago, Illinois
(War Conference)

1945 Cincinnati, Ohio (Board Meeting)

1946 Cincinnati, Ohio

1947 Washington, DC

1948 Kansas City, Missouri

1949 Los Angeles, California

1950 Boston, Massachusetts

1951 Atlanta, Georgia

1952 Oklahoma City, Oklahoma

1953 St Louis, Missouri

1954 Dallas, Texas

1955 Atlanta City, New Jersey

1956 San Francisco, California

1957 Detroit, Michigan

1958 Cleveland, Ohio

1959 New York, New York

1960 St. Paul, Minnesota

1961 Philadelphia, Pennsylvania

1962 Atlanta, Georgia

1963 Chicago, Illinois

1964 Washington, DC

1965 Denver, Colorado

1966 Los Angeles, California

1967 Boston, Massachusetts

1968 Atlantic City, New Jersey

1969 Jackson, Mississippi

1970 Cincinnati, Ohio

1971 Minneapolis, Minnesota

1972 Detroit, Michigan

1973 Indianapolis, Indiana

1974 New Orleans, Louisiana

1975 Washington, DC

1976 Memphis, Tennessee

1977 St. Louis, Missouri

1978 Portland, Oregon

1979 Louisville, Kentucky

1980 Miami Beach, Florida

1981 Denver, Colorado

1982 Boston, Massachusetts

1983 New Orleans, Louisiana

1984 Kansas City, Missouri

1985 Dallas, Texas

1986 Baltimore, Maryland

1987 New York, New York

1988 Washington, DC

1989 Detroit, Michigan

1990 Los Angeles, California

1991 Houston, Texas

1992 Nashville, Tennessee

1993 Indianapolis, Indiana

1994 Chicago, Illinois

1995 Minneapolis, Minnesota

1996 Charlotte, North Carolina

1997 Pittsburgh, Pennsylvania

1998 Atlanta, Georgia

1999 New York, New York

2000 Baltimore, Maryland

2001 New Orleans, Louisiana

2002 Houston, Texas

2003 Miami, Florida

2004 Philadelphia, Pennsylvania

2005 Milwaukee, Wisconsin

2006 Washington, DC

2007 Detroit, Michigan

2008 Cincinnati, Ohio

2009 New York, New York

Appendix F

Lift Ev'ry Voice and Sing

by James Weldon and Rosamond Johnson

Lift ev'ry voice and sing,
'Til earth and heaven ring,
Ring with the harmonies of Liberty;
Let our rejoicing rise
High as the list'ning skies,
Let it resound loud as the rolling sea.
Sing a song full of the faith that the
   dark past has taught us,
Sing a song full of the hope that the
   present has brought us;
Facing the rising sun of our new day
   begun,
Let us march on 'til victory is won.

Stony the road we trod,
Bitter the chastening rod,
Felt in the days when hope unborn
   had died;
Yet with a steady beat,
Have not our weary feet
Come to the place for which our
   fathers sighed?
We have come over a way that with
   tears has been watered,
We have come, treading our path
   through the blood of the slaugh-
   tered,
Out from the gloomy past,
'Til now we stand at last
Where the white gleam of our bright
   star is cast.

God of our weary years,
God of our silent tears,
Thou who has brought us thus far on
   the way;
Thou who has by Thy might
Led us into the light,
Keep us forever in the path, we pray.
Lest our feet stray from the places,
   our God, where we met Thee,
Lest, our hearts drunk with the wine
   of the world, we forget Thee;
Shadowed beneath Thy hand,
May we forever stand,
True to our God,
True to our native land.

Index